Paul Wilkinson

THE NEW FASCISTS

Pan Books London and Sydney

First published 1981 by Grant McIntyre Ltd
This revised edition published 1983 by Pan Books Ltd,
Cavaye Place, London SW10 9PG
© Paul Wilkinson 1981, 1983
ISBN 0 330 26953 4
Printed and bound in Great Britain by
Richard Clay (The Chaucer Press) Ltd, Bungay, Suffolk

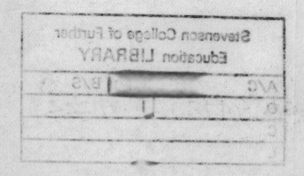

THE NEW FASCISTS

Paul Wilkinson is Professor of International Relations at the University of Aberdeen, and a long-standing expert on international terrorism. He acts as an adviser to several western governments, international organisations and large corporations, and is the author of several books on the subject of terrorism including *Terrorism and the Liberal State*.

CONTENTS

To my father

In the nightmare of the dark
All the dogs of Europe bark,
And the living nations wait,
Each sequestered in its hate.

W. H. Auden
In memory of W. B. Yeats

PREFACE

My aim in writing *The New Fascists* was to alert the general public, and particularly the young generation, to the resurgence of neo-fascist and related movements of the ultra-right, and the implications for the liberal democracies. It is above all a book concerned with political ideas and beliefs and the horrifying results, past and present, of the fascists' attempts to put their ideas into practice.

The sometimes impassioned tone of my writing reflects my belief that fascism is fundamentally evil. In some ways its most dangerous votaries are not those who openly flaunt the swastika banner: rather it is those fellow travellers and crypto-fascists of extreme right-wing regimes and parties who use their political influence, and in some cases considerable power, to convert their visions of racialism and national supremacism into reality. What makes fascists so different from other extremist groups active within our liberal democracies is their *ideological* commitment to the denial of the basic human rights of other racial and national groups. Like Hitler and the Nazi movement, with which they so ardently identify themselves, the new fascists perceive other racial groups as inferior; as sub-human creatures to be suppressed, enslaved or eradicated.

The book also seeks to break down the astonishing insularity of view which assumes that the electoral demise of the National Front in 1979 meant that fascism need no longer be regarded as a threat in Britain or in the world at large. This study is not mainly about fascism in Britain (though this subject is touched on in the general survey, and it is shown how neo-Nazi groups have mushroomed and spread their poison of race hatred and violence in our multiracial cities). My main attention has been focussed on the resurgence of the ultra-right in other countries, where it is not very difficult to show that it is alive and kicking. Recent and current events in the Middle East, Spain, South Africa and Latin America show all too clearly how basic human rights and freedoms in many parts of the world are far more directly threatened by quasi-fascist regimes, and in some cases by ultra-right military and foreign policies pursued by self-professed democracies, than they are by the Soviet Union. Since the original edition of this book appeared events in Latin America and the Lebanon may have at last brought this home to western politicians and publics previously mesmerised by the bogey of bolshevism. In its warning against acceptance of a creeping fascism from within infecting the democratic countries, and in its plea for a return to liberal internationalism, the book may have some claim to prescience. The generally enthusiastic reception of the first edition, from such a wide variety of philosophical, political and religious positions, in itself gives me some slight encouragement. For if more of the politically conscious and active wake up to the dangers of fascist resurgence there is some hope that they will actively resist fascist ideas, propaganda and violence, perhaps on the lines suggested in the final chapter.

Some political science colleagues in the universities have gently chided me for not dwelling on the large social scientific literature on fascism. A highly selective bibliography from this vast literature is appended. It includes works and articles quoted and cited in the text. However, the general reader should be warned that much of the social science is extremely dry, and very little of it deals with fascist ideas, movements and violence today.

I warmly acknowledge the encouragement and assistance of Adam Sisman of Grant McIntyre publishers, and David Kewley of Pan Books. Their faith in this project and publishing talents made it possible.

Washington DC   P.W.
September 1982

1 THE ENIGMA OF FASCISM

Ludwig Klages once boasted that the Nazis were working 'for the extinction of mankind'. When one remembers the millions who died at the hands of the Hitler regime and its collaborators, and the millions more who died fighting to overthrow the Nazi tyranny, Klages's claim was really a terrible prophecy. Nazism defiantly rejected all the universalist claims of morality, humanity and reason, in favour of a policy of brutal subjugation, mass extermination, and enslavement.

The recent resurgence of fascist movements on the streets of many British cities, the obscene daubings of synagogues and attacks on immigrant communities, and the neo-fascist bombing outrages at Bologna, Munich and Paris, are tragic reminders that the devastating military defeat inflicted on the fascist powers in the Second World War has not been able to totally extinguish fascist beliefs, attitudes and ambitions. Obscene and crazy though it may seem, there still exist, 38 years after Hitler's suicide in the Berlin bunker, small groups of neo-Nazis preaching their poisonous doctrines of racial supremacy, anti-Semitism and world conquest to new generations of recruits. There they are, in Italy, Spain, West Germany, France, Britain, the USA, Belgium, Norway, like so many tiny cancerous cells in the body politic of Western democracies, still working 'for the extinction of mankind'.

When one remembers the crimes against humanity committed in its name is it any wonder that fascism has become for many people a term of abuse, a synonym for those who combine race hatred and a love of brutality with a desire for power? But the problem with using the term merely as a slogan or a curse is that it tends to lose its force. On 28 May 1958, for example, a large crowd marched through the French capital, from the Place de la Nation to the Place de la République, in protest against the moves to bring de Gaulle to power. Mingled with slogans such as *De Gaulle au musée!*, *La girafe au zoo!*, *Vive la République!* and *Front populaire!* was a call that might have startled some foreign observers, *Le fascisme ne passera pas!* Surely, one would ask, the demonstrators knew that de Gaulle was the self-appointed leader of the Free French forces who fought with the Allies against the fascists during the War? Perhaps what they were expressing was a sense of apprehension lest the General might be seeking to turn himself into a dictator like General Franco, or their fears about the extreme right-wing elements that had helped to engineer the coup in Algiers which had brought de Gaulle out of the political wilderness. Some of them may have recalled the strikingly undemocratic character of de Gaulle's post-War right-wing political movement, Rassemblement du Peuple Français (RPF), with its huge para-military style rallies and its personality cult of the General. But even if some of the demonstrators were influenced by these factors, is it really useful to use the term fascist so loosely that it covers any case of a General achieving political leadership, or any right-wing movement exploiting the personality of a charismatic figure?

Events proved that fears of the Fourth Republic giving way to a fascist dictatorship were groundless. De Gaulle went out of his way to secure constitutional legality. His first cabinet was like a roll-call of leading figures from the traditional parties of the Fourth Republic. In the debate in Parliament over de Gaulle's new constitution-making powers as Prime Minister, the crypto-fascist Tixier-Vignancour and Pétain's lawyer, Isorni, bitterly opposed the General. Tixier-Vignancour reminded deputies that he had been disgraced for voting away his powers to another military saviour, Marshal Pétain; how could he now do the same thing again at the orders of the man who had previously condemned him? The French and Algerian fascists and the Organisation de l'Armée Secrète (OAS) ended up by hating de Gaulle more than any other French political leader, not only because of his determination to ensure the continuance of democratically accountable civilian government but also, of course, because of his key role in negotiating the independence of Algeria at the Evian talks.

There are many other examples of misuse of the term 'fascism'. For the far left it is often used as a pejorative for any policy or government they believe to be strongly anti-communist, oppressive or authoritarian. When Socialist Workers' Party demonstrators accuse Mrs Thatcher or Mr Reagan of being fascist we know that it is really a knee-jerk reaction to the policies of these leaders. Used in this way the term is clearly meaningless, and ought to be ignored.

Others sometimes use the term to denote a regime which may show one major trait of fascism very clearly, but which certainly does not see itself as wittingly following fascist ideas, and which has many other features that depart radically from the fascist models. For instance, when General Pinochet took power in Chile the communist front organisation, the International Union of Students, issued posters saying 'Stop the Fascist Terror in Chile!' Now it happens that the Pinochet regime has been one of the most repressive in Latin America. It has a shocking record of torture, imprisonment without trial, and other major violations of human rights. But does this make it a fascist regime? If brutal oppression is to be the major criterion, then would it not be fair to describe a state such as the Soviet Union, or East Germany, or Kampuchea, as fascist? Or Amin's Uganda? Or Bokassa's Central African 'Empire'? All these tyrannies used (or still use) state terror as a routine method of social and political control. But one looks in vain for any evidence that the leaders of these ghastly dictatorships have retained explicitly fascist beliefs, created fascist parties or movements, or consciously identified with the fascist leaders of the past. Pinochet and his collaborators appear to be motivated by the traditional rationale of the *caudillo*, 'national salvation' and 'the restoration of order'.

There has indeed been a fascist movement in Chile for many years, though Pinochet and his colleagues were never part of it: it was called the National Socialist Movement (MNS), or *Nacis*. It was founded in 1932 by a Hispano-German, Jorge González von Marées, who was initially inspired by Hitler's seizure of power in Germany. In 1937 von Marées broke with German National Socialism, claiming that Hitler had become a tyrant, and that henceforth his Chilean movement would follow the path of democracy. Nevertheless, the movement kept its fascist character, claiming that violence was a 'defensive necessity'. It staged an abortive coup against Alessandri's traditional rightist government, with the result that over 50 captured *Nacis* were massacred. Thereafter the *Nacis* supported Aguirre Cerda and the Chilean Popular Front. The MNS was later reconstituted as the Popular Socialist Vanguard, and a tiny Chilean fascist party has survived throughout the post-War years, never succeeding in building a mass base of support and increasingly irrelevant in the traditional left/right dichotomy of Chilean politics of which the Pinochet reaction to Allende is a manifestation. One leading authority has characterised the Pinochet regime as 'strictly pretorian syncretic or semipluralist', and not attempting 'significant new political mobilisation' (Payne, 1980), meaning that it does not evince the degree of centralisation or totalitarian ideology that one finds in true fascist regimes. Even Pinochet's dictatorship leaves some room for interest group conflict and pragmatic change.

The cases of France and Chile illustrate the hazards of using the term fascism loosely and inconsistently or merely as a term of abuse for brutally repressive regimes. Hence it is important to try to define the quintessential beliefs and doctrines common to all fascist movements, old and new. But, in doing this, we must be aware of a number of pitfalls. First we must beware of assuming all these movements conform to a single historical model. It is broadly the case that fascists in America, Latin America and elsewhere have looked to European models and that most of the contemporary new fascist movements enthusiastically emulate Nazism, regard Hitler as their great 'lost leader', and preach virulent anti-Semitism as well as racist propaganda against other chosen scapegoats such as the immigrant communities in Britain, West Germany, and elsewhere. Even the numerous small Italian neo-fascist groups, such as the Avanguardia Nazionale (National Vanguard) or Ordine Nero (Black Order), are blatantly pro-Nazi. For example, Ordine Nero, which claimed responsibility for the bombing of the Rome-Munich express near Bologna in August 1974, killing 12 people and injuring 48, issued a declaration that:

'The Nazi flag did not die in Berlin in 1945. It still lives for a powerful fascist and Nazi Italy. Nazism will return for the salvation of a renaissance Italy (sic).'

Nevertheless in the past there have been other types and styles of fascism, quite different from each other and from the Nazi version, for example in Spain, Italy, Brazil and Argentina. We must be careful to distinguish these different subtypes, as the ways in which they diverge from the German experience may be important to assessing their historical implications and possible influence. Many contemporary new fascisms have attempted to trick themselves out with new labels, styles and tactics in order to pass themselves off as respectable political parties engaged in legitimate electoral competition. For example, this has been the policy of the National Front in Britain, and of the Movimento Sociale Italiano (MSI) in Italy, which has built up a base of mass support to make it the fourth largest political party. But we need to probe beneath the surface to identify the true basic ideas, attitudes and policies of such formations, and to trace the past involvements of their leaders.

The new-found desire for respectability on the part of some of these parties is not merely the result of Machiavellian cunning or artful propaganda: in Italy and West Germany the constitution forbids the reconstituting of a fascist or Nazi political party. Hence legal constraints compel the leaders in these countries to hide their real aims, roots, and connections. Yet, ironically, if they hide their true face too well they stand to lose their traditional hard-core support from fascist militants on which the movements depend. In effect, as we shall observe later, these new fascist umbrella parties are linked in all kinds of ways with the small violent neo-Nazi cells that have been mounting spasmodic terrorism and which have engaged in racist attacks, intimidation, arms robberies and other criminal activities over recent years.

Another problem familiar to the serious student of contemporary extremist movements has been the attitudes of some influential groups to the whole subject of the new fascisms. One must remember that in West Germany and Italy there are still many, some occupying high positions in government and industry, who are embarrassed about their past relations with the fascist regimes and about their activities during the Second World War. War crimes, trials and purges of the ranks of the administration and the professions no doubt weeded out a large number of the major Nazis, especially in the case of West Germany where the occupying powers continued to exert pressure to cleanse the system of National Socialist elements. But they did not begin to touch the large numbers of middle-ranking and lower-level officials who had knowingly and willingly served the Hitler regime, and who by virtue of their professional knowledge and experience as, say, lawyers or civil servants, were needed in post-War Germany. They could easily adjust to working under the new political system under Adenauer, but some never lost their sneaking regard for National Socialist beliefs; anti-Semitism, the *Führerprinzip*, the yearning for a new national dictator, and contempt for parliamentary democracy. Despite the fact that large numbers of returned prisoners-of-war and others were 're-educated' under Allied reconstruction programmes, many

Nazi followers and sympathisers remained outside the net. In Italy, because of the different circumstances of the fascist defeat, there was no equivalent attempt to eliminate all traces of fascist influence, and hence it was even easier than in Germany for the committed and unrepentant fascists to lie low, regroup and launch their post-War movements when the opportunity arose. The same is true of fascists who have survived the fall of the Salazar, Franco and 'Colonel' regimes in Portugal, Spain and Greece.

After the War traditional conservatives, liberals and social democrats in both Italy and West Germany, strongly supported by their colleagues in the industrial and business sectors, were naturally anxious to achieve the most rapid possible rehabilitation of their political and economic systems, in order to gain the maximum benefits of international economic co-operation and alliance in the Western camp against the widely perceived threat of Soviet expansion. To these people the survival of fascist individuals and tendencies was an embarrassment. It was not that politicians like Adenauer or de Gasperi had themselves anything to hide. They simply did not want anything to spoil their countries' progress towards full re-acceptance into the international community. Thus in these quarters any threat of neo-fascist extremism or resurgence was either played down or ignored altogether. Such attitudes were, and still are to some extent, supported by the 'wishful thinkers' who fondly imagine that fascism is really dead in their countries, who cannot conceive of anybody other than a few lunatics and veteran Nazis actually working for a fascist resurgence. Thus there has been considerable complacency concerning threats from the extreme right. People have missed the point that when fascism got started in the 1920s it was almost universally regarded by foreign observers as nothing more than a comic opera performed by a handful of cranks. It tends to be forgotten that fascists have never believed in waiting for a democratic mandate: they believe, as Karl Mannheim once expressed it, that 'History is made neither by the masses, nor by ideas, nor by "silently working" forces, but by the elites who from time to time assert themselves.' One does not need a mass movement to organise a *coup d'état*. Equally, a deadly and destructive campaign of terrorism can be waged by quite small cells. Hence it would be foolish to be lulled into a false sense of security by the repeated inability of fascist movements in most western countries to win more than derisory electoral support. They have a more sinister potential to carry out violence and terrorism in the streets and to provoke conflict in our multi-ethnic urban communities.

Although fascism originated in Europe between the World Wars, reaching its peak of influence and power in Germany and Italy in the 1930s and early 1940s, it would be a cardinal error to assume that fascist doctrines and movements are historical phenomena limited to a particular historical period or to specific countries. I hope to make it clear that the new fascists are currently active, to varying degrees, in almost every western country, in most of Latin America, in South Africa, and even, in a somewhat mutated form, in Japan.

There has been a widespread assumption since the late 1960s that the only serious internal threat to western parliamentary democracies has been from extremists of the left. Only a few brave and determined voices, such as the journal *Searchlight* in Britain and the leaders of the minority communities, have warned repeatedly of the dangers from the revival of racism, anti-Semitism, and neo-Nazism. Not surprisingly, among those who have been the most concerned and best informed regarding these threats have been the religious leaders and spokesmen of the Jewish communities in Western countries, and such organisations as the Anti-Defamation league of B'nai Brith, the Institute of Contemporary History, and other specialist research organisations.

But gathering information which proves, beyond doubt, the widespread occurrence of these sinister tendencies is only the beginning of analysis. How does one *explain* the survival of all these small fascist and neo-Nazi cells and the larger new fascist political parties? What makes them tick? Surely, it will be said, they must realise that they cannot gain any power in a democracy. What rational purpose is served by continuing their clandestine struggles? If they organise and commit acts of violence, they will inevitably become outlaws, constantly in danger of arrest and imprisonment. So why do they bother? After all, it is 40 years since any new fascist regimes were set up in Europe, and they were only the creatures of Nazi Germany's military occupation.

Most political commentators and scholars researching into political violence and extremism have been, perhaps understandably, baffled by the survival of fascist and neo-Nazi extremism 38 years after the defeat of Hitler's Germany. It defies all the established theories and models of political participation and rational political choice elaborated by the political scientists. We perhaps come closer to understanding the durability of these tiny groups if we view them as ideological-religious cult movements sustained by a crude set of irrational dogmas and paradoxically strengthened in their fanaticism by their total alienation from the norms of the modern democratic societies in which they exist. Thus, their obsession with *Führer* figures. Swastika emblems and other *bric-à-brac* of the Nazi period, ritual celebration of Nazi festivals, and their constant preoccupation with violence can be seen both as a means of sustaining the 'Nazi way of life' in a hostile world, and as a preparation for the collapse of democracy, providing the opportunity for an ultimate fascist coup they so ardently believe will occur 'one day'.

The new fascists reject the values and institutions of democracy from the right as totally as the Red Army Faction and the Red Brigades reject them from the extreme left. These people stubbornly believe that democracy and elections are signs of the 'weakness' and 'corruption' of 'the national spirit'. They hanker for a strong man, a national saviour figure who will sweep away the compromises, the slow and peaceful bargaining of democracy, in favour of absolute authority of the leader, a system of regimented discipline and blind obedience, warrior-like virtues, and the determined pursuit of racial or national supremacy through the use of violence. Mussolini enjoined his followers *Credere, Obbedire, Combattere!* ('Believe, Obey, and Fight!') as the fascist answer to the old revolutionary slogan *Liberté, Egalité, Fraternité.* Mussolini's dictum is perhaps the neatest encapsulation of the fascist mentality.

These beliefs present an obvious challenge to democracy, but in this respect they do not differ from the anti-democratic doctrines of the extreme left, or indeed from the key ideas of the traditional authoritarian right. Moreover these beliefs are quite openly, indeed stridently, expressed: they see no point in hiding their hatred and contempt for the system of parliamentary democracy, and their desire to abolish it on gaining power. (Of course, they often simultaneously adopt the tactic of legality, fighting elections as a means of making their cause known, recruiting, and exploiting social and political divisions and discontents. But in no case has a fascist or new fascist movement actually disavowed its ultimate aim of dispensing with parliamentary democracy and free elections.) However, what is infinitely more dangerous about fascism is its racist character. Fascist parties, by actively preaching racial 'purity' and 'supremacism', promote racism, prejudice and discrimination. These evils inevitably and understandably provoke a defensive reaction by the victimised communities. Any group which, in a multi-ethnic society, advocates the ostracism of a scapegoat group or demands its 'repatriation' or deportation is bound to be conducive to political violence. This, of course, is just what the fascists desire, for they believe in violence as a way of life and as living proof of their 'right' to dominate or subjugate other groups. They believe that 'might is right' and that in the struggle for racial survival the 'weakest' must go to the wall. This notion of racial exclusiveness and supremacism is thus inextricably linked with the idea of identifying the alien, the scapegoat, the 'enemy of the people' (*Volksschädling*). In the 1930s and 1940s the scapegoat was primarily the Jews; but although anti-Semitism remains strong, the main victims of the new fascists are immigrants from the West Indies, Asia, and Africa.

Thus an integral part of fascist ideologies is the mission to suppress, enslave, banish, even destroy, any minority cultures. Fascists seek to make some ethnic minorities non-nations, to destroy even their sense of national consciousness and identity, in the frenetic process of glorifying and expanding pursuit of their own national or racial supremacy. Within 'the Fatherland' they seek to centralise control under the leader and impose a total cultural uniformity (*Gleichschaltung*), using the methods of totalitarian social control. All ideas of cultural pluralism and heterogeneity are anathema to them: they wish to eliminate ethnic-culture differences and elements of autonomy just as completely as they desire to abolish independent institutions such as free trade unions, free churches and free universities. In practice the only case of a fascist regime at least partially establishing a thoroughgoing system of totalitarian control was Nazi Germany. Italy, Romania and the other fascist regimes never even began to attain that degree of centralisation, standardisation, and social control. Nevertheless this intolerance of pluralism and cultural diversity is built in to the fascist mentality. A contemporary illustration is to be found in the fanatical opposition of the largest Spanish Falangist movement, Fuerza Nueva (New Force), to the Statute of Autonomy for the Basque region and to other regional autonomy movements such as the Andalusian and Catalonian. In some cases quasi-fascist para-military groups have sprung up to wage terrorism against the separatist para-militaries, as in Corsica and the Basque region.

Fascism is not only intrinsically opposed to the pluralism of secondary groups: it is also in direct conflict with individual rights and freedoms. According to fascist doctrine every individual must be dedicated to the service of the fascist state, personified in the Leader. There is to be no room for individual conscience or critical independence or other individual rights. According to fascism, every citizen's duty is total obedience to the state: the individual should willingly sacrifice everything, including life itself, if it is demanded for the greater glory of the fascist nation as interpreted and directed by the *Führer*. This is spelt out with appalling clarity in the Nazi *Beamtenkalender* (1937):

'Since there is, in the national-socialist state, no difference, let alone opposition, between the state as a separate legal structure and the totality of citizens and the individual citizen; since the state consists here of the totality of citizens united in a common destiny, by a common blood, and a common philosophy of life and comprised in a single organisation, it is neither necessary or possible to define a sphere of freedom for the individual citizen.'

Mussolini's article on 'The Doctrine of Fascism', published in *Enciclopedia Italiana* (1932), contains a similar assertion:

'The keystone of fascist doctrine is the conception of the state .... For fascism the state is an absolute before which individuals and groups are relative.'

Yet even this transcendentalist view of the state as the highest realisation, to which all other groups, individual and social institutions must be subordinated, is not unique to fascism. It was first fully articulated by the German philosopher Hegel, and later developed by the French 'integral nationalism' of Charles Maurras (1868–1952) and Auguste-Maurice Barrès (1862–1923). Maurras, one of the founders of the integral nationalist review *L'Action Française*, anticipated fascist doctrines with his emphasis on the supremacy of the state and the primacy of the interests of his own nation-state above those of all other nations. In common with the fascists the 'integral nationalists' believed that, in a certain sense, the state is prior to the nation, and that the state itself, through its leader or ruling elite, is engaged in a continuous process of heightening national expansion and glory. These were precisely the same beliefs that drove extreme nationalists to clamour for war in nineteenth century Germany, Austria, Hungary, Russia, and elsewhere. Sometimes this chauvinism led to jingoist attempts to expand overseas empire, as with Britain in eastern and southern Africa, France in the Mahgrib, and Italy in its disastrous first attempt at the conquest of Ethiopia. But in central and eastern Europe attempts at national expansion were made at the expense of neighbouring states' territory, and hence provoked a succession of wars, culminating in the catastrophe of 1914.

No portrayal of fascism's core ideas would be adequate if it did not identify those beliefs and attitudes that differentiate fascism from these corrupt and aggressive nationalisms so fashionable in the late nineteenth century. One of the distinctive attitudes of all fascist movements, and a major source of their appeal to certain groups, is their all-consuming hatred of communist parties and regimes, and their claim that they are the only ones capable of saving the nation from the horrors of a Bolshevik revolution. The communist doctrine of class struggle is anathema to fascists for fairly obvious reasons. They see it as dividing and weakening national solidarity, and ultimately leading to the destruction of national sovereignty and identity. Proletarian internationalism is a concept diametrically opposed to the fascist doctrines of the natural inequality of nations, and the inevitability and desirability of the struggle for national supremacy. Fascists regard communist doctrines of equality and the brotherhood of man as subversive of a healthy and warrior-like national spirit. In the fascist's mind men and nations are born unequal: it is for the 'supermen' or super-race to rule, while it is the task of the masses to obey blindly and sacrifice to the greater glory of leader and nation.

In the 1920s and 1930s fascist movements were particularly successful in playing on the fears of the lower middle classes that their status would be destroyed in the impending cataclysms of economic collapse and communist revolution. In the devastating depression of the 1930s it was fairly easy for the fascist leaders to find a recruiting ground among those who felt in imminent danger of proletarianisation. ·

Moreover they were skilful enough as propagandists to try to outbid communist and socialist appeals to the masses by promising a 'third way' to restore prosperity and economic self-respect. Fascist economic programmes were always a hotch-potch, so full of contradiction and ambiguity that they do not bear serious economic analysis. Yet in political *propaganda* terms they often worked quite effectively by deceiving sections of the working classes that they, the fascists, could deliver economic justice – something that what they disparagingly termed the 'old gang', the traditional parties of left and right, had failed to do. Thus Hiltler's National Socialist *Workers* Party was decked out with promises of full employment and economic security, and ambitious public works and national welfare schemes.

It was not merely the Nazi Party that wooed the working classes in the name of promoting class solidarity as a key to national regeneration. The founder-leader of the Spanish fascist movement, the Falange, José Antonio Primo de Rivera, provides one of numerous examples of fascist leaders making a powerful populist appeal for support among the industrial urban masses:

'Finally, the liberal state came to offer us economic slavery, saying to the workers, with tragic sarcasm: you are free to work as you wish; no one can compel you to accept specified conditions. Since we are the rich, we offer you the conditions that please us; as free citizens, you are not obliged to accept them if you do not want to; but as poor citizens, if you do not accept them you will die of hunger, surrounded of course by the utmost liberal dignity . . . . Therefore socialism had to appear, and its coming was just (for we do not deny any evident truth). The workers had to defend themselves against a system that only promised them right and did not strive to give them a just life. However, socialism, which was a legitimate reaction against liberal slavery, went astray because it resulted, first, in the materialist interpretation of life and history; second, in a sense of reprisal; and third, in the proclamation of the dogma of class struggle . . . . '

Primo de Rivera went on to summon all classes in Spain to join in 'total unity' in the *Patria* which 'cannot be in the hands of the strongest class or of the best organised party.' And later in the same speech he said:

'Henceforth let no one think that we recruit men in order to offer rewards; let no one imagine that we join together in defence of privileges. I should like to have this microphone before me carry my voice into every working-class home to say: yes, we wear a tie; yes, you may say of us that we are *senoritos*. But we urge a spirit of struggle for things that cannot concern us as *senoritos*; we come to fight so that hard and just sacrifices may be imposed on many of our own class, and we come to struggle for a totalitarian state that can reach the humble as well as the powerful with its benefits . . . . '
(quoted in Weber, 1964)

There is much that is reminiscent of the early fascist propaganda of Mussolini in these passages: the same allegations that the liberal state has cheated the working class, and the same explicit call for a totalitarian state. But the whole emphasis on working-class appeal is a feature of all fascist movements. As one authority on the history of fascism observes:

' . . . we should do well to remember that fascism never denied its early social radicalism. On the contrary, it considered itself a form of socialism, freed of humanitarian sentimentalism and Marxist dialectic, truer to fundamental socialist aims in that it tried to adapt itself to a changing historical reality which the old Marxist interpretation no longer suited . . . . ' (Weber, 1964)

It is not really so surprising that fascist movements should have been so anxious to steal some of the more attractive promises of socialism for their own programmes. Many fascist leaders had, after all, sprung from socialist parties and groupings. Mussolini had been a socialist newspaper editor and agitator. The French fascist leader, Jacques Doriot, leader of the PPF (French Popular Party), was a renegade communist. Marcel Déat, his main fascist competitor and leader of the Rassemblement National Populaire, was a former socialist, as was Oswald Mosley, who from 1929 to 1930 held ministerial office in Ramsay MacDonald's Labour Government, only three years before forming his new fascist party in Britain. In a period of acute economic depression and mass unemployment throughout western Europe fascist leaders were well aware of the potential to exploit growing discontent and despair in the coming struggle for power on the streets. In doing so they adapted many techniques of mass political propaganda and organisation that they had learnt from the socialists. Hitler confesses in *Mein Kampf*:

'With what changed feeling I now gazed at the endless columns of a mass demonstration of Viennese workers that took place one day as they marched past four abreast! For nearly two hours I stood there watching with bated breath the gigantic demonstration slowly winding by.'

He goes on to explain how this dramatic demonstration of the influence of the social democrats in Vienna impelled him to read its press, and study its techniques. Hitler is repelled by socialist ideas, yet cannot suppress his admiration for the socialists' skill in mass propaganda and mobilisation, and their use of the trade union weapon:

'By my twentieth year I had learned to distinguish between a union as a means of defending the general social rights of the wage-earner, and obtaining better living conditions for him as an individual, and the trade union as an instrument of the party in the political class struggle.

The fact that social democracy understood the enormous importance of the trade union movement assured it of this instrument and hence of success; the fact that the bourgeoisie were not aware of this cost them their political position.'

Not only did many fascist *leaders* have a previous history of involvement in socialist organisations. In some cases one can also trace a connection between workers' organisations and fascist groups. For example, one of the Spanish groups which formed JONS (Juntas de Ojensiva Nacional Sindicalistas) was La Conquista, led by Ledesma Ramos. This group was anti-bourgeois, anti-clerical and anti-Marxist. It was ultra-nationalist, advocating a return to the Spanish grandeur of the Golden Age, but it also demanded the expropriation of estates, and the syndicalisation of the masses. Ledesma's group and Onesimo Redondo's Liberty Movement, which joined to form JONS, merged with the Falange in 1934. Ledesma drafted a programme which alienated traditional Spanish conservatives because it included promises of radical reform and social justice.

However, only a fool would have been deceived by these trappings of socialism. Despite its mixture of confused and contradictory declarations the Falange was in reality a para-military organisation dedicated to the establishment of a centralised and all-powerful Spanish state. Like all true fascist parties it was passionately eager to use terror to defeat its enemies on the left and to impose a totalitarian system on society. The fact is that every fascist movement sees itself performing a special mission to 'save' the nation from the 'horrors' of Marxism and communism. Most are ready to use the most brutal violence to suppress these movements. Fascists hold them responsible for the 'evils' of class struggle, egalitarianism and internationalism. In addition those fascist movements which share the anti-Semitic beliefs of the Nazis also portray international communism and socialism as products of a worldwide Jewish conspiracy. Fascism and Nazism are implacably opposed to socialism and communism, and always have been. Alan Bullock's masterly summary of Hitler's attitude towards Marxism and communism applies with equal force to the position of every fascist movement, past and present, on this question:

'While Hitler's attitude towards liberalism was one of contempt, towards Marxism he showed an implacable hostility. The difference is significant. Liberalism he no longer regarded as a serious threat; its values had lost their attraction in the age of mass politics, especially in Germany, where liberalism had never had deep roots. Marxism, however, whether represented by revisionist social democracy or revolutionary communism, was a rival *Weltanschauung* able to exert a powerful attractive force over the masses comparable with that of Nazism. Ignoring the profound differences between communism and social democracy in practice and the bitter hostility between rival working-class parties, he saw in their common ideology the embodiment of all that he detested – mass democracy and a levelling egalitarianism as opposed to the authoritarian state and the rule of an elite; equality and friendship among peoples as opposed to racial inequality and the domination of the strong; class solidarity versus national unity; internationalism versus nationalism.'

It cannot be emphasised too much that the fascists have a quite different conception of the nature and role of ideology from that of the Marxists. In the Marxist lexicon, ideology is only adequately understood as a manifestation of 'false consciousness' reflecting the prevailing conditions of material production, and as a rationalisation and self-legitimation of the ruling class. For the classical Marxists ideology was thus something to be overcome, outgrown and discarded, as the revolutionary movement broke free into the true science of

Marxist theory. But for fascist leaders and propagandists, man has an intrinsic and over-riding need for meaning, a sense of purpose, a guide to collective action and individual conduct, an inspiration to struggle and sacrifice 'for the glory of the nation'. The fascists are not only willing to recognise the irrational element in this notion of political ideology as a surrogate religion or creed: they positively embrace its mythic and anti-intellectual character. Hitler and Goebbels were particularly adept at exploiting fascist ideology as a potent political weapon, and using the full repertoire of necromancy, indoctrination and terror, created and manipulated myths and blatant lies, in order to control the masses.

Hitler's cynical conception of ideology is shown in his description in *Mein Kampf* of the technique of 'scapegoating', which he and his Nazi followers applied to the Jews with such horrifying consequences:

'The more unified the application of a people's will to fight, the greater will be the magnetic attraction of a movement and the mightier will be the impetus of the thrust. It belongs to the genius of a great leader to make even adversaries far removed from one another seem to belong to a single category, because in weak and uncertain characters the knowledge of having different enemies can only too readily lead to the beginning of doubt in their own right. Once the wavering mass sees itself in a struggle against too many enemies, objectivity will put in an appearance, throwing open the question whether all others are really wrong and only their own people or their own movement are in the right. And this brings about the first paralysis of their own power. Hence a multiplicity of different adversaries must always be combined so that in the eyes of one's own supporters the struggle is directed against only one enemy . . . . '

But it would be quite wrong to assume that the fascist's preoccupation with mass propaganda and techniques of manipulation is evidence of a complete ideological promiscuity, a willingness to trade in any idea or policy that could help them in their relentless struggle for power. This would be a fundamental misunderstanding of fascist ideology. For while the overwhelming majority of fascist leaders play on mythic themes such as *Patria*, *Volk* or 'Race', which they believe will appeal to the instincts of the masses, and *select* their policies and slogans to serve more immediate goals, they are passionately committed to establishing a fascist order and way of life, pursuing power often with a demonic violence and terror. Hitler's assertion, when he invaded Czechoslovakia, that this was his 'last territorial demand in Europe' is just one example of his readiness to lie when it was politically expedient. There is also a kind of finality to fascist beliefs. Few, if any, examples have been recorded of fascist leaders, hierarchs and intellectuals having renounced their fascism, though the post-War German and Italian experience shows that rank-and-file support and mass sympathy for fascism *can* be destroyed by the defeat of the fascist regime and the destruction and discrediting of its leaders.

Yet fascism cannot be understood adequately in terms of its central beliefs and aims. Fascists have never been content to articulate a passive *Weltanschauung*. Flamboyantly anti-intellectual, they constantly proclaim the superiority of action over theory, of will over metaphysics. Their essential vehicle for their activism is, of course, the fascist party or movement. Every fascism manifests itself in some political organisation purpose-built to attain fascist objectives. It is not a characteristic of fascists simply to establish study groups or philosophical cells. Nor are they content merely to serve as undercover fascists in other political parties: their only aims in regard to other parties, political movements or pressure groups are either to destroy them completely, or, if they believe they can be made useful to a fascist regime, to take them over completely and convert them into mere organs of their own rule. (The Nazis employed the latter technique to the German labour and youth movements in the 1930s.) Nevertheless, there is a constant contradiction between the fascists' emphasis on the importance of the party as being something considerably more than a mere political party – the movement of the elite activists, the chosen instrument of the leader and the master race or nation – and the drive towards ruthless centralisation and a totalitarian monopoly of state power in the hands of the leader. Though Mussolini never succeeded in attaining totalitarian control over Italian society, he was often in conflict with the impatience and ambitions of the militants in the fascist squads he himself had helped to create. Ultimately under fascist dictatorships the party faithful become mere agents of ritual leader-worship, mass mobilisation and social control. Any official or local organiser who even appears to represent a potential challenge to the central control of the leader is ruthlessly eliminated, and thus any notion of the party as being the keeper of the pristine doctrine or the arbiter of policy is out of the question.

This 'conveyor-belt' model of the role of the fascist party breaks down, however, in the case of the fascist-supported regime, when the leader brought to power by *coup d'état* is at the head of a broader coalition of the armed forces, big business, and other groups. In such cases (for example Franco's Spain or Peron's Argentina) the fascist movement remains an increasingly frustrated and impatient minority pressure group, some of whom may be silenced by being 'co-opted' into posts within the regime while others become seen as a threat to the dictatorship and are therefore imprisoned, executed, or forced to flee abroad.

A third model, the one which has become characteristic of fascist movements since the Second World War, is the tiny marginal party of still tinier coteries. In this type of party the lack of a single *Führer* figure generally recognised as such by all the activists and supporters is both a manifestation and a partial cause of their powerlessness. What happens is that a handful of would-be leaders vie for control of the party, as in the case of John Tyndall's pathetic attempts to become the British *Führer*. Megalomaniac contenders typically compete with each other to build up personal followings and to gain control over party structures, funds, and publications. Differences over interpretation of fascist ideology, choice of tactics and programmes are often important, but they are also closely interwoven with the in-fighting of the leading personalities, and it is the latter who, by the nature of fascism, arrive at the revised formulations and applications of the fascist doctrine and impose them on their followers by diktat.

These tensions between fascist ideology, policy and leadership are clearly demonstrated by their attitudes towards economics. Here again the fascist movements of the past, particularly if they came to power, were faced by contradictions. In practice there was no universally accepted fascist economic programme. Every movement tended to follow its nose, making up the policy as it went along. Fascist leaders always claimed to be on the side of the ordinary man against the concentrations of power in the hands of capitalists. They promised that when in power they would establish control over the economy for the good of the nation as a whole. Mussolini, in his article on 'The Political and Social Doctrine of Fascism' (1932) asserted rather grandiosely:

'The fascist state has drawn into itself even the economic activities of the nation, and through the corporative social and educational institutions created by it, its influence reaches every aspect of the national life and includes, framed in their respective organisations, all the political, economic and spiritual forces of the nation.'

While it is certainly true that Hitler managed to create full employment with his public works and rearmament, and to make Germany more self-sufficient, in fascist regimes generally economic policies have been a succession of improvisations and reactions to crises adapted to meet different national ambitions. In no case has a fascist regime attempted to suppress capitalism. Big firms that are prepared to work co-operatively with the fascist leadership have been allowed to continue much as before, sometimes with fewer restraints and curbs on profit than existed in pre-fascist times, and often, as in the case of the armaments industry, with the added 'incentives' of a huge rearmament programme and even the provision of slave labour from concentration camps. In Hitler's Germany the giant industrial manufacturers soon became locked in an incestuous relationship with the Nazi regime, and by the mid-1930s they were pouring cash into Nazi coffers to show their appreciation to their new masters.

Practically the only economic doctrine the fascists formulated which could be said to have been original to them was that of the corporatist state. The doctrine had its origin in a fusion of fascist and syndicalist ideas. In Italy, and to a lesser extent also in France and Spain, some of the early fascist leaders had enjoyed intimate links with the syndicalist workers' movements which developed so strongly in the period 1906–21. Mussolini had cut his political teeth in this wing of Italian socialism, and a section of the syndicalist movement in Spain became a part of the earliest fascist movement. When in power some fascists adapted the syndicalist concept of workers' associations expressing the collective, as against the individualist, needs and aspirations of the workers, to the needs of a centralised ultra-nationalist fascist state. Mussolini and the Italian fascists found this a particularly convenient notion. But of course they did not want workers' organisations that were genuinely autonomous. What fascists sought was an organisational structure for industrial control which, under the firm direction of the leader, could apply and police the application of the fascist government's norms and priorities while appearing to be carrying out the corporate decisions of the workers themselves. One of the leading Italian fascist exponents of this approach was Alfredo Rocco, who explained it thus:

' . . . Any idea of abolishing the syndicalist movement is inconceivable. It is a phenomenon of so far-reaching an extent in the life of our times as to be irrepressible, and on the other hand, it must be judged for itself and not in its aberrations .... The state must return to its traditions, interrupted by the triumph of liberal ideology, and treat the modern syndicates exactly as it treated the medieval corporations. It must absorb them and make them part of the state .... On the one hand, syndicates must be recognized as essential and on the other they must be placed firmly beneath the control of the state, which must lay down their precise functions and ensure that their role of watchdog and guardian should be held within fixed limits .... above all it is necessary to change them from aggressive bodies defending particular interests into a means of collaboration to adhere to common aims.' (Rocco, 1920)

Rocco went on to outline the fascist pattern favoured by the Italian movement: workers' and employers' syndicates joined together within each industry to form a single 'functional' syndicate, in which managers, technicians and all other grades would be 'represented'. However, this industry syndicate was not to function democratically or autonomously. In order to achieve 'common aims' actions must be directed by a single committee or board of directors. In reality every corporatist organ in the Mussolini regime had to conform to the norms on wages and production dictated by the fascist government. The fact is that the whole economy was riddled with inconsistencies, due to the inefficiency and confused policies of the fascist regime itself. No other fascist party saw fit to take over the Italian corporatist doctrine, though partially corporatist frameworks for the organisation of industry were adopted in very different forms in Pétain's Vichy regime in France (1940–4), and in Franco's Spain.

Thus, the fascists had few original ideas on economics. In bidding for mass support they claimed to offer an alternative to 'failed' capitalist-individualism and the bogey of socialism-communism, yet in practice the fascist regimes found it expedient to allow capitalism to provide the economic power for their wars of expansion.

Contradictions also inevitably arise in the relations between fascist ideology and foreign policy. As each movement identified with its own nation and national mission of expansion, it is not really surprising to find that it is only at the most basic level that there is any evidence of a shared outlook among fascist movements and regimes on foreign policy. Their doctrines of national or racial superiority and the necessity of war as a struggle for the survival of the fittest naturally dispose them to justify and promote wars of annexation and imperial conquest. Mussolini believed he had a mission to rebuild a new Roman Empire in north Africa and the Mediterranean. Until the defeat of the Axis powers, Franco planned to develop a new Spanish sphere of influence in the Mahgrib. The militarist-imperialist group who took control in Japan in the 1930s and whose ideas had so much in common with European fascism set their sights on creating a 'Greater South-East Asian Co-prosperity Sphere' (a new empire in the Far East). Hitler's aims included the establishment of the Germans as a master race with a vast new land empire, enslaving of the non-German peoples of eastern and central Europe and then occupying their land as 'living-space' for the *Reich*.

Not all fascist movements, thank God, have taken up the terrifying annihilatory doctrines of full-blown German National Socialism. But without exception they do present themselves as the champions and would-be saviours of aggrieved 'have-not' nations, peoples 'robbed' of their 'right' to colonisation, or 'victims' of unjust imposition of frontiers or of economic discrimination. Thus, without exception, fascists are opposed to movements of universalistic internationalism and co-operation, such as the United Nations, or its predecessor, the League of Nations. They seek conflict rather than peace, and national or racial dominance over others rather than equality of peoples, and the only *formal* bond that held the fascist powers together for a brief period was the Anti-Comintern Pact. Italy, Germany, and Japan had all walked out of the League of Nations when the organisation tried to impede their expansionist plans.

Last, but by no means the least important of the characteristics common to all fascist movements is their subordination of women. Every fascist movement and regime has viewed women as unfit to occupy the leading positions in the party and the state. The female role is seen to be almost entirely centred on the home, family, and the bearing and upbringing of children to sustain the purity and strength of the nation or the race. Women are assumed not to have the warrior virtues necessary to engage in the constant wars of expansion necessitated by the mission of national glory. Fascism is a world of men who believe in a world run by supermen. The solitary exception sometimes mentioned is Evita Peron in Argentina, though the Peron regime was not fascist in the full sense, merely fascist-supported.

It will have become clear from the above discussion that fascism is an extremely broad concept embracing a great diversity of movements and regimes, each of which will emphasise different elements of fascist doctrine in their appeal. Historically, the major division within fascism has been between German-style National Socialism and the Mussolini model of latin fascism. The Nazi movement can obviously be differentiated from the latin movements by virtue of its fanatical anti-Semitism, and its belief in the racial superiority of the 'Aryan' or Nordic race; the German race in particular, who were to be the *Herrenvolk* in a new world order based on a hierarchy of racial domination. The Nazis' hatred of and violence towards the Jews culminated in the Holocaust, which was an act of genocide unparalleled in European history. Moreover, in pursuit of these terrifyingly evil aims the Hitler state achieved a degree of totalitarian control over society unequalled by any other fascist system before or since. Nazism can therefore be viewed as the most fully developed form of fascism; and thankfully not all fascist parties or regimes, even then or subsequently, share the same qualities and characteristics.

However, when one surveys the contemporary fascist movements which are the subject of this book, one is struck by the fact that the overwhelming majority have fully assimilated and identified with Nazi ideas. They regard Hitler as the greatest ever fascist leader and unquestioningly accept Nazi doctrines of anti-Semitism and all the other Nazi mumbo-jumbo of race 'theory'. Even in the Latin American fascist movements, which in the 1930s and 1940s were almost wholly guided by the *Hispanidad* model imported from the Spanish Falange, Nazi ideas have taken root. Perhaps the single exception to this is the Japanese mutation of fascism, in which doctrines of anti-Semitism and Aryan race purity inevitably make no sense whatever (though they have an interesting Japanese analogue).

One of the modern trends, however, has been for movements seeking a mass following or fighting democratic elections to drop the terms 'Nazi' or 'Fascist' entirely from their vocabulary. The fascist label is of course unacceptable for constitutional reasons in Italy and West Germany. But in other countries fascists often seek to avoid the designation fascist as they fear the title would undermine their efforts to establish an image of respectability and moderation among the electorate. We should not allow ourselves to be misled by these surface tactics or image-building devices of certain fascist movements. I shall be including in this survey many movements that are sailing under quite different names, but this is done on the basis of strong evidence about the fascistic nature of their ideas, attitudes and record.

There are two other matters of usage that must be disposed of briefly. First, many commentators have been using the term fascism very loosely in recent years to describe much of the vandalism and sheer thuggery that has appeared in the football terraces and streets of our major cities. I believe this is a misuse of terms. It is only really accurate to use the term 'fascism' to refer to such violence when the perpetrators are clearly affiliated to or consciously motivated by fascist political aims and beliefs. Similarly the term 'fascism of the left' has often been applied by commentators such as Professor Hugh Seton-Watson and others. This is also, in my view, unhelpful to our understanding of fascism as such. Of course it is true that some extreme left groups share with fascists a hatred of democracy, a love of street confrontation and violence for its own sake, and, in some cases, a propensity for terrorism. But this does not make those of the extreme left fascists. We must take some account of the political beliefs and aims of the groups involved, and, needless to say, it is precisely because the extreme left and extreme right loathe each other's ideas that they fight each other on every possible occasion.

2 FASCISM'S GOLDEN AGE

What were the political, social and economic conditions which led to the rise of fascism in its original inter-war phase? By what means did fascist movements succeed in gaining power in Italy, Germany, and in other countries, such as Hungary and Romania? How influential were these as 'models' for fascist movements in other countries? This chapter will address these important historical aspects of fascism quite briefly, in the knowledge that there now exists a vast and authoritative literature on almost every phase which the reader can consult. Nevertheless, it is important to emphasise that it is impossible to understand the meaning and implications of contemporary fascism unless one commands some basic knowledge of those movements that rose to the zenith of their power in the 1930s and 1940s, together with their historical legacies. One does not have to be a believer in Marxist historical determinism to be persuaded that history sometimes repeats itself, and our present grave economic crises, international and domestic, are, alas, sowing the seeds of instability and extremist reaction in ways alarmingly similar to those fostered by the world slump of 1929–34. Moreover, the rise of fascism to power is such a relatively recent phenomenon, and its effects on the political psychology of those who experienced it directly so traumatic, that its direct and indirect effects on domestic politics and international relations are still working through. As for the contemporary fascist movements themselves: almost without exception they stridently proclaim their belief that 'Hitler was right'. So it is helpful to have some knowledge of the historical record which they so stridently defend and with which they so proudly identify themselves.

One major factor conducive to the growth of fascism, with its ultra-nationalist appeal, was the deep sense of bitterness and frustration left in a number of countries as a result of the territorial settlement following the First World War. This resentment was not confined to the defeated powers. Some of the smaller states among the victorious powers also felt cheated by the peace treaties. The Italians, for example, had hoped for far greater gains following its war-time sacrifices and strains. Orlando, the Italian representative at the peace conference in Paris, returned without any tangible rewards to show in the form of colonies, mandates, or guaranteed access to raw materials essential to Italy's industrial development. Yet in the broader sense Italy should have been relieved at the results of the War. The removal of her traditional opponent to the north, the Austro-Hungarian Empire, gave her (as Count Cforza, Italian foreign minister from 1920 to 1921, fully understood) much greater national security than ever before, and the prospect of playing the leading role in the international politics of the Balkans. Unfortunately, many of those Italians who, like Mussolini, had been vociferous advocates of Italian entry into the War on the Allies' side, now felt that they were being treated as a second-class nation by plutocratic major powers, and robbed of their just rewards. Frustration over the outcome of the War was all the greater because Italy had entered the War against the wishes of the majority in parliament and the country. The *interventisti* had only prevailed because they had the consent of the King and support from a powerful group of idealists, democrats, some ex-socialists under Mussolini's leadership, trade unionists, and a powerful conservative group led by Salandra. Popular discontent was aggravated by the grave socio-economic strains imposed by the War. The government's economic policy during the War had been to allow all available resources to be handed over to the major industrial firms with booming war-time production needs. A huge budget deficit and rampant inflation confronted the politicians with unprecedented economic difficulties. While big business interests had been allowed to prosper mightily, the general population became increasingly impoverished, and the government failed to keep its war-time promise to hand over land to poor peasants. Industrial wage-earners had also been very hard-hit during the War. Thus, after the War in many areas industrial workers and poorer peasants combined forces to demand a revolution that would remove the bourgeoisie from power. As for the middle classes and intellectuals, many of those who had supported entry into the War were now disillusioned by the results of the peace conference and alarmed at the prospects of a social revolution that would threaten them with proletarianization. Thus, so far as Italy was concerned, the effects of the War were conducive to fascism not as the result of a psychosis of defeat and territorial losses but through its exacerbation of latent social tensions and economic stresses which, even without the problems of war, would have been the inevitable concomitant of Italy's efforts to modernise her backward, unevenly developed economy.

Nazism as a mass movement can also be seen as, in large part, a protest at the outcome of the First World War and the diktat of Versailles. In *Les Enfants Humiliés* Georges Bernanos observed that Hitler was a man who, at the outset of the Second World War, was still re-fighting the First. Hitler was obsessed not only with his desire to exterminate the Jews, but also with the aim of avenging Germany's disastrous defeat and humiliation in the First World War. He exploited the psychosis of German resentments and frustrations about the War with all the rabble-rousing oratory he could command. In *Mein Kampf* and in speech after speech he claimed to speak for the German front-line soldiers who had sacrificed their lives in the War. He bitterly attacked the politicians in Berlin, elaborating the myth that they stabbed an undefeated German army in the back by capitulating to the Allies, and claiming that this was the result of a conspiracy of Jews, socialists, and other 'foreign' elements.

'Was this the meaning of the sacrifice which the German mother made to the fatherland when with sore heart she let her best-loved boys march off, never to be seen again? Did all this happen only so that a gang of wretched criminals could lay their hands on the fatherland?'

Hitler argued that Germany was compelled to sign the dictated peace of Versailles at the point of a sword. This humiliation was, he claimed, the result not of a defeat by arms but of a betrayal by the civilian politicians, the financiers, and the Jews. These people, Hitler asserted, were always those who put profit before country. The Nazi propaganda against Versailles squeezed every drop of latent frustration and hurt national pride out of the myth of the victimisation and betrayal of Germany. Even while the Treaty was being negotiated, Germany was excluded from participation and her children were being wantonly massacred by the Allies' blockade. The diktat was designed by the malevolent Allies to ruin Germany. Hallowed German soil was stolen from her. Her land was cut in two. She was robbed of her colonies and her industries and markets were smashed. Intolerable burdens of reparations were heaped upon her. Forcibly disarmed, she was left a prey to both external enemies and internal disorder. And, as if these humiliations were not enough, Germany was compelled to accept sole blame for the War. So Hitler argued.

Hitler made enormous political capital out of his repeated attacks on Versailles and the 'system' of the Allies which had imposed it. He presented himself as the only person who could save the German people from this humiliating defeat. He alone would unite and redeem them, and win back the dignity of arms and the respect and status commensurate with Germany's true role as a great power. This line of argument was by no means sufficient in itself to bring the Nazis to power, but it is important to understand the key role this challenge against Versailles and the 'system' played in Hitler's message to the German masses. It provided a ready-made justification for an aggressive policy of rearmament and the use of force: this was the only way of restoring Germany's just rights. She must take back what was rightly hers. It provided a convenient defence of the remilitarisation of the Rhine, the Anschluss with Austria, the invasion of Czechoslovakia and Poland. Was not Germany just reclaiming what already belonged to her?

In eastern Europe also, fascist movements were able to exploit popular resentment against the post-War settlements. For instance, Ferenc Szalasi's Arrow Cross movement, which developed a mass base in the 1930s, found ready support for its militant rejection of the Treaty of Trianon (1920). The latter had effectively reduced Hungary from a population of 21 million to one of 8 million. (The amount of territory Hungary was forced to cede to Romania, Transylvania and half of the Banat, actually amounted to a larger area than that which remained to Hungary! Hungary also lost Croatia and the Vojvodina to Yugoslavia, and Ruthenia and Slovakia to Czechoslovakia. She was forced to limit her army to 35,000 men, and was made liable for reparations.) And the Croatian Ustase, who with Italian help mounted an international terrorist campaign against Yugoslavia in the 1920s and 1930s and in 1941 set up an 'Independent Croatia' which became notorious for its atrocities against other Yugoslav nationalities, mounted its own challenge to the peace settlement. The struggle of the Ustase in their fascist phase was concentrated against the Yugoslav kingdom, which had been granted sovereignty over their region in the post-War peace treaty.

The Japanese form of fascism, too, was spurred on by a fierce resentment against China and the western Allies for blocking the Japanese attempt to impose a protectorate over China between the Wars. Indeed, resentment and rebellion against the Versailles system was the major common denominator among all the successful fascist movements, i.e. those that actually achieved power over their respective states. On the other hand it was by no means a necessary condition for the development of fascist movements as such. The existence of such movements as Mosley's British Union of Fascists and the American Nazi Party in the 1930s are evidence that these phenomena could take root even in modernised industrial 'victor' states. And, of course, the growth of indigenous fascist movements in countries like Spain, Portugal, Ireland, Brazil, Argentina and Chile, shows that not even participation in a major international war was a necessary condition for such ideologies to grow.

A second conducive factor for the development of fascism was the depression. This was more far-reaching than any other economic recession before or since (though it is conceivable that the present recession will ultimately bring comparable economic collapse and chaos unless appropriate international action is taken to pull the world economy out of its nosedive). In 1928–9 there was a dramatic fall in agricultural and timber prices, partly brought on by over production of wheat in the USA and Canada which forced down grain prices worldwide. This agricultural recession was worsened by a general financial collapse, in which, again, events in the USA provided the trigger: a fever of Wall Street speculation led to a withdrawal of funds from Europe and thereafter, in October 1929, to the Wall Street Crash. French banks withdrew short-term credits to Credit Anstalt, a major Austrian bank, which then failed to meet its obligations. As a result many institutions in eastern and central Europe went bankrupt. German bankers felt compelled to repudiate foreign liabilities by a moratorium, and this hit British bankers very badly, as they had heavy investments in Germany. All through 1931 there was a run on the pound. Shortage of capital led to a fall in exports and internal consumption in all industrial countries. This led to widespread factory closures, and also to big cutbacks in shipping and shipbuilding, because of the resulting fall in trade. Every industrial country inevitably faced dramatic rises in unemployment, with all its attendant social problems and political protest and frustrations. In 1932 unemployment reached 2.8 million in Britain, 13.7 million in the USA, and 5.6 million in Germany. In the latter, and in certain other central and eastern European countries, the economic crisis led to intensified political instability and provided an enormous boost in support for fascist parties promising panaceas of radical authoritarian economic nationalism aimed at *autarky* (economic self-sufficiency) and the creation of a war economy. Hitler had begun exploiting the psychosis of fear and economic insecurity in 1930, as the German unemployment figure reached 3 million. He promised the desperate masses work, bread and a better future. By 1932 the middle classes in Germany were flocking away from the traditional conservative and centrist parties to vote for Hitler's National Socialists, both because they saw the Nazi's as a bulwark against communist revolution and because they believed in Hitler's promises of decisive and effective measures for economic salvation. In the three years 1929–32 the Nazi Party (NSDAP) attracted 75 per cent of the former centre and rightist party voters, so that in the election of July 1932 they were able to capture 37.4 per cent of all votes cast. This phenomenal switch is best shown in tabulated form (Broszat, 1980):

The decline of the middle-class parties and the rise of the fascists in Germany 1928–32

Reichstag elections	Socialist parties (per cent)	Nazi party (per cent)	Centre party (per cent)	Other middle-class parties (per cent)
20.5.1928	40.5	2.6	15.1	41.8
14.9.1930	37.6	18.3	14.8	29.3
31.7.1932	36.2	37.4	15.7	10.7

Yet even the most severe economic depression is not a sufficient or even a necessary condition for the rise of fascism. We have already noted that in the USA, where the depression may be said to have had its origins, unemployment reached as high as 13.7 million in 1932, yet the American fascist movement remained a tiny lunatic fringe. And fascism made little or no headway in Britain, Australia, Canada or the Scandinavian countries, despite the fact that they all experienced relatively high levels of unemployment in this period. In Spain and Portugal fascism did not really get well under way until the worst effects of the depression had passed; even then, despite their coalition with powerful authoritarian forces and the help they received from fascist regimes abroad, neither fascist party succeeded in taking complete control of the government and applying a comprehensive fascist policy. And in Italy fascism came to power long before the depression, and it was the economic stresses created by the War that provided the fertile ground in which fascism could grow. Italian industrial workers were actually worse off in 1918 than they had been before the War. While wages had generally increased, the average level of income for the whole population was slightly lower than it had been in 1914, and a severe inflation, resulting in part from the heavy borrowing of the state for its war debt, had eroded real living standards to the point where the poorest workers needed government price controls, especially on food, in order to survive. This war-induced economic crisis was serious enough, but it was gravely exacerbated by the end of the War and the sudden cancellation of the weapons contracts that had kept iron, steel and machine production booming in the northern cities. Thousands were thrown out of work, and they were joined in 1919–20 by the 2.5 million demobilised from the Italian armed forces. Poorer peasants were clamouring for the portions of cultivable land they had been promised during the War. The whole country was in a ferment. Yet although these socio-economic conditions constituted a promising seed-bed for fascist recruitment and pursuit of political power, it was only when they were combined with skilful exploitation of Italy's crisis-ridden liberal-democratic political system that

Mussolini and his fascist followers had their real opportunity of grabbing power.

Indeed Italy provides an interesting illustration of the third conducive factor for the rise of fascism: insecurely based liberal–democratic institutions. Every country in which an indigenous fascist movement succeeded in taking power – Italy, Germany, Hungary, Romania and 'Independent Croatia' – had only relatively brief experience of operating parliamentary democracy, and all had been deeply marked by their long experiences of government by reactionary authoritarian regimes. Germany had a far more advanced science, technology and industrialised economy than Italy, but entirely lacked the stronger intellectual tradition of liberalism which Italy had developed since the Risorgimento. Italy, on the other hand, had a far greater burden of socio-economic backwardness. It is estimated that in 1914 half the population were illiterate, and the per capita income for the country was less than half that of Britain. As one historian has observed:

'. . . accustomed to deprivation, and dulled by ceaseless toil, whole regions were innocent of the most elementary education and were consequently not equipped to participate in the challenge [of modern civilization].' (De Felice, 1963)

But these factors were not the immediate cause of the Italian political crises of 1920–1. The traditional political class was already deeply divided during the War into the *interventisti* (those in favour of the War) and the *disfattisti* (those opposed to it), led by Nitti and Giolitti respectively. Although this split was gradually healed in 1919–20, other deep divisions appeared to dog the efforts of the Giolitti's last government (1920–1). In the general election of 1919 suffrage was more broadly based than it had been in 1913, and proportional representation was used. One result of this was to make the old combined parliamentary majority of liberals and conservatives impossible. Now a far more militant force, the socialist party, succeeded in trebling its share of the seats in Parliament (156, compared to 50 in 1913), and in the local elections of 1920 thousands of communes returned socialist governments. These were fiercely opposed to the traditional parties, and thus the political system was more sharply polarised than even before. Moreover, a new mass party called the Popular Party, founded after the War by a Sicilian priest, won 100 seats in Parliament. Its domestic programme was basically populist, its major demand being the break-up of large estates into small property holdings, and it was closely bound up with the Catholic agricultural leagues.

Simultaneous with these developments was a large increase in trade union membership. For example, the General Confederation of Labour, under a far more left-wing leadership than before, had expanded to 2,200,000 members (compared to 321,000 in 1914). Almost 1,000,000 of these were farm workers. The nationalist trade unionists, mainly syndicalists, founded a new movement, the Italian Union of Labour, which also grew very rapidly in 1919–20. Finally, there was a rapidly-growing cluster of war veterans' groups. One of the most militant and aggressive of these was Associazione degli Arditi d'Italia, which fostered a kind of romantic nationalist programme and had a strong tendency to use political violence. Another, more moderate group was Associazione Nazionale Combattenti, which focused mainly on the issues of more land for the peasants and constitutional reform. Benito Mussolini's Fasci Italiani di Combattimento, which attracted many veterans and some ex-revolutionary syndicalists and socialists to its banner, was founded on 23 March 1919.

Mussolini did not have a fully worked out and consistent programme. Doctrines, slogans and policies were made up very much as he went along, always with one eye on opportunities to bring him closer to power. In part the fascists' initial programme was ultra-nationalistic, demanding the integration of all Italian 'national' territories (such as Fiume) into the nation, vigorously opposing the imperialism of other nations that might be harmful to Italy, and promising to sabotage all neutralist politicians of whatever party. Their domestic programme was in some respects liberal, even radical, at the outset: universal suffrage, referenda on major continuing questions, a constituent assembly, a republic with regional and communal autonomy, elimination of the Senate and all noble titles, conscription to be ended, state intervention to be reduced, speculation and monopoly profits to be ended, an eight-hour day, land to the peasants and workers' participation in factory management. From the start the fascists took part in counter-demonstrations and demonstrations against internationalist socialism, which they regarded as being unpatriotic. On 15 April 1919 they took part with other veterans and students in a 'counter-demonstration' in Milan which turned into a physical attack on an anarchist–socialist march, and ended with the sacking of the offices of *Avanti*, the socialist newspaper once edited by Mussolini. By this time it had already become clear that the parliament and the King would not be powerful enough to stop the political system dissolving into a chaotic struggle of extra-parliamentary groups. Unable to cope with these swirling and conflicting tides of political mobilisation, the constitutional authorities were not so much overturned as rendered helpless, as real initiative and power passed to the armed bands in the countryside and the streets.

In Germany there was an even more dangerous and blatant hostility to the Weimar Republic's parliamentary constitution. The extreme right saw it as an alien imposition of the Allied powers, hopelessly compromised by its capitulation to the 'system' run by the USA, Britain and France, and lacking in the authoritarian power and efficiency of the old *Reich*. The far left, on the other hand, yearned for the day when the Weimar system could be overturned so that capitalism could be replaced by communism and the German working class could take its proud part alongside the Soviet workers in the march of proletarian internationalism. In the period 1928–32 it was the two parties fundamentally opposed to the system – the NSDAP and the communist party – that were making the greatest electoral gains. This did not bode well for the Weimar Republic. And once Hermann Muller's coalition of social democrats, liberal and catholics had broken up in face of a deteriorating economic situation, it became increasingly difficult to stitch together any workable parliamentary majority. The next Chancellor, Brüning of the centre party, got the support of President Hindenburg to invoke Article 48 of the Weimar Constitution which enabled him to govern by decree, without the backing of parliament. This only tended to increase the irresponsibility of the traditional political parties: government by decree effectively absolved them from the need to negotiate workable and stable coalition agreements in parliament. Hence the social democrats still failed to hammer out any common positions with the moderate catholic centre party, even though both were faced with the ever more dangerous challenge from the Nazis against the whole basis of the constitutional system. The truth is that Brüning's government was increasingly isolated. It could no longer provide strong enough leadership to reassure people that the economic ills of the country – fast-rising unemployment, farmers being ruined by the collapse of world agricultural prices, a breakdown of law and order, and fear of renewed inflation – could be tackled. By January 1933 the Weimar political system was so febrile that Hitler, once invited to join a right-wing coalition, found it child's play to dispose of his partners, liquidate the opposition parties and establish a totalitarian regime based on a monopoly of power by the Nazis.

A fourth condition for fascist success appears to have been widespread fear among the middle and lower-middle classes of a communist revolutionary takeover in their country. Each of the fascist parties which took power was able to play on that fear to great effect. At the time of writing it does not appear that this particular condition for fascist growth that prevailed in Europe between the Wars has any close parallel today.

Even if all these conditions prevail there is no real threat of a fascist rise to power unless the movement has one other vital component: a charismatic leader with the political cunning and ruthless ambition to achieve absolute power over the fascist movement and ultimately over the regime. In the eyes of most foreign observers, Mussolini appeared a rather absurd figure: plump and pompous and festooned with self-awarded decorations, he did not look as though he had the stuffing to survive as a dictator. Yet survive he did for twenty years. How did he succeed in maintaining his position as leader? He was not a resolute or courageous figure, and often hesitated and procrastinated, both before and after his seizure of power. But he was a skilful popular agitator who put his experience as an orator and political journalist to effective use: he has been described by one leading Italian historian as 'a cunning corrupter of men, who could play on their faults whenever he had the chance to do so.' (Carocci, 1975) He was quite an adroit political tactician in his handling of the politics of the fascist movement and his domestic power-base, but his knowledge of international relations was hopelessly inadequate and he became mesmerised by his own heady imperialist rhetoric and adventurism. His greatest, indeed ultimately fatal, mistake was to throw in his lot with Hitler. In the earlier phase of the development of Nazism, Mussolini seemed to have the sense to realise the gulf between Italian fascism and National Socialist ideology. In the early 1930s he described German National Socialism as 'one hundred per cent racism: against everything and everyone: yesterday against Christian civilisation, today against latin civilisation, tomorrow, who knows, against the civilisation of the whole world.' Alas, he soon forgot this prophetic assessment of the Hitler movement, and his ambitions for territorial aggrandisement led him to overestimate Nazism's potential. In the end he gambled on Hitler's belief that Germany and its satellites could take on the rest of the world and win. In 1935–6 Mussolini, frustrated by the opposition of the west and the League of Nations to his conquest of Abyssinia and mesmerised by Hitler's brazen challenge against Versailles, began to talk of a Rome–Berlin Axis. And in 1939 Mussolini took another irrevocable step down the Nazi road by introducing anti-Semitic laws in Italy (though these were not implemented with anything approaching the ruthlessness of the Nazi regime until the Gestapo *razzia* in Rome and the atrocities committed under the final puppet 'Italian Social Republic'). Italy entered Hitler's war in June 1940, but her military inefficiency and economic backwardness were soon revealed, and Mussolini and his fascist movement were swept away in the Allied victories.

Mussolini appeared to make up his ideology and policies as he went along, making constant compromises with other powerful forces in Italian society such as the Roman Catholic Church. Hitler sought and achieved a far greater degree of totalitarian control over German society and pursued his anti-Semitic and racial supremacist ambitions with a brutal fanaticism unique in recent history. Like Mussolini he was a brilliant agitator, only half-educated and equipped with a muddle of ideas picked up in the streets of Vienna, yet capable of considerable feats of mass necromancy, propaganda and manipulation. Hitler's *Mein Kampf* (1925) provides the most revealing exhibition of Hitler's prejudices and ideas. If only western statesmen and liberal-minded Germans had read it in time they might have realised that they were dealing not simply with a power-hungry ex-corporal, but with a megalomaniac obsessed by a demonic mission which threatened the future of humanity. In its pages Hitler showed himself obsessed with the idea of history as a struggle between the 'spirituality' of the German race and the 'poison' and corrupt materialism of the Jewish race. From the anti-Semitism he had picked up in Vienna, from Houston Stewart Chamberlain and other racist writers, he developed the obsessive idea that Germany had to defeat the Jewish race in order to realise its 'world destiny'. The Jews were made the scapegoat, the enemy, on whom all Germany's major ills could be blamed. The book is also full of the crude pan-German nationalism Hitler had acquired from such influences as Dr Leopold Potsch and Georg von Schonerer's Pan-German Nationalist Party. *Mein Kampf* revealed his total commitment to the idea of re-uniting all the German-speaking peoples in one *Grossdeutschland* (Greater Germany), as a precondition for colonial expansion into the vital *lebensraum* (living-space) in the east:

'And so we National Socialists consciously draw a line beneath the foreign policy tendency of our pre-War period. We take up where we broke off six hundred years ago. We stop the endless German movement to the south and west, and turn our gaze towards the land in the east. At long last we break off the colonial and commercial policy of the pre-War period and shift to the soil policy of the future.
If we speak of soil in Europe today, we can primarily have in mind only Russia and her vassal border states.'

Thus Hitler, in contrast with Mussolini and many other major fascist figures, did not acquire his key ideas after seizing power. His hate-filled credo was fully formed long before. In *Mein Kampf* he wrote on the 'Jewish question':

'There is no such thing as coming to an understanding with the Jews. It must be the hard-and-fast "either-or".'

And in the founding programme of the Nazi Party, announced on 14 February 1920, Hitler stated:

'We demand the union of all Germans, on the basis of the right of self-determination of peoples, to form a Great Germany. . . . All men and women of German blood, whether they are living today under Danish, Polish, Italian, or French rule, must be united in a German *Reich*. We shall not renounce a single German in the Sudetenland, in

Alsace-Lorraine, in Poland, in the League of Nations colony of Austria, or in the successor states of the old Austrian empire.'

We must be thankful that, so far, fascist history has not thrown up any other leader who could match Hitler's demonic powers and beliefs. Fascist movements in the post-War phase are constantly riven and weakened by personality squabbles among would-be *Führers*. And in many cases the fascist parties have lost their founder-leaders, through political violence or other causes, at the crucial stage, just when they might have achieved greater power. For example, the Romanian fascist leader, Corneliu Codreanu, was murdered on 30 November 1938, leaving his Legion of the Archangel Michael movement leaderless and vulnerable so that eventually it was crushed in 1941. And the Spanish Falange lost their enigmatic but powerful leader José Antonio Primo de Rivera in 1936, when he was executed by extreme left-wing militants at Alicante in the early stages of the Spanish Civil War. The movement never found a fascist leader who could fill his place.

Last but by no means least of the conditions for the rise of fascism is anti-Semitism and other forms of racism, discrimination and prejudice. Hitler knew he could exploit a long tradition of virulent anti-Semitism in Germany and Austria, and the war-time occupation showed that such attitudes were prevalent in other European countries such as France, Belgium and the Balkan states. Today, a similar background of racial tension is very much a feature of many Western societies. In Britain the influx of coloured immigrants has provided a new target and focus for race hatred. Admittedly this racism is forced 'underground' and is condemned in all official pronouncements. But fascist groups such as the National Front and other similar movements in Europe and America have directed all their racist propaganda and intimidatory violence at the immigrant community. Latent racial tensions and conflicts, when combined with the severe economic and social problems of inner-city areas, provide a fruitful environment for fascist movements to recruit and provoke conflict.

While there remains debate among historians on the necessary conditions for fascist success, there is far less controversy concerning the *methods* employed by fascist movements in the past. All of them have used four major means of achieving, maintaining and expanding their power: political violence and terrorism; tactics of electoral party competition, and, where expedient, coalition with other political groupings of the right; intensive campaigns of mass propaganda, including a particularly strong effort to mobilise youth; and enlistment of covert or overt financial support from big business. Fascists see the first two of these methods as perfectly compatible, and generally conduct their struggles for power at all four levels simultaneously.

Mussolini and his Italian followers did not use political violence and terror to anything like the same extent as the Nazis. But it would be a grave mistake to assume that they managed without them. From autumn 1920, in Tuscany, the Po Valley and Emilia, and increasingly also in other areas, the fascist squads used ruthless violence to smash the socialist co-operatives, peasant leagues and labour unions. Later they turned their terrorism against the *Popolari* organisations as well. The *Squadrismo* (from which the Mussolini Action Squads of the 1970s take their name) comprised young men, mainly students and petty-bourgeoisie, hooligans, misfits and demobilised officers. One recent historian of fascist violence has described their activities as follows:

'Truckloads of fascists would arrive in a community, attack the headquarters of the workers' organisations, beat up anybody foolish enough to stay around, throw files and furniture into the street, sprinkle with gasoline, and burn them. . . . Then the fascists would seek out union, league, or co-operative officers, socialist communal officials and bully or beat them into resigning, "banishing" them from the region.' (Tilly, 1975)

In the first half of 1921 alone, fascists were reported to have destroyed 17 newspapers or printing plants, 110 Chambers of Labour, 83 Peasant leagues, 151 Socialist Circles, 59 *Case del Popolo*, and 151 cultural circles. While socialist organisations crumpled under the increasing attacks, fascist membership grew from 190 *fasci* in October 1920 to over 800 by the end of that year, 1,500 in May and 2,200 in November 1921. Often local officials and the *carabinieri* simply turned a blind eye when the fascist *Squadri* drove into town. Sometimes they even supplied weapons to the fascist squads.

Hitler used terror on the streets, on an even bigger scale, in order to suppress any opposition. In *Mein Kampf* he makes this policy quite explicit:

'What we needed and still need were and are not a hundred or two hundred reckless conspirators, but a hundred thousand and a second hundred thousand fighters for our philosophy of life. We should not work in secret conventicles, but in mighty mass demonstrations, and it is not by dagger and poison or pistol that the road can be cleared for the movement, but by the conquest of the streets. We must teach the Marxists that the future master of the streets is National Socialism, just as it will some day be the master of the state.'

Even though Hitler's jackbooted stormtroopers were unleashed to clear the opposition parties from the streets, it is a striking fact that the Nazis did not succeed in terrorising the electorate into anything approaching total submission in the period 1930–2, and Hitler's party never received an overall majority of the votes cast in any election. What Hitler did was to get himself taken into partnership with a right-wing coalition, then rapidly disposed of the partners and liquidated the opposition parties to clear the way for himself. After 1930, when the NSDAP became the second most powerful party,

Hitler for a time pretended to be observing fully all the constitutional proprieties, and sued anyone who accused him of undemocratic ambitions. He kept his para-military organisations on a tight leash in order to help preserve this image of democratic respectability, for he calculated that his best chance of power was to obtain the Chancellorship by the legal process: only then did he immediately suspend democracy and establish dictatorship.

Hitler's tactics of mass propaganda were of great significance in providing him with fanatical support. One of the most potent features of the Nazis appeal was their image as the movement of the rising generations. Nazi rallies, symbols, films and displays constantly sought to evoke both youthful energy and total devotion to Hitler, while inculcating into the *Hitler Jugend* (Hitler Youth) the warrior-like virtues of physical strength and blind loyalty which prepared them for the Nazis' mission of war. It is in the Nazis' systematic corruption of youth that one sees Nazi ideology for what it really is, the defiant rejection of liberalism, Marxism and capitalism, indeed of all the humane values inherited from Judaeo-Christian civilisation. In its place the Nazis substituted anti-intellectualism (the burning of the books, for example), sensuality, and total devotion to and worship of the *Führer*.

Finally, a very important element in Hitler's political strategy was the wooing of right-wing industrial magnates for big financial contributions to meet the costs of organising the party and its para-military organs. By 1930 the Nazis were rapidly running short of cash. It was at this stage that negotiations with leading industrialists, such as Emil Kirdorf and Baron Fritz von Thyssen, brought huge direct subsidies which, in effect, guaranteed the Nazi Party its debts and financed its major election campaigns. Major financial support of this kind would make any modern fascist party that so benefited a much more dangerous force. The absence of any such backing to contemporary European fascist parties must be taken as a healthy and reassuring sign.

Both the German and Italian models of fascism had considerable influence abroad, then and subsequently. The deference of modern fascist movements to Nazi ideas, over 38 years after the defeat of Hitler's Germany, is striking evidence of this. We also need to recall the vast array of fascist movements that mushroomed in the 1930s in every European country, and in both north and south America. It even reached into Manchuria, where in the 1930s the All-Russian Fascist Party (VFP), under the leadership of Konstantin Vladimirovich Rodzaevsky, nourished the belief that it would become the successor to the communist party in Russia. The Russian fascists were basically an *emigré* movement, drawing its cash and other support from Russians in America and elsewhere. But the first and largest of their Russian fascist organisations developed in Manchuria, where it held the first congress of the Russian fascist groups in May 1931. As the historian Erwin Oberlander explains, its leader Rodzaevsky:

'looked forward to an alliance between fascist Russia, Japan, and National Socialist Germany (astonishingly enough completely overlooking Italy, in so many respects his model fascist state). Only such an alliance could solve all world problems, establish lasting peace, and break the world domination of the Jews and freemasons.' (Oberlander, 1966)

Any such alliance with Germany seems somewhat far-fetched when one bears in mind the policy towards Russia outlined in *Mein Kampf*!

Nor was it only the Nazi model that found eager yet bizarre bedfellows. Some of the Irgun, a Jewish nationalist movement in Palestine in the 1930s, were attracted by Mussolini's fascist ideas, and even advocated setting up a Jewish nationalist youth movement modelled on the Italian fascist youth organisation. In its early period, prior to the forging of the Rome-Berlin axis, the Italian fascists had shown no interest in promoting Italian anti-Semitism. Indeed at that stage some

Italian Jews held leading positions in the fascisti. Thus it is not really so surprising to find some pre-War Palestinian Jews looking admiringly to Mussolini's ideas. As the anti-Semitic thrust of Hitler's movement had become more apparent and more threatening, they soon abandoned these philo-fascist ideas.

The Spanish Falange model also had its admirers, and, particularly after 1936, one sees the interesting influence of the Hispanidad movement. This pro-Spanish cultural movement became a vehicle for the advocacy of fascist-style dictatorship, militant suppression of communism, and a doctrine of total subservience to the state, with all democratic pretensions discarded. This new style ultra-nationalism was able to exploit the concepts of the essential unity of Spanish culture and institutions. The influence of these ideas on Argentinian leaders such as Ramirez and Peron was to prove considerable. In its period of Second World War isolation, Spain was able to count on invaluable aid in the form of food and weapons supplies from Argentina. Besides the latter, Peru, Venezuela, Paraguay and Bolivia were all responsive to the export of fascism through the vehicle of Hispanidad.

It is easy to exaggerate the depth and extent of the popular appeal of fascist ideas. Though they certainly travelled over almost every national frontier in the world in the 1930s and 1940s, in most cases they remained the preserve of small, politically marginal groups. Even in the occupied countries of Europe, where Nazi ideology and methods were imposed by force of arms, the indigenous fascist collaborators remained despised and rejected by the majority of their fellow-countrymen. In Romania and Hungary the existence of sizeable native fascist movements gave somewhat broader bases of support to the Axis-dominated regimes, but in France, the Low Countries, Norway, Denmark and the greater part of occupied eastern Europe, typical popular reaction to the new dictatorship ranged from sullen acquiescence to courageous armed resistance.

3 WAR'S AFTERMATH

The Second World War, unleashed by Hitler when he ordered his forces to attack Poland on 1 September 1939, was the most total and terrible in history. The human suffering and material devastation inflicted as a result of the conflict, and the systematic terror inflicted by the Nazis and their collaborators on the peoples of occupied Europe, can never be calculated. It is estimated that over 24 million civilians were killed in Europe alone, and that roughly 25 million soldiers, including 6 million Russians, lost their lives.

The Nazis set up huge concentration camps, the most notorious of which were Auschwitz, Treblinka and Sobibor in Poland, Buchenwald, Belsen and Ravensbruck in Germany, Mauthausen in Austria, Vught in Holland, and Theresienstadt in Czechoslovakia. Millions of men, women and children, the majority of them Jews, were transported by train to these camps. The fittest were generally put to work as slave-labourers. Those unfit for work were gassed and burned. Special units of the SS were established to carry out what Hitler termed 'the Final Solution', the extermination of the Jewish people. Under this policy 6 million Jews, more than a third of all world Jewry at the outbreak of War, were murdered by the Nazis. In the extermination camps gas chambers were disguised as shower-rooms. The gas, Zyklon B, killed its victims in twenty minutes. Special gangs scoured the corpses for gold teeth and hidden valuables, and then the bodies were burned. In the summer of 1944, at Auschwitz, about 9,000 corpses were being burned in the crematoria each day.

The testimony of the Nuremberg Trials (1945–7) and the thousands of war crime trials held since, including the trial of

Adolf Eichmann in Jerusalem in 1961 (brilliantly analysed by Hannah Arendt), reveal in horrific detail the way in which fanatical Nazi ideology was combined with modern bureaucracy and technology to produce genocide on a totally unprecedented scale. Even now it is difficult to grasp the degree of evil embodied in the Nazi tyranny. And when the defeat of Hitler finally came, with such sudden speed in 1945, there was an inevitable and understandable desire on the part of many survivors to try to forget the nightmare from which they had just been saved. There was an almost frenetic keenness to restore normality, and to try to rehabilitate the shattered economies of Europe. Yet the nightmare could not be easily dispelled. Two events in particular brought the Nazis' atrocities to the forefront of the world's attention. First there were the terrible discoveries by the Allied troops when they entered the camps, the emaciated ghost-like survivors among the piles of corpses. Secondly, there was the battery of evidence produced at the Nuremberg trials. These constituted a major innovation in international law, as the first trials ever held of a whole war-time leadership. In rejecting the Nazis' defence pleas of 'superior orders', the judges upheld the basic rights of civilian populations, even in times of total war. The leading Nazis were convicted of crimes against humanity, and in a series of trials a total of 175 German and Austrian Nazis were indicted, of whom 25 were sentenced to death, 20 to life imprisonment, 97 were given shorter sentences, and 35 were aquitted. One of the leading Nazis sentenced to life imprisonment at the original Nuremberg trial, Rudolf Hess, is still imprisoned at Spandau.

However, the effort to bring the Nazis and their collaborators to book for their war crimes was soon to run completely into the sand. A practical difficulty was that, in the chaos of the Nazi capitulation and the division of Germany into four Allied occupied zones, large numbers of the Nazis responsible for committing atrocities fled to safe havens in Latin America, Spain and elsewhere, some with the systematic assistance of an underground network of former SS men. Others, like Klaus Barbie the Gestapo 'Butcher of Lyons' who escaped to Bolivia, managed to get protection from military dictatorships.

Another difficulty was the vexed question of defining complicity. Allied officials, keen to restore Germany to normality as quickly as possible, argued that one could not prove full knowledge of the Holocaust in anyone beyond the inner circle of war criminals convicted at Nuremberg. The British in particular were anxious to restore Germany to a position of strength as a bulwark against the new danger from her former ally, the Soviet Union.

In fact these excuses did not hold much water. Despite the practical difficulties, one could in fact identify certain leading officials, lawyers, industrialists and others who had known what was being done to Jews, Poles, Russians, Czechs, Serbs and other peoples of the Nazi-occupied countries, as well as political opponents of the Nazis in Germany. All the boards of directors and management of German firms such as IG Farben, Krupp, and Flick, should have been implicated, as the latter used slave labour and even ran their own concentration camps. It would have been easy to identify and prosecute far more individuals than actually were.

This issue caused deep dissension among the Allies. As a recent major study of war crimes policies has concluded:

'Essentially, British and American policies were so at odds that the intended victims of de-Nazification became its beneficiaries. While both Allies were agreed on the destruction of Germany's military power, they disagreed on the destruction of the German economy. The Americans wanted a harsh, penal peace settlement. The British did not want to crush Germany and make it dependent on other countries for support.' (Bower, 1981)

Thus there was a clash of interests between those who wanted the speediest possible construction of the Germany economy and industry on the one hand, and those who wanted to cleanse Germany thoroughly of Nazi elements on the other. The latter objective was made even more difficult by yet another practical difficulty. Neither the United Nations War Crimes Commission nor the Allied forces in Europe had the personnel or resources adequately to pursue the task of rounding-up Nazi war criminals. Prolonged inter-departmental wrangles occurred within each Allied government as to which agency should have major responsibility for making and interpreting war crimes policy. Further complications resulted from conflicting interpretations of the punishment of war crimes under international law. It is significant that in a speech on behalf of the British government announcing the setting-up of the UN Commission, Lord Simon specifically limited the scope of the new body to crimes committed against the 'nationals of the United Nations'. This exempted the Allies from the necessity to prosecute those who had committed crimes against stateless persons, including German Jews (because the Nazi regime had deprived them of their nationality) and gypsies. There was a bitter split between the American and British governments on this issue, but the Foreign Office chiefs clung to their view that the Commission should not deal with crimes against such stateless persons, or with crimes committed before the outbreak of the War. The Allies stuck to the line that the prosecution of war criminals had to be restricted to those who had committed crimes against civilians or military from countries belonging to the United Nations, in order to conform to existing international law. This was all the more reprehensible when one considers the unprecedented nature of the atrocities concerned, and the fact that the draft terms of surrender gave the Allies 'supreme authority with respect to Germany'.

If the confused and ineffectual approach of the Allied powers to the prosecution of war criminals led to former Nazis remaining in high positions in industry, banking, the judiciary, and every other important profession, the record of Allied attempts at 're-education' as a method of de-Nazification was just as unsuccessful. Supreme Headquarters Allied Forces in Europe set its Psychological Warfare Division to the task of touring Germany displaying films and photographs of the concentration camps. Almost invariably the reaction of the individual German was to protest his innocence and to lay the blame on 'the Nazis'. Opinion polls at the end of the War showed that 50 per cent of Germans thought 'National Socialism was a good idea badly carried out', and that 70 per cent rejected any responsibility for the War. The failure of Allied propaganda is conveyed by the fact that polls conducted three years later (in 1948) showed almost identical results.

In Britain the Foreign Office was responsible for an ambitious programme of 're-education' of German prisoners-of-war, aimed at countering Nazi indoctrination. It had to undermine the Nazis' blind devotion to Hitler, group identification and their belief in the concept of the 'Master race'. One modern British historian has emphasised the importance of this programme as follows:

'The real long term danger of Nazism was not the handful of bloodthirsty fanatics who led the country to destruction, but the identification of the mass of ordinary, decent citizens with the lower moral standards and social behaviour of a paranoid leadership!' (Fergusson, 1973)

A full study of the British prisoner-of-war programme has shown that the generation aged between 27–35 in 1945 were those who had most wholeheartedly supported Hitler. This group found it extremely difficult to shake off the influence of National Socialism. Many were deeply resentful of the world's condemnation of Hitler and Nazism. Those over 35 at the end of the War, on the other hand, were those most easily able to revert to another social ethic, usually the one they adhered to before 1933. These findings on generational attitudes towards Nazism are interestingly confirmed by recent West German opinion surveys.

The difficulty in converting people from deeply-held beliefs is well-known to social scientists and historians. It is no surprise to find that hard-core Nazis and fascist supporters survived the rather confused and short-lived efforts of the Allies to 're-educate' them. Those who were in their teens when Hitler gained power were, after all, intensively indoctrinated. Many who had served in the German forces without being taken prisoner by the Allies had no opportunity to question their Nazi beliefs. And even of the German prisoners-of-war, probably less than 10 per cent of them ever experienced an intensive re-education programme. In the turbulence of post-War Germany, with such disparities of policy between Allied powers' occupation zone authorities, and given the ineffective methods employed for 'de-Nazification' in Germany, it is easy to understand how remnant groups of Nazis and unrepentant believers managed to survive in the Federal Republic.

In Italy the conditions for a fascist movement to resurface were even more propitious. Because the Italians were knocked out of the War earlier, the Allies had neither the resources nor the inclination to purge the whole Italian establishment and social institutions of fascist elements. Moreover Italy's defeat did not inflict the same degree of devastation and social dislocation as happened in Germany. Many of Mussolini's followers comforted themselves with the belief that it was not *Italian* fascism that had failed. Mussolini had been careful to avoid a direct conflict with the Catholic Church, and so had avoided alienating supporting in the traditional rural areas, like Sicily, where fascism continued to flourish after the War.

The constitution of the new Italian Republic prohibited any attempt to reconstitute the Fascist Party. Yet as early as 1946 the Movimento Sociale Italiano (MSI) had been formed, a party which clearly set out to attract the traditional Fascist Party vote. Paralleling Mussolini's own tactics in the 1920s, the MSI claimed to be a conventional political party working within the norms of the new democratic constitution. It claimed to support the Christian Democrats as a bastion against 'the communist threat'. Simultaneously, however, some MSI leaders privately favoured the re-emergence of para-military fascist groups favouring illegal means of struggle. Their propaganda boasted that the zenith of Italian political achievement was the 1943–45 Italian Social Republic, and implied that eventually the new-fangled democratic system would fail, and would then need to be replaced by a full-blooded fascism building on the methods and policies of Mussolini. The leaders of the new movement had all been enthusiastic and in some cases senior supporters of the defeated Fascist regime – for example, Prince Junio Valerio Borghese, the former fascist Militia commander, and Augusto de Marsanich, Mussolini's Under-Secretary of Posts and Telegraphs.

In its first electoral trial in 1948, MSI's candidates received a total of 525,408 votes, an astonishing figure when one takes account of the smashing defeat of fascist regimes throughout Europe only 3 years before. Even more astonishing was its showing in the 1953 election, when it gained 1,579,880 votes, 5.9 per cent of the poll. By the early 1960s, the party had acquired a formal membership estimated at about 200,000. However, it was already apparent by this stage in its development that supporters were polarised on tactics and methods between the young fascist tyros who had never lived through a fascist regime, and the 'old guard' who held the leading posts in the party.

Another development during this period was that clandestine Italian groups began to establish direct links with other European fascist and neo-Nazi organisations, such as Thiriard's Jeune Europe, based in Belgium, Georges Bidault and his colleagues in the OAS, the German neo-Nazis and the SS escape network Odessa. They began to participate in neo-Nazi international meetings and training-camps held in

Spain, Belgium, Germany and Holland. The links of Ordine Nuovo with the OAS appear to have been of quite a close and practical nature: Bidault and other OAS men were sheltered by Italian fascists when they were on the run from the French authorities, and Ordine Nuovo also helped the OAS in dissemination of propaganda and by providing documents and weapons. This is a harbinger of the close links between fascist movements in the two countries in 1979–81.

The record of France in the struggle against Nazism was profoundly ambivalent. On the one hand, the collapse of the French Army in 1940 had been followed by the establishment of a collaborationist regime, Vichy, under Marshal Pétain, which took power with the connivance of a parliament and a French public unwilling to continue the struggle. On the other hand, although France did not liberate herself, she did, as the War progressed, produce increasing numbers of resisters willing to fight Nazism. And in 1944, General de Gaulle, the symbol and self-proclaimed leader of Free France, was able to reclaim Paris. During the Vichy regime, the government could be described as a blend of authoritarianism and diluted fascist corporatism. But with the exception of the tiny fascist leagues under Doriot and Déat, the occupied French had no stomach for Nazi ideas and rejected or ignored them. That is to say that collaboration for the majority was grudging and coerced rather than willing. In the euphoria of liberation a very thoroughgoing anti-fascist, anti-collaborationist purge was launched and it is estimated that more than 40,000 'collabos' were executed.

These events had a somewhat ambiguous effect on the post-War climate for the development of the extreme right in France. Hard-core Nazis who survived the purge, by lying low or by fleeing abroad, were not converted to the Liberation. They continued to await the next civil war, when they believed their ideas would triumph once again. They became beleaguered but fanatical tiny cults, convinced of their own absolute rectitude and confident that their time would come.

The hard core blotted out the uncomfortable truth that they were on a hiding to nothing preaching fascism in France. Liberation had brought with it a feverent desire to bury the painful and embarrassing memory of Vichy, and for any post-War politician, a record of collaboration was the mark of Cain.

But even despite the enormous wave of anti-Vichy and anti-Nazi revulsion in France in the Liberation period, tiny explicitly fascist groupings, using all the symbols, salutes and uniforms of Nazism, re-appeared in France almost immediately. The groups were constantly changing their labels, so that very often one is seeing the same small group of fascists re-emerging in reconstituted groups. For example, Mouvement National Citadelle re-emerges as Parti Socialiste Français, then as the Phalange Française, and (in 1958) as Mouvement Populaire Français (MPF). These movements attracted both young Nazis and former members of the war-time French fascist organisations led by Doriot and Déat. Another French fascist grouping, Jeune Nation, was founded in 1951 by the four Sidos brothers, whose father had been a fascist militant henchman of the Vichy collaborator Darnand, shot in 1945 for his war-time activities. Jeune Nation's rallying call was 'Power into the hands of the nationalists'. Ultra-right publications also re-appeared soon after the War ended. *Rivarol* (founded in 1951) was the most extreme. The Action Française magazine *Aspects de la France* had a tiny readership, but the *Paroles Françaises* magazine, which was not affiliated to any particular political group, reached a circulation of almost 100,000.

However, French fascism in the immediate post-War period remained a very tiny and isolated political force. Most of the activists who had survived the Liberation purges were despised and hated, and those who were found guilty of war-time collaboration had their civic rights taken away from them.

But the real opportunity for the French fascists to re-establish themselves and bid afresh for popular support sprang out of the right-wing fury and resentment at the reversals suffered by French forces in the colonial wars in Indo-China and Algeria. Jeune Nation, for example, exploited these situations to the full. Very early on it linked up with the Indo-China war veterans' organisations and joined with them in condemning the government for the defeat in Dien Bien Phu. The fascist group staged an ugly scene at the wreath-laying ceremony at the Tomb of the Unknown Warrior in April 1954, when Ministers were jeered at and jostled by the crowd. Jeune Nation also had intimate connections with the OAS, and joined with the strong right-wing elements in the army in campaigning against a 'sell-out' in Algeria. Some of the young fascists hoped that conflict between the Algerian nationalists and those who supported *Algérie Française* would reach the point of a civil war in France, in which they could intervene. These hopes were badly set back by the ultimate peace settlement with the Front National de la Libération (FLN) at Evian, for this robbed them of the emotive claim that they were rallying to defend an integral part of France. Jeune Nation's real long-term aims remained unrepentantly Nazi. In 1958 the group was banned, but it was reconstituted a year later in combination with several other fascist groups under a new heading, Parti Nationaliste.

The other major development on the French extreme right in the 1950s was the growth of a populist movement with strong fascistic elements, Pierre Poujade's Union de Defense des Commercants et Artisans (UDCA), founded, in 1953. This, as the name implies, was an organisation designed to express the needs and grievances of the shopkeepers, small businessmen and artisans. The militancy of the movement was undoubtedly fuelled by growing disenchantment with the Fourth Republic's major parties and governments, and an economic crisis exacerbated by the financial strain of the colonial wars. But the major plank in UDCA's programme was a root-and-branch opposition to the tax system. They managed to obtain 52 seats in the Chamber of Deputies in the

January 1956 elections, with 2,600,000 votes. But in November 1958 their share of the poll had dropped disastrously, from 11.58 per cent in 1956 to 1 per cent.

There is strong evidence of the Poujadists' fascistic tendencies. Many of their leading figures (for example, Tixier-Vignancourt, de Carbuccia, Benoist-Mechin and Serge Jeanneret) were former collaborators or ex-Vichy officials. Moreover, alongside Jeune Nation they established close links with the OAS and the right-wing of the French army.

Parti Nationaliste, formed in 1959, was an amalgam of some Poujadists, monarchists, and several *Algérie Française* movements with Jeune Nation. The new grouping saw itself as the new ultra-nationalist elite rather than as a democratic party seeking electoral support. Its real purpose was to co-ordinate all the fascist groups in France, with the aim of achieving the destruction of the democratic system of the Republic, the establishment of a fascist corporatist state, the expulsion of all 'aliens', and of course the defence of the French colonies. The Parti Nationaliste helped arrange the violent street demonstrations in Algiers in February 1959, which were intended to drive the French army into taking the side of the rioters. This tactic failed, and the new grouping was banned by the authorities for making an 'attack on the interal security of the state'. *Algérie Française* continued as the one rallying-call which temporarily united all the French ultra-right. These groups intensified their violent campaign as the pressure for Algerian self-determination, within Algeria and from the French left, grew in strength. Although the right-wing alliance managed to exploit this issue to win sympathisers and allies in the army, they did not succeed in winning over sufficient senior and middle-ranking officers to bring about the desired military coup in France. The generals' coup in Algiers was not followed up on the French mainland: hence the fascists were already relishing the possibility of a major civil war in France. Possible major loss of civilian lives did not concern them, for, in typically fascist manner, they despised the ordinary population as decadent and passive. In the same way they believed the left would be incapable of offering any major resistance to their plans.

French fascists were heavily involved with kindred movements in Europe. In 1950–51 for example, some French fascists attended international assemblies – in Rome and Malmo. At Malmo the so-called moderates like Mosley, Per Engdahl (a Swedish Nazi), and the Frenchman, Bardeche, advocated a strategy of stressing the communist menace and playing down racialism, while the more militant participants wanted an undiluted Nazism. The latter elements became the basis of the Nouvel Ordre European (NOE) formed in September 1951 at a meeting in Zurich. Using their magazine *Europe Réelle* as a propaganda vehicle for their violent racism, this group was among the earliest post-War attempts to disseminate Nazi myths and lies about the Holocaust. It championed neo-Nazi groups everywhere, and constantly harped on 'threats to the white race', the dangers of cross-breeding, and the 'virtues' of the Peron and Salazar regimes. There were four Frenchmen among the NOE organisers: Josseaume (a Breton autonomist), Binet and Jeanne (former Waffen SS members), and Cavallier (of Phalange Française).

In 1962 a splinter group of Nazis from Jeune Nation formed the Associations des Vikings de France. They began to establish closer links with the most extreme Nazi groups abroad. Under the new label Parti Proletarian National-Socialiste they joined the World Union of National Socialists (WUNS), and thus developed closer links with Colin Jordan and Lincoln Rockwell, the British and American Nazi leaders. In 1963 Yves Jeanne became the leading French member of WUNS, and WUNS propaganda began to be imported from the USA into France. Jordan, 'world *Führer*' of WUNS, and his fellow-Nazi Françoise Dior appointed Jeanne chief of the Fédération Ouest Européene (FOE) to represent WUNS in French-speaking countries: Jeanne was made to take an oath on an *Sturmabteilung* (SA) dagger. The FOE remained a tiny group of fanatics, probably no more than 50 strong, until September 1964, when it was broken up following the arrest of its leading officials.

Another attempt to establish a new Nazi grouping was Cercle National et Socialiste Européen, but this only lasted nine months because its efforts to evade the law forbidding 'vindication of crime' were too ambivalent. (It attributed the crimes of the Nazis purely to 'administrative errors'.)

A terroristic breakaway group from Europe-Action (formerly Jeune Nation) emerged in 1964. It was called Occident and was responsible for a number of brutal assaults on the left-wing students and organisers. And in April 1966 Fédération d'Action Nationale et Européene (FANE) was founded. Like the other fanatically Nazi groups it was of insignificant size, but did become a source of provocative racialist propaganda. The extreme right-wing candidate Tixier-Vignancourt's presidential election campaign was considerably aided by young people from Europe-Action, and much of the propaganda was provided by Société d'Etudes de Relations Publiques (SERP), founded in 1962 by a former Poujadist deputy, Jean-Marie le Pens, later also to become an extreme right presidential candidate. Yet another French fascist grouping, started in Spring 1966, was Mouvement Nationaliste du Progrés (MNP), which tried to present itself as a responsible nationalist party, recruiting mainly among students, and kept itself at arms' length from the overtly neo-Nazi movements while preserving its international links with fascists abroad. MNP claimed to have over 300,000 sympathisers and around 3,000 activist members. Despite its ambitious political plans and pretensions of becoming a mass party, it remained an insignificant feature of French electoral politics. The main fascist initiative in France in this period came from organisations such as FANE and Delta, another small and mysterious group of anti-Semitic terrorists.

In Germany, political movements were covertly but determinedly peddling Nazi ideas while the Allied occupation authorities were still in charge of their zones. Wirtschaftliche Aufbauvereingung (Economic Reconstruction Association) (WAV), founded and led by the demagogue Alfred Loritz, attracted many old Nazis to its banner and made a strong political impact in south-east Germany. Deutsche Reichspartei (German Rights Party) (DRP) and WAV both had deputies elected to the new post-War German parliament. DRP had 5 members returned from its power-base in lower Saxony, while WAV had 12 deputies elected from Bavaria. In fact 5 constituencies in lower Saxony gave over twenty per cent of their votes to DRP, and in 2 this party came near to obtaining one-third of the total vote. Both these, however, were to some extent catch-all parties, attracting old-style conservatives, farmers and the petty bourgeoisie in addition to the overtly Nazi elements. (The same thing was true of certain other groups, like the Refugee Party.)

A far more explicity and self-assertive Nazi party emerged in 1949. This was the Sozialistische Reichspartei (SRP), started and led by former Nazi Dr Fritz Doris, who had sided with the Otto Strasser more working-class oriented faction in the Nazi Party. The SRP was very closely modelled on the Nazi Party and sprouted a para-military auxiliary called Reichsfront. It also succeeded in penetrating the DRP and another extreme right party, Deutsche Partei (DP). In 1951 the SRP caused democratic observers some alarm when it scored eleven per cent of the total vote in the lower Saxony elections, and later scored successes in Bremen. At the height of its impact, the SRP attracted nearly 40,000 members. But its successes were short-lived, and it began to lose its support well before it was banned in 1952 under the law forbidding the reconstitution of a Nazi Party. From the mid-1950s to the mid-1960s the radical right in Germany declined almost to vanishing-point, while the main recipients of the conservative vote remained the Christian Democrats and, to a lesser extent, DP.

The dramatic decline of the Nazi right in Germany in this period is difficult to explain. The increasing affluence of

Germany's recovery period was beginning to percolate through to all strata of society and to all regions. Dr Adenauer provided a reassuringly strong anti-communist stance, which pleased the conservative right. And from 1958 the German membership of the European Common Market provided fresh opportunities for economic growth and a fresh source of success, security and international recognition and rehabilitation for the German people. But if all these factors explain the absence of any strong neo-Nazi challenge in this period, how does one explain the successes of Adolf von Thadden's National Democratic Party in 1965? How is it that, after almost 15 years without any significant electoral representation, the radical right suddenly became mobilised in 1965? If most of the conservatives had now reconciled themselves to Adenauer and his system, where was support for any new radical right party going to come from?

A possible factor was the growing sense of political frustration and confusion felt after the strong hand of Adenauer had been removed by his retirement. Cracks in the western Alliance and a sense of hopelessness over the possibilities of German re-unification, combined with a fear of economic recession, created the 'politics of anxiety' which, ever since Hitler's political successes, fascist movements in Europe have made every effort to exploit. Small businessmen and farmers, who felt particularly vulnerable to these changes, were precisely those who rallied to the mixture of populism and extreme nationalism preached by von Thadden and his NPD. Von Thadden's new party was able to get its organisation launched in time to take advantage of these tendencies. And the NPD absorbed the old faithfuls of the DRP as well as other ultra-right elements. In addition, the NPD leader was shrewd enough to present the party as a much broader new right coalition, emphasising constantly the NPD's formal acceptance of the norms of the Federal Republic's Constitution. Von Thadden had realised that by the mid-1960s there was no real electoral mileage remaining in an exclusivist neo-Nazi party. This new strategy was surprisingly effective. Von Thadden's anti-foreigner emphasis struck a response chord, especially in the old Nazi strongholds, but he was careful not to bring the anti-Semitic message of his DRP days to the fore. Instead he was able to work on popular irritation over the *Gastarbeiter* (guestworker) programme, antipathy to 'Americanisation', and an atavistic yearning for discipline and authority. It is this strategy and the change of mood in a more nationalistic direction that offers the best explanation for the NPD's ability to obtain 2.1 per cent of the second votes cast in the 1965 Bundestag elections, only a year after the founding of the party. Although four years later the NPD did not succeed in getting the 5 per cent of the total vote in the national elections necessary to secure representation, it did gain 4.3 per cent of the votes cast (1,422,054), and it won useful footholds in the *Landtag* of Hesse, Bavaria, Schleswig-Holstein, Rhineland-Palatinate, lower Saxony, Bremen and Baden-Wurtemberg. The surprising fact is that the NPD increased its share of first votes in every electoral district, doubling or tripling its share in the majority. In 1969 it crossed the magical 5 per cent barrier in Bavaria, Hesse, and Rhineland-Palatinate. But it remained an insignificant political force in comparison with the centrist parties, the CDU, FDP, SPD and CSU, which collectively *increased* their share of the vote from 71 per cent in 1949 to 94.3 per cent in 1969.

The experience of the 1970s was to show that the NPD had no great future as a political party. On the other hand, despite the failure of the fascist mass party strategy in West Germany, small and sinister neo-Nazi para-military and terrorist groups still survived, and kept in contact with other fascist movements in Europe and even further afield.

The puzzle about the fascism since the War is that it has survived at all. Even in the defeated fascist states, the climate after 1945 was overwhelmingly hostile to the extreme right.

Fascism carried the stink of humiliating defeat and destruction, and the memory of the colossal crimes committed by the Nazis was still fresh in the minds of millions who had suffered at their hands. There was no great Nazi comeback, not even any political conspiracy by former Nazi leaders. They were too busy trying to evade capture and prosecution for war crimes, or trying to find a safe haven where they could get rich 'in retirement'. Odessa, the network of former SS officers, specialised merely in trying to help Nazis escape and survive undetected. The people involved in leading the new European fascist movements, when they began to creep out of hiding, were by and large those who had been small fry in war-time, middle-range officials and local party organisers.

4 FASCISM IN THE 1970s

Italy was perhaps the one European country where a neo-fascist mass party seemed to have some chance of making real headway in the 1970s. They had already shown that they could enlist support both from the 'old guard' of the Mussolini era and from the young. And this gradual electoral progress did not appear to have been checked or even seriously damaged by popular revulsion at fascist acts of indiscriminate terrorism, from the bombing at Piazza della Fontana in Milan on 12 December 1969, which left 14 dead and 80 wounded, to the Brescia explosion at an anti-fascist rally on 28 May 1974, in which 7 were killed and 93 injured, and the bombing of the Rome-Munich express just outside Bologna on 4 August 1974, which killed 12 people and injured 48.

The Italian fascists continued to operate their dual strategy with limited success in the early 1970s. Giorgio Almirante, who had become MSI leader in 1968, strove desperately to shake off the party's image of the parliamentary pariah. He and his leading spokesmen insisted they were not a fascist movement, which in any case would have been contrary to the constitution, but a truly 'democratic' party officially opposed to violence and in favour of 'strong government', the restoration of authority, and traditional values. Yet under the respectable facade of the pin-striped suit the movement's black shirt showed all too clearly. In reality Almirante made every effort to cement his hold on both the old guard of fascist sympathisers still hankering after the Mussolini era, and a new influx of youthful supporters, many of whom were attracted precisely by the anti-democratic, anti-parliamentary image of the MSI, and the glamour of its implicitly illegal fascist past and beliefs. Indeed it was these same young fascists who spawned a whole cluster of fascist secret societies to mount a terrorist war against the liberal democratic institutions of the Republic and against their deadly enemies, the communists of the Italian Communist Party (PCI) and the neo-Marxist terrorist groups of the extreme left. There is nothing odd about the Italian fascist terrorist groups so consistently going for communist targets. Of course the PCI leadership has consistently held aloof from extra-parliamentary violence and has indeed joined with the christian democrats and socialists in condemning terrorism. This, however, only increases the loathing the fascists feel towards 'the system', and the communists in particular, for what they dread most of all is that by consolidating its position in the Senate and the Chamber of Deputies, using its organisational and trade union strength in the country to increase its share of the vote, the PCI might come to power, legally, as a dominant force in its own right or as a major coalition partner. Fascists also see the PCI as standing in the same relationship to the terrorists of the extreme left as the latter holds that the MSI does to the fascist secret societies like New Order and the Mussolini Action Squads – that is as a source of funds, weapons and other forms of covert support, though in reality there is no evidence of this.

In the early 1970s, however, MSI seemed at one stage to be on the verge of breaking through to much larger electoral support. By pushing its anti-communist, anti-trade union and ultra-nationalist ideas, and by playing on growing frustration, particularly strong in certain regions, over the stagnation of the economy, the endemic corruption and the inefficiency of the cumbersome bureaucracy, the MSI had a considerable boost of electoral support. In parts of Rome, Bari, and in Sicily, traditionally a strong base for Italian fascism, the MSI managed to increase its share of the vote in the 1971 regional and provincial elections to as high as 16 per cent. Over the previous 20 years they had rarely achieved more than 5 per cent of the vote. In Sicily the neo-fascist vote more than doubled as compared with the 1970 regional elections, from 7.2 to 16.3 per cent. In Rome, another area of traditional neo-fascist support, they pushed up their vote by 4.5 per cent. Most of their votes probably came from former monarchists (this party was now defunct), and from disgruntled Christian Democrats and Liberals.

The fascists' successes were in fact very unevenly distributed, and can largely be attributed to local circumstances. For example, in Sicily, the population

'. . . never suffered the tragic experiences of the Fascist Social Republic, set up in the North from 1943–5; even the *Squadrismo* of the early days of Fascism in 1921–4 was not as ferocious and had nothing like the same impact on Sicily as in the Po Valley and elsewhere in northern and central Italy. In Sicily, moreover, the MSI has consistently presented itself as a party of socially advanced views, never failing to stress the contrast between the massive revival of Mafia power, rendered possible by the acquiescence of the christian democrats and their allies and the (alleged) achievements of Fascism under Mussolini who, it is claimed, had virtually liquidated the Mafia. Sicily is also, despite recent efforts, an educationally and politically backward region (a considerable percentage of its inhabitants have remained illiterate) and the younger generation is unaware of the infamies committed by Mussolini's Social Republic, while working-class and trade-union organisations are weak owing to the island's lack of industry.' (Giovana, 1972)

Nevertheless, how can one account for the fact of the MSI's even partial success? One important factor was its ability to exploit the political and economic difficulties of the country to the full. It was already becoming clear in the mid-1960s that social tensions and conflicts were intensifying to a dangerous level, fuelled by the stresses of rapid industrialisation in the north, the continuing problem of backwardness in the south leading to heavy migration to the already overcrowded urban industrial centres of the north, the problems of adjustment to competition in the EEC, and, last but not least, the desperate plight of the agricultural sector.

Another important factor behind MSI's electoral gains was Giorgio Almirante. His record as an Under-Secretary in Mussolini's Social Republic, and before that as editor of the militant fascist journal *Difesa della Razza* (Defence of the Race) does not seem to have denied him a parliamentary career. After the war he was cunning enough to avoid taking sides in the furious disputes between, on the one hand, the militant *Squadrismo* and the tearaways who wanted terrorist and para-military action groups to be the order of the day, and, on the other, those favouring the building of a popular neo-fascist political party. Hence he avoided a break with the clandestine extremist groups. Indeed there is evidence that he acted as spokesman within the MSI for many of their ideas, and in the years 1970–2 he was quite successful in winning over many of these splinter-groups to the party.

Almirante achieved this, typically fascist, feat of being all things to all men by combining a moderate, reasonable tone in press conferences, parliamentary debates, and on television, while speaking to the party faithful at party meetings and rallies in the most violently aggressive terms, pandering to all the inflammatory impulses of the hardliners.

This explains the bizzare contradiction of Almirante publicly disavowing violent anti-Semitism and racism, while neo-fascist literature produced by groups within the MSI was still ranting about racial purity in traditional fascist terms. What Almirante and his circle appear to have had in mind was to present themselves as a kind of Italian Gaullism reminiscent of de Gaulle's RPF days, appealing to the army, civil service, and important sections of the middle class, and promising strong leadership and national salvation. Despite MSI's rather dramatic gains in the 1972 elections, increasing their share of seats in the Chamber from 24 to 51, Almirante's strategy did not come off. Even when they were

augmented by the merger with Destra Nazionale in 1973 and
their total strength reached 400,000 members, 14 senators and
35 deputies, they still looked miles away from challenging the
parliamentary strength of the christian democrats and the
PCI. Mario Giovana believes this was mainly because the
neo-fascists were too antiquated and rigid in their thinking:

'Even if Italy were to drift towards the authoritarian right, it would
hardly do so under the auspices of a neo-fascist party. It is far more
likely that this operation would be carried out under the aegis of the
clerical and conservative right with the support of sections of the
establishment. The MSI would play a secondary role. Authoritarianism in the 1970s, in an industrially advanced country, certainly
cannot revive the former ideas of fascist totalitarianism. Moreover,
the Christian Democratic Party, having the means and the power to
bring back disaffected conservatives into its own orbit, has no
intention of handing over the right-wing leadership to the MSI.'
(Giovana, 1972)

Yet there is a more fundamental reason for the MSI's
ultimate failure to succeed as a major parliamentary force. It
is simply that the transformation of the party into a respectable Gaullist-style movement has not been credible to the
Italian electorate. Considerable doubt has been thrown on
Almirante's claims of strict democratic propriety. They know
that MSI members have covertly worked hand-in-glove with
sinister terrorist groups such as Ordine Nero (Black Order),
Avanguardia Nazionale (National Vanguard) and Squadre
Azione Mussolini (SAM). The Italian press has quickly
exposed the Movement's violent links. An MSI senator and
the party's youth organiser were discovered at the scene when
a hand-grenade was thrown at a policeman, injuring 30
people, at a left-wing demonstration in Milan on 12 April
1973. When the matter was raised in the Chamber the next
day deputies almost came to blows. Following this the judiciary applied to the Chamber of Deputies to lift the parliamentary immunity of Almirante so that he could be put on trial for

trying to reconstitute the Fascist Party. The deputies voted to
do so by 485 votes to 69. Almirante protested his complete
innocence, and claimed his party disavowed the violence of
the fringe groups. He was not convicted, and his claims were
lent some credibility by the police discovery that the neo-
fascist Compass Rose Group arrested at La Spezia for organising a right-wing coup attempt had included Almirante
(along with 1,617 names, including Berlinguer, the PCI
leader) in their assassination list. This phase in the development of the MSI is so murky and confused, with secret service
and senior officers' conspiracies so closely interwoven, that it
is impossible to be sure whether Almirante and his leading
colleagues were personally involved. Often the fragmented
fascist groups worked against each other. But there is overwhelming evidence that the MSI's party offices have served as
'base camps' for groups of young fascist thugs roaming the
streets in search of left-wingers to beat up.

Another sinister aspect of the Italian political scene in this
period was the way in which MSI and other fascist groups
tried to establish themselves as champions of the police and
armed forces. Often they would mount 'revenge' attacks
following the death of a member of the security forces. More
intimate links, of an almost routine nature, were revealed by
the series of trials of neo-fascists accused of terrorist attacks
between 1969–74. Evidently successive Italian governments
had permitted and even actively encouraged the Italian
security services to penetrate the extreme right. This incestuous relationship was administered by General Vitor Miceli,
who was later accused of conspiring to carry out a *coup d'état*,
and who later still became an MSI deputy. Who was watching whom, one wonders?

By 1974 the MSI's electoral effort and the violence of the
fascist terrorist groups were both losing steam. In that year
the leaders of the extreme right lost their valuable links with
their former protectors in the security forces when leading
plotters were arrested, and the initiative in political violence

switched to the Red Brigades and other groups on the far left. The right did not regain the initiative until 1980. Meanwhile Almirante has had to content himself with trying to cultivate a new-style role as a kind of leader for a 'classic European right' as opposed to a strictly fascist European right.

The only other case among the western democracies of a neo-fascist movement making some progress towards creating an effective mass party with at least a chance of winning some leverage, is the National Front (NF) in Britain. It is interesting that the NF, like the MSI, has tried to develop a 'two-track' strategy. On the one hand it follows an opportunistic policy of attempting to present itself as a respectable political party appealing by argument and peaceful persuasion for the support of the British electorate. On the other, its leadership is deeply imbued with Nazi ideas, and though they try to play down their past affiliations with more blatantly Nazi movements, such as Colin Jordan's British National Socialist Movement, they covertly maintain intimate connections with small neo-Nazi cells in Britain and abroad, because all their beliefs and motives make this not only tactically expedient but instinctive.

While the MSI was quite effective, at least for a time, in exploiting the endemic social conflicts and regional tensions in Italy, the NF has had what from a fascist point of view is infinitely more promising ground to cultivate: the intensifying racial tensions in the many British cities which had experienced a large influx of immigrants in the 1950s and 1960s from the 'New Commonwealth' countries. The British Nazis have largely, though not entirely, redirected their racist hatred against this new group of scapegoats, in place of the Jews. The National Front sees the new immigrant communities as the major enemy of the British race and way of life and calls for compulsory repatriation of all immigrants.

The Front was formed in 1967 out of a merger of the League of Empire Loyalists, the majority of the Racial Preservation Society, and the British National Party. In 1968 Tyndall's

Greater Britain Movement, formed in 1964 as a splinter from the British National Party, joined the party. Though they could only claim 2,000 members when they were launched, they soon received a considerable, though unanticipated, boost from the after-effects of Enoch Powell's notorious April 1968 speech on immigration in which he warned of 'rivers of blood'.

Yet another speech by Enoch Powell, only five days before polling-day in the 1970 election, gave aid and succour, no doubt unwittingly, to the National Front campaign. Yet the 1970 National Front election results were a grave disappointment to their leadership. Their overall average vote was a mere 3.6 per cent and the best share they got in any constituency was 5.6 per cent.

Personal squabbles and splits among the NF hierarchy have plagued the movement. These are a traditional feature of fascism in Britain ever since the departure of its 'lost leader', Mosley, to retirement on the continent. The first Chairman of the NF, A. K. Chesterton (who had previously led the League of Empire Loyalists), resigned his office, ostensibly uneasy about the Nazi position of John Tyndall. Chesterton's successor, John O'Brien, resigned in 1972 for similar reasons. Yet despite these organisational problems, the Front began to make considerable improvements in its electoral showing. At the West Bromwich by-election in 1976, in an area with considerable social problems and latent anti-immigrant sentiment, the NF candidate, Martin Webster, managed to achieve 16.2 per cent of the poll. It is true that this occurred shortly after the controversy over the admission of Ugandan Asians to Britain, an issue which the racist propaganda of NF exploited to the full; but it was a danger-sign to the major parties that National Front support was on the increase in certain areas, and that the Front was capable of whipping up racial tension to electoral advantage. In the same year an NF candidate in the local government elections in Leicester increased the NF share of the poll to 18 per cent.

Many conditions in Britain in the mid-1970s seemed to be propitious for a big push by the NF for public support. Severe economic recession was hitting hardest at areas with heavy concentrations of immigrants among their populations, worsening housing situations, and severely over-strained educational, health, and social welfare services. These conditions

'. . . threw up exactly those social dissaffections and difficulties which traditionally have profited fascist organisations. The National Front asserted vigorously that economic hardships, inflation, unemployment, housing shortages, declining standards in education and welfare generally, the breakdown of law and order and all manner of associated problems were to be traced to the doors of black immigrants. . . .' (Tomlinson, 1981)

They also exploited several other factors. The NF cashed in on the growing unpopularity of British membership of the Common Market by demanding British withdrawal. And they parroted many other populist slogans that always find a ready hearing at the hustings: a 'crack-down on law and order', 'bring back hanging', 'stop the sponging on the social security' and so forth.

Their next big electoral opportunity for NF gains came in 1974, when they entered 90 candidates for the Autumn election. Yet the Front's capacity to exploit all the opportunities created by earlier campaigns in the midlands, parts of Greater London, and the north, was seriously hampered by the continuing internecine war for control over the movement among its leading figures: John Tyndall (who lost his position as chairman as a result of an internal schism), Martin Webster and Andrew Fountaine were rivals for leadership. John Tyndall was a Nazi of long standing, who had once been a member of A. K. Chesterton's League of Empire Loyalists. In 1960 he worked with Colin Jordan, running 'Spearhead', the para-military wing of the British National Party (BNP). (*Spearhead* later became the title of Tyndall's

National Front journal.) Tyndall and Jordan caused a split in the BNP as the result of their blatant Nazi style, and formed the short-lived British National Socialist Movement. Martin Webster joined Tyndall and Jordan's new movement early on, but has tried very hard to disguise this since. When the NF was formed in 1967 he and Tyndall became two of its leading organisers. Andrew Fountaine had, with John Bean, founded the National Labour Party in the 1950s, and later had started the BNP, which in turn was subsumed into the NF along with several other organisations.

Despite squabbles among these three the NF went into the elections with a membership that had tripled over the previous two years, and, because they had fielded sufficient candidates, they qualified for broadcasting time on television. Again the NF failed to make any major breakthrough. Every one of their candidates lost his deposit, and their total UK vote was 113,625, only half what Tyndall had been privately hoping for. The one key area where they got a significant rise in support was Greater London, particularly in the northern and western districts. Overall, however, the picture showed that though the NF had become the fourth largest political party in England, it was still a long way from winning even one parliamentary seat. And despite the deepening recession in Britain, the party registered yet another total failure in the general election of 1979.

How can this political failure be explained? In the first place, the mass media rapidly established the facts about the NF leaders' Nazi past and doctrines, and conveyed these clearly to the public. Secondly, both the major political parties took steps to equip themselves with a policy on immigration. Some argue that such policies are racialist and themselves exacerbate racial tension, but poll evidence suggests that the majority of the population see them as fair and reasonable, and thus an important NF plank has been taken away. Last, but not least, the movement was plagued by schisms and leadership struggles. These diverted energies, disrupted organisation and continuity, and created an image of disarray and weakness which tended to destroy its credibility as a political force. In Autumn 1979, Fountaine and Paul Kavanagh, another of the NF's leading members, were dismissed from the executive after making an abortive attempt to dismiss Tyndall. Tyndall was later forced to give up the chairmanship. The NF lost a court action over misrepresentation of the usage of Excalibur House (their Headquarters), and party membership has slumped. To add to their difficulties, a major split has now occurred, with Tyndall setting up the New National Front in 1980. In August of that year the National Front magazine *Spearhead* bemoaned the fact that:

'What our enemies could not accomplish over 13½ years of increasing endeavour had now been accomplished by the efforts of nationalists themselves: the NF has been smashed to pieces.'

However, the probable demise of the NF as a viable political force following the electoral lane of the 'two-track' strategy should not be equated with the collapse of British fascism as a whole. What has happened since 1978–9 is that a major switch of neo-Nazi effort has occurred, away from the attempt at electoral respectability or the tactics of 'legality' used with such effect by Hitler in the 1930s, and towards para-military recruitment and activity. Since 1980 the British Movement, founded in 1968 by Colin Jordan, has been channelling much of the fascist effort away from the National Front. Since 1975 the Movement has been led by Michael McLaughlin who took over after Jordan had to resign following a conviction for shoplifting. The organisation claims to have 25 branches in the UK, and probably has over 1500 members. Leaderguard, a para-military auxiliary group of the British Movement, has a grim reputation for violence. Its propaganda is blatantly Nazi. Its journal *British Patriot* describes itself as the 'Voice of Britain', is anti-Semitic, and totally scorns the electoral system. The Movement has a

'British Patriots [B.P.] Publications' outlet based in Clwyd, North Wales, distributing films, tapes, records and militaria, as well as Nazi books. Its 1980 catalogue bears the legend on its cover 'Eind Volk, Eind Reich, Eind Führer' (sic), and it lists numerous books and pamphlets eulogising Hitler and German Nazi history, in addition to staple anti-Semitic propaganda such as *The Protocols of the Elders of Zion*. An advertisement for the James Murphy translation of *Mein Kampf* claims: 'Read the book that became a bible to hundreds of millions of National Socialists as they fought to stem the communist avalanche'. British readers may be surprised to find a hagiographic biography of Herman Goering advertised, describing the head of the Luftwaffe as 'the founder of the Brownshirts; the power behind the world's most formidable air force who won the very heart of millions'. B.P. Publications also offers for sale *The Future Calls*, an analysis of Hitler, National Socialism, and where America's future lies, by the leader of the US Nazi Party, Koehl; *Our Nordic Race* by Richard Hoskins ('Every White Person should have a copy'); and *Auschwitz* by Christopherson and Roeder, described as 'an unbiased eyewitness report of the real life in a concentration camp. There were no gas chambers! Only fumigation chambers for delousing clothes'. It is a horrifying fact that the British Movement and its propaganda have been penetrating Britain's secondary schools and increasing their recruitment of young teenagers. The implications of the activities of this ugly movement are discussed in chapter 6.

Other fascist propaganda organisations active in Britain throughout the 1970s were the British League of Rights affiliated to the fascist World Anti-Communist League and specialising in low-key racist propaganda, and the League of Saint George, found in 1974, which serves as an umbrella organisation for British fascist groups. It has made special efforts to cultivate European and other Nazi organisations, such as the German Deutsche Burgerinitiative, the American NSDAP-AO, the Flemish VMO and the French FANE.

Two other worrying developments in Britain in the 1970s were the emergence of Column 88 and SS Wotan, clandestine Nazi groups organised and trained for terrorism. A recent authoritative study found evidence that Column 88 had infiltrated military units and established weapons training-camps and exercises. SS Wotan has been responsible for fire-bomb attacks on left-wing and immigrant targets.

If the electoral strategy of the neo-fascist parties in Italy and Britain appeared to have gone badly wrong by the mid-1970s, in other west European countries they were making little or no running at all. For example, in France the vote for the neo-fascist candidates in the 1974 Presidential election (Le Pen, Renouvin, and Royer) was derisory. Le Pen received 189,304 (0.75 per cent), Renouvin 42,719 votes (0.17 per cent), and Royer 808,825 (3.22 per cent). This makes a total of only 1,040,848 votes (4.14 per cent) for all the candidates of the extreme right, compared with a 1956 extreme right vote totalling 2,483,813 (9.2 per cent). This gradual decline in electoral support for the extreme right seems to have continued throughout the 1970s. Furthermore, it is worth noting that by no means all the extreme right groupings and voters are fascist in orientation: some are traditional authoritarian right. Poll evidence suggests that nearly 50 per cent of their supporters are over 50, and very few of them (only 14 per cent) are working class. Many of the potential voters for far right candidates have been attracted instead to the Gaullists, who combine full-blooded nationalist policies with a greater chance of achieving parliamentary representation and influences, if not power.

In West Germany, similarly, the neo-Nazi NPD, which made such surprising gains in the affluent 1960s (see chapter 3), has totally failed to follow up its earlier successes. The party declined in influence throughout the 1970s, with many of its members moving to the extreme right of the Christian

Democratic parties. However, once again it is essential to remind readers that the ebb and flow of electoral support is not a reliable gauge for assessing the potential of a fascist movement for damage and disruption. In France and West Germany, as in Britain, there has been a dangerous escalation of fascist terrorism, racist propaganda, and anti-Semitic attacks in the last few years.

By the mid-1970s neo-fascism was on the retreat, at least in electoral terms. The most dramatic setback to fascism internationally came in 1974, when the fascist-supported military dictatorships in Portugal, Greece and Spain collapsed in quick succession. These regimes had been important to fascists for a number of reasons. They provided a sanctuary for Nazis on the run from War crimes proceedings. Fascist movements within these countries could enjoy greater status and influence because of their historic support for the ruling regimes. The Spanish fascists under Franco, for example, could remain in touch with each other and indoctrinate up-and-coming generations with fascist doctrines. Finally, the fascists in these countries looked upon military dictatorship as a last bastion against communism and 'red terror'. Thus they saw the collapse of these systems as a major disaster, even though many of them had had reservations about the policies the dictators had actually followed.

The first collapse came in Portugal on 25 April 1974, when the Armed Forces Movement staged a military coup against Dr Marcello Caetano, successor to Salazar, who had applied a form of fascist-corporatist dictatorship to the country 'to save the nation from the government'. A possible communist takeover was forestalled on 25 November 1975 and a stable social democratic parliamentary government established, with the first free elections being held on 25 April 1976.

The regime of the Greek Colonels, set up in 1967 (the fascist elements of which have been referred to earlier), was eventually overthrown in 1974 as a result of increasing unrest in Athens and the government's failures in handling the crisis with Turkey over Cyprus. The experienced democratic politician, Mr Karamanlis, formed a fresh government in August 1974, pending elections the following November. Karamanlis' New Democracy Party won a safe majority, and once more a fascist-supported regime was firmly routed.

In Spain the transition to parliamentary democracy came surprisingly peacefully. In 1969 Franco nominated Prince Juan Carlos, grandson of King Alfonso XIII, to succeed him as Head of State. This occurred peacefully in November 1975, and the new King set about dismantling the controls used by the dictator. Political parties, including the Communist Party, were legally re-established, and other changes included a return to the independence of the judiciary and the freedom of the press, and the establishment of procedures for free elections, the first in Spain for over 40 years. At these elections in July 1977 the Democratic Centre Party won an overall majority with 166 seats, the Socialist Workers' Party 116 seats, and the communists 20 seats. The fascists' fears that democracy would open the floodgates to red terror were shown to have been exaggerated.

Spain is the only one of these countries to have experienced a significant fascist reaction since the establishment of parliamentary democracy. It is true that a small group of Greek army officers still loyal to the military junta plotted a coup a few months after its collapse in July 1974, but this conspiracy was foiled by the Karamanlis government on 24 February 1975. The ensuing purge of the armed forces was relatively cautious, to avoid the forces being taken over by the Marxist left. The heads of the navy and air force, who had been appointed by the junta, were replaced, and 37 army officers were arrested on charges of collusion in insurrection and similar crimes. In June 200 officers were either cashiered or retired. And after 3 weeks of rallies by groups, some led by senior officers, demanding a restoration of the monarchy, 21 former officers appeared in court accused of plotting rebellion.

The junta leaders and those alleged to have administered torture during the rule of the Colonels were put on trial, as were army and police officers charged with taking part in the storming of the Athens Polytechnic building in July 1974, when 30 of the occupying students, who were demanding the resignation of the junta, were killed and 1,000 injured. All these moves have made the Karamanlis government very popular, and although some small extreme right-wing organisations have survived, such as Fourth of August (date of the 1936 military take-over) and New Order (connected with the Italian Ordine Nuovo), the neo-fascists no longer constitute a serious threat to stability in Greece. Meanwhile in Portugal no significant regrouping on the extreme right has appeared, and its new democratic constitution follows the Italian and West German by declaring (under Article 46.4) that 'organisations which adopt fascist ideology shall not be permitted.'

There are special reasons why Spain has experienced an upsurge of fascism since the establishment of parliamentary democracy. Firstly, Spain under Franco was never a fascist state in the proper sense of the term. The dictator certainly enjoyed full-blooded support of the Falange movement in the Civil War, and this fascist element in his National Movement helped him considerably in enlisting military support from the Hitler and Mussolini regimes, which gave his forces the decisive edge in that war. Certainly Franco remained on very friendly terms with the fascist powers right up until 1943. But when the tide began to turn towards the Allies he rapidly began to distance himself from his fellow fascists overseas, realising that the strong taint of fascism would jeopardise the rehabilitation of Spain in a post-War world dominated by the Atlantic Alliance. Thus within the increasingly senile corporate state Franco presided over in the post-War years the Falange were excluded from power. Military chiefs, technocrats and industrialists carried the main weight in running the

Franquist system, while the Falange were confined to staging their annual ceremonies commemorating their colleagues slain in the Civil War. Hence, by the 1970s, the Spanish fascists were already looking to the death of Franco as a new opportunity to achieve the power that they had been so long been denied.

It is important to remember that Spanish neo-fascist groups such as Partido Espanol Nacional Sindicalista (PENS), Guer-rilleros de Cristo Rey (Warriors of Christ the King), Circulo Espanol de Amigos de Europa (Spanish Circle of the Friends of Europe), and Adolf Hitler 5th Command, were already actively engaged in violence and propaganda before Franco's death in 1975. Several of these groups, such as PENS and the Guerrilleros de Cristo Rey, were closely linked. Blas Pinar's Fuerza Nueva (New Force) party, formed before Franco's death, had ultra right-wing policies, and attracted support from traditional Spanish fascist groups which became deeply involv-ed in street violence and murder after the return to democracy in 1976–7. However, many of the more militantly neo-Nazi groups have been contemptuous of Pinar's party. For exam-ple, Juan Rubio Gomex of the Nazi Juventud Nacionalista Revolucionaria was reported in *Interviu* in May 1979 as declaring that Hitler had the right ideals. He dismissed Pinar's party as a reactionary faction!

Fascists have increasingly turned to violence and terrorism to oppose the King's constitutional reforms and to block or reverse the moves to democracy. One of the most dangerous groupings is Alianza Anticomunista Apostolica (AAA), op-erating in different cities as Benito Mussolini Commando, Adolf Hitler Commando, and so forth. Such fascist terrorists are undoubtedly sheltered and encouraged by the fascist old-guard and the *emigré* Nazi community in Spain. AAA terrorists assassinated four leading left-wing lawyers in Ma-drid on 24 January 1977, and in September killed two people when they bombed a Barcelona newspaper. In February 1977 the Prime Minister was advised to move his place of residence out of central Madrid because of threats from fascist terrorists.

One should not exaggerate the scale of public support for fascism in Spain. Despite the long period of indigenous and foreign fascist influence in the country the extreme right as a whole succeeded in mobilising only 2.5 per cent of the entire Spanish electorate to vote 'no' in the referendum of 15 December 1976 on whether or not to proceed with constitutional reform. The extreme right in party political terms is isolated, demoralised and ineffectual. But one cannot measure the dangers posed by fascism in Spain purely in such terms. The Spanish experiment with the new constitution is young and vulnerable, and the country is beset by acute economic problems. Francoists and crypto-fascists still occupy strategic positions in the armed forces, police and administration. And, most significant of all, the new democracy has been weakened by the severe and protracted terrorist campaign by the separatist organisation Euzkadi ta Azkatasuna (ETA) in the Basque region, a conflict in which many army, civil guard and police officers have been murdered. Left-wing terrorists from ETA and Grupo de Resistencia Antifacista Primero de Octubre (GRAPO) have been brazen enough to murder senior army officers in the heart of Madrid during broad daylight. Those senior elements in the military who have always disliked the idea of democratic reforms use the problem of terrorism to argue for the suspension of democracy and the emergency of military government. Moreover, as we have observed earlier, fascists have never been worried about constitutional proprieties and lack of democratic support. In a state with such a well-established tradition of *golpismo* (proneness to coups), attempts by fascists, in concert with others on the extreme right, to seize power cannot be discounted, as the Tejero coup attempt in February 1981 (discussed on page 133ff.) has shown. Spain is the former military dictatorship most vulnerable to a violent fascist reaction.

A very significant trend in the 1970s was the development of closer and more extensive international links between fascist movements throughout the western world. It is important not to exaggerate the degree of co-operation implied by these inter-connections. After all, one of the cardinal features of fascist ideology is the emphasis on the primacy of the 'nation' or 'race' and the supremacy of one's own nation or race over all others. This doctrine is not conducive to an atmosphere of fraternal internationalism. Tensions between fascist movements in different countries, along with the endemic personal squabbles and rivalries of the *Führer*-figures of the various movements, mean that the path of international fascist co-operation seldom runs smoothly.

Despite the difficulties mentioned above, the phenomenon of international links between fascists is by no means an entirely new one. In the earlier phase of fascism, Hitler and Mussolini ardently cultivated and aided client fascist movements in other countries as a means of extending their own power and influences (see p. 48). In the aftermath of defeat European fascists gravitated towards certain countries which became havens for wanted Nazis, such as Argentina, Brazil and Spain. For example, in Spain the Circle of Spanish Friends of Europe (CEDADE), formed in 1965 and based in Barcelona, became a forum and a source of propaganda and encouragement for fascists from other countries.

Nevertheless, the 1970s saw three new forms of linkage between fascists in different countries. First, there were bilateral links between movements with similar aims and ideological stance, such as the links between the Greek and Italian New Order groups, and the neo-fascist arms smuggling trade from Greece to Italy during the mid-1970s. Another example is the link between the Italian Black Order and the Italian Armed Revolutionary Nuclei (NAR) and FANE. Sometimes there has been a link with a sponsor state, as between Libya and the Italian-Libyan Friendship Groups, which have acted as a channel for cash aid to neo-fascist organisations in the early 1970s. The second type of link is the effort to establish international fascist organisations with grandiose European-wide or global aims. European National Fasces (FNE), the successor to FANE, is an example of this type, although in this case the leadership and activities of the leadership and activities of the group are entirely French. Another example is the World Union of National Socialists launched by the self-proclaimed world *Führer* Lincoln Rockwell, the American Nazi who was later murdered (see chapter 3). Third, there are the rallies held annually under the sponsorship of the Flemish Militant Order (VMO) at Diksmuide, Belgium. These are largely of ceremonial or symbolic significance to the fascist movements from all over the Western world who attend them. Here they parade in black uniforms to commemorate members of the SS slain in the Second World War. These Belgian gatherings are not generally used for any international political meetings or planning. The groups do meet informally in bars after the rally, but even then the language barrier prevents them from using these occasions for any serious co-ordination.

The late 1970s saw more collaboration in para-military training or 'manoeuvres', of the kind organised by the VMO and the Sports Group Hoffman in Germany. Occasionally the groups exchange 'troops'. Other multilateral contacts of this kind have been organised in Spain, under the sponsorship of CEDADE. There has also been a growing international trade in fascist publications. For example, the *Volkischer Beobachter* has been printed and distributed in Belgium. When the police there stopped the presses, printing was taken over by British fascists with their own publishing outlet. In the recent big raid by West German police on neo-Nazi homes thousands of anti-Semitic and neo-Nazi publications produced by extremists in the USA and Canada were discovered. Ernst Christof Zundel, a Canadian from Toronto, runs the 'Samisdat Publishers Ltd', a main centre for producing this propaganda. Zundel, who emigrated to Canada in the 1950s, is the son of Black Forest lumberjack. He made contact with escaped

Nazis and began producing cassettes of books for German customers on such themes as: 'Hitler at the South Pole', 'Hitler, the Bible and the Six-Million-Jews-Lie', and 'Allied War Crimes' (which has an introduction by the Nazi Hans Ulrich Rudel). Another major entrepreneur of Nazi propaganda, based in the USA but exporting all over Europe, is Gerhard Lauck, an American of German descent who is based at Lincoln, Nebraska. At the age of 18 he founded the NSDAP – Auslands- und Aufbauorganisation (National Socialist Workers Party – Foreign and Development Organisation). He specialises in distributing swastikas, photos of Hitler, handbills ('Death to the Reds', 'Out with the Jews'), and Nazi flags and badges. He works for the American Nazi Party and publishes both the *New Order* in the USA and its German counterpart *N S – Kampfruf*. Lauck is obsessed with his mission as a Nazi propagandist. He distributes 1,000 copies of his bi-monthly Nazi tract throughout West Germany: it is dated from the year of Hitler's birth and rages about the 'Holocaust swindle', describing the Federal Republic of Germany as the 'occupiers of what remains of Germany'. Typical of this publication is the following comment on a bomb attack by Spanish fascists: 'five reds kick the bucket'. Elsewhere he writes of 'five communist lawyers eliminated', and enjoins his readers 'the following reds are to be earmarked for special treatment.' In another passage he comments: 'it would have been better if another six million Jews had allegedly left the world via a "gas chamber".'

The links between American and European neo-Nazis are two-way. Colin Jordan of the British Nazi movement and Manfred Roeder, the German Nazi organiser who spent many years among sympathisers in other western countries before returning to Germany on a false passport, are among the many European fascists who have made fund-raising trips to the USA. The American Nazis also have links with the Swedish neo-Nazi headquarters at Malmo and with the Spanish CEDADE. Veteran German Nazis like Thies

Christopherson (author of *The Auschwitz Lie*) have conducted lecture tours in the USA and Canada, trying to strengthen links between the Nazi groups. In their turn American Nazi and Ku Klux Klan leaders have visited Europe, and the latter have succeeded in starting new sympathiser groups in West Germany and Britain.

Another fascist group having close connections with fascist extremist groups abroad is the League of St George in Britain, founded in 1974. One spokesman for this body, Mike Griffin, interviewed on Dutch TV, tried to present the League as merely an anti-immigrant group. In reality it is an organisation of neo-Nazis. Its *League Review* preaches anti-Semitism and most of its members also belong to other fascist organisations such as the British Movement and the National Front. The group has specialised in developing links with European and other fascist parties, such as Fane, NSDAP-AO, the Ku Klux Klan, the VMO, and the Dutch Nazi Northern League. They have invited leading Euro-Nazis – such as Arnd Marx of the Hoffmann 'Sports Group' and Manfred Roeder of the German Deutsche Burgerinitiative – to address their meetings and contribute articles, and they also represent British fascists at the VMO rally in Belgium. With the aid of the British Movement, they co-ordinate this annual pilgrimage of British fascists to Diksmuide.

In the 1970s there were a number of major efforts made by European fascists to bid for a wider base of support and a greater acceptability among the 'classic' or traditional right. One example was the meeting of the 'European Right' hosted by Tixier-Vignancourt in Paris. But to 'sell' themselves as members of the legitimate right the fascists have to make great efforts to disguise their Nazi ideas and interconnections. This is not only difficult; it is highly unpopular with the more militant Nazi propagandists. Leon Degrelle, the war-time Belgian fascist leader, who was condemned to death in his own country but who escaped to Spain, is one of several who have attempted to woo the traditional right. In a recent book he pleaded with them to accept the war-time fascists as honourable allies. In an 'Open Letter' to the Pope, included in the book, Degrelle claims that Auschwitz did not have extermination chambers. Yet another European fascist who has attempted to unite the fascist parties with the traditional right is Giorgio Almirante of the Italian MSI. His party attended a combined rally with Blas Pinar's Fuerza Nueva in Spain to commemorate the third anniversary of Franco's death, which attracted a 200,000-strong crowd. Almirante and Pinar have made frantic efforts to broaden the base of their support and to get on better terms with traditional parties of the right. Not surprisingly all these approaches have been rejected by the conservative and Christian democratic parties of western Europe, but the legitimate right has to remain on its guard against neo-fascist attempts at penetration or subversion.

Yet it was not only in Europe and the USA that fascistic movements, so long written off for dead, began to surface again in the 1970s. At the beginning of the decade, on 25 November 1970, a bizarre and horrifying event in Japan awoke the Japanese public and the rest of the world to the fact that the peculiarly Japanese 'military-imperial' mutation of fascism (which took root in Japan, with such dire consequences, in the 1920s and 30s) was still alive in the minds of a tiny fanatical cult on the extreme right. Informed opinion abroad was certainly aware of the vociferous extremism at the opposite end of the Japanese political spectrum: pacifism, unilateral disarmament, and ultra-left ideas on the future of Japanese society, were deeply and widely held among Japanese students and the younger generation as a whole. Indeed it was from this quarter that Japan experienced most political violence, including pitched street-battles with the police. The most extreme form of neo-Marxist revolutionary violence was manifested in the ruthless terrorism of the Japanese Red Army.

At 11 a.m. on 25 November Yukio Mishima, accompanied by four of his disciples, forced his way into the Army Headquarters in Tokyo. He made an emotional speech from a balcony over the parade square, calling upon the soldiers to rise and demand rearmament from the government and bitterly condemning the Japanese people for being 'drunk with prosperity'. Mishima addressed the soldiers for eight minutes before realising that they were not responding to his appeal, then unsheathed his Samurai sword, stripped to the waist, knelt down and disembowelled himself. Thereupon one of his followers, Kazumasa Morita, decapitated Mishima, and then slit his own stomach, before being beheaded in his turn by another disciple.

To many Japanese this came as a terrible shock, for Mishima had already built up a reputation as Japan's greatest living novelist. It was as if Hemingway had committed suicide in a public demonstration in the centre of Washington. Yet to those who knew Mishima's writings intimately, and had understood the passionately romantic and reactionary nature of his nationalist political beliefs, it was a gesture entirely in character. After all, he did not confine his nationalism to his writings. In 1967 he had founded a tiny fascist-style private army called the Shield Society, consisting of less than 100 hand-picked ultra-rightist officers and dedicated to protecting the life of the Emperor (whom they believed to be sacred), to reviving the Samurai tradition, and to overturning the decadent 'peace constitution' imposed by the Americans after the War. Ironically, the passive Japanese Self-Defence Force, the only armed body permitted under the Japanese constitution, provided military training for the Society. With its emphases on blind obedience, military discipline and warrior-virtues, Mishima's Shield Society was a replica of the Japanese secret societies of the 1930s and the fascistic German Frei Korps of the inter-War period.

We have earlier observed that the mutation of fascism that afflicted Japan did not follow the German and Italian models very closely. The leader-worship was not directed at a charismatic political *Führer* or *Duce*, but at the figure of the God-Emperor himself. The powerful Jushin group, emboldened by the success of their expansionist drive into Manchuria, harnessed its ultra-nationalist and imperialist aggressiveness to the struggle to create a new empire for Japan (the Greater East Asian Co-Prosperity Sphere) in the 1930s and 40s. Radical and liberal voices in Japan were silenced. Expansionist militarism was welded together with a Shinto Emperor cult, rather than into an explicitly fascist ideology or structure.

Following the Meiji Restoration of 1868, Shrine Shinto was elevated into what really amounted to a national cult, to which all other religions were subordinated. The Emperor, as the High Priest of the Shrine Shinto, was made the focus of worship, along with his unbroken line of ancestors. In the 1930s the Japanese militarists used the Emperor cult to tighten their hold on the people, claiming that because of their unique God-Emperor system the Japanese were superior to all other races and were therefore predestined to dominate the rest of the world. The similarities between this doctrine and the German Nazis' concept of themselves as the *Herrenvolk*, linked to the powers of the ancient Teutonic gods, should not need to be laboured.

What may be less well-known abroad is that despite the post-War constitution imposed by the Americans, and their instruction to the Emperor to renounce the attributes of divinity, the God-Emperor cult still quietly survives, and is thus a potential rallying-point for the extreme right. The emperor continues his custom of rendering account to his spiritual ancestors at Ise, and prays to his deified grandfather in the Tokyo Meiji Shrine. And he performs many of the other rites and ceremonies of Shinto tradition. There is considerable discrepancy between the official public relations statements and the reality of religious practice. It would be the aim of right-wing extremists to publicly restore the Emperor cult to its previous position in Japanese society. Again, it is hardly necessary to point out the anti-democratic and authoritarian implications of such a move.

It is somewhat reassuring to learn that most of the soldiers who heard Mishima's tirade seemed totally unmoved, while many jeered. However, we should not be under any illusions: many senior officers and officials who served in the Second World War nostalgically approved of Mishima's act of *seppuku*, seeing it as a link with the warrior virtues of the Samurai and the traditional Japanese army. The welter of press comment and public reactions to the event showed that the fascistic attitudes symbolised by the Shield Society were shared by student groups and others. They are a small minority, but they nevertheless keep these dangerous beliefs alive. Thus the anti-Americanism and anti-Soviet sentiments that have sometimes erupted into street violence in post-War Japan could conceivably, given a major economic crisis or threat, be channelled by the extreme right into a more general xenophobic ultra-nationalism. Indeed Mishima and his followers had themselves hoped to exploit such opportunities in June 1970 when they expected a huge uprising against the security treaty with the United States. In the event the riots Mishima anticipated did not transpire, but the right-wing extremism he represented is still a potentially explosive force.

Nor can we assume that the *attitudes* represented by Mishima only reached a tiny and insignificant audience, for he was, in the estimation of most Japanese and foreign critics, the most powerful Japanese novelist of the post-War period, and his novels and short stories provided him with a medium for exploring his ideas on Japanese nationhood and history, the Emperor, and the moral and physical cult of the Samurai. His writings do not hide his contempt for Japanese parliamentary politics, which he saw as degrading and corrupt. His *After the Banquet* (1960) was a widely read tragi-comedy on the nature of Japanese politics. Parts of it were so thinly disguised that they led to an action for libel. Mishima's short story 'Patriotism', also published in 1960, describes a group of the young officers involved in a 1936 revolt against a corrupt government. One of the officers has been recently married, and is therefore excluded from the plot. When the conspiracy fails and he sees that he will be forced to take military action against his brother officers, he spends a final ecstatic night with his wife, and then commits *seppuku*. His young wife, who has witnessed his suicide, then slits her own throat and dies.

These obsessions with loyalty, patriotism, and violence recur in book after book. For example, in *The Voices of the Heroic Dead* (1966) the 1936 rebel officers' group reappears when their ghosts, in the company of those of the *kamikaze* pilots of the Second World War, rise up to reproach the Emperor, claiming that he has betrayed them by declaring he is not a god.

In the police investigations following Mishima's *seppuku* it transpired that there was originally more to it than patriotic gesture. The first plan had been to bring about a *coup d'état* by getting the 32nd Infantry Regiment to rise in their support. Mishima had apparently only discarded this plan on the day before, when he discovered that the commander of this regiment would be away from Tokyo on the planned date of the coup. How many potential supporters or sympathisers does the extreme right have in the Japanese Self-Defence Force? And, if the other western allies get their way and encourage Japan's military to take on a larger and more powerful role in the alliance, may it be the case that they could release the genie of Japanese militarism from the bottle after all these years of domesticity?

Japan is an example of a country where fascist trends have long been in eclipse, though have by no means been extinguished. A complete contrast is the case of the Republic of South Africa, where a powerful fascistic secret society, the Afrikaner Broederbond, formed in 1918, has completely penetrated and now tries to manipulate the government, the armed forces, and every important institution in the state. As we have seen (in chapter 3), members of this group had intimate links with Nazi Germany, vehemently opposing South Africa's participation in the Allied cause. In 1942 J. G. Strijdom, later to be a Nationalist prime minister, felt able to declare:

'German national socialism strives for race purity. That philosophy is most certainly the nearest to our national-Christian philosophy in South Africa.'

Dr Malherbe, General Smut's Director of Military Intelligence in the War, observed that 'a number of prominent Afrikaner leaders became openly pro-Nazi and found expression of their ambitions in flamboyant organisations such as the Grey Shirts and the Ossewabrandwag (Ox-Wagon Sentinel). Malherbe and other observers noted the disturbingly high proportion of Dutch Reformed ministers, teachers and Afrikaner students involved in the Broederbond and concluded:

'Racial separation, which had been a part of South Africa's way of life for generations, received a new impetus from Nazism and German-orientated Afrikaners . . . a number of leading Afrikaners had become impressed by Hitler's success in propagating the doctrines of national socialism in Germany. The Nationalists, particularly, found themselves in sympathy with his ideas of building up a pure Nordic race which would rule Europe after getting rid of Jews and capitalists. Hitler's regimentation of the German youth and particularly his use of symbol slogans and national rallies to create a feeling of national consciousness were soon copied in building up an exclusive Afrikaner nationalism. Behind it all was the thoughtful planning and pervasive organisation of the Broederbond.' (Wilkins and Strydom, 1979)

The essentially racist and fascist message of the movement

was reiterated in a speech by Dr Treurnich, head of the Broederbond since 1972, in a speech he made at the secret *Bondsraad* meeting in 1968:

'I believe that the Afrikaner nation and the Broederbond must again be called on to resist the blurring of the Afrikaner consciousness in a kind of white unity which will be neither Afrikaans nor English; the overwhelming of our beliefs by liberalistic ideas; a temptation to yield as the tide is turning against us.' (ibid.)

One difference between this and the Nazi message is the Afrikaans stress on the absolute truths of the Dutch Reformed Christian faith. It is also, of course, more an exclusivist secret society and pressure-group operating within the South African power structure than a mass movement or party. In 1977 the Broederbond claimed to have 11,910 members, of whom 18.81 per cent were farmers, 20.36 per cent teachers, 7.12 per cent clergymen, and 4.35 per cent public service officials. It is important to notice that the Broeders monopolise all the top positions in the education system, with 24 university and training-college rectors, 171 professors, 176 lecturers, 468 headmasters and 121 inspectors of schools among their membership. Also in their ranks are 16 judges, 67 magistrates, 16 managers of newspaper groups and 22 editors. The vetting and preparation of candidates is a protracted and complicated process, taking as long as 3 years in some cases.

Induction into the society is by means of a ceremony which takes place in a darkened room lit only with two candles. A table is draped in a South African flag, and the flag of the Republic is used, the symbol of Union Jack in the flag is always blanked out. The recruit has the aims of the Broederbond read aloud to him and then takes a solemn oath to serve the Afrikaner nation through the Broederbond, to maintain complete secrecy about the Broeders and his own membership, never to join any other secret society, and to obey the orders of the organisation. The organisation even has a junior or cadet branch, the Ruiterwag, with identical aims to the Bond, which serves as a training and recruitment channel for the senior organisation.

In a speech at the Broeders' 50th anniversary, Professor A. N. Pelzer claimed:

'The understanding [between the government and the Bond] has always been of the best. This fortunate state of affairs can be attributed to the fact that the political leaders were normally members of the Afrikaner Broederbond and the problems were discussed in a spirit of brotherhood.' (ibid.)

There are close links between Cabinet members and business chiefs in the Bond. The present prime minister, Mr P. W. Botha, is a member, and there was no doubt that he was coming under increasing pressure from his fellow Broeders in 1980. He is already being seen as a dangerous and disruptive 'liberaliser' by many of the hardliners, and there are signs of a major split in Afrikanerdom with a new political party, the Herstigte Nasionale Party, being formed to stop Botha's policies 'undermining' the apartheid system. Moreover, in 1980 a new fascistic terrorist group called Witkommando (White Commando), claiming to be acting in the 'true interests of Afrikaner nationalism and race purity', was founded. In May 1980 it tried to blow up the prime minister, and in August 1980 it tried to kill Professor Lombard of the South African Institute of Race Relations.

Meanwhile developments on the 'intellectual' right were to significantly influence the outlook for fascism in the USA and Western Europe in the late 1970s and early 1980s. In the 1970s propaganda efforts by fascists and philo-fascists to revise or even entirely rewrite the history of the Second World War along neo-Nazi lines were considerably intensified. Of course pamphlets and books by neo-Nazis and former Nazis white-washing Hitler and claiming the Nuremberg trial to be a gigantic confidence trick by the Allies had been the stock-in-trade of fascist groups throughout the post-War years. Perhaps the most brazen of all these propaganda efforts was the anonymous *The Myth of the Six Million* (1969) which alleged that the Holocaust never happened. It was in the crudest tradition of anti-Semitic tracts, a direct descendant of the notorious forgery *The Protocols of Learned Elders of Zion*.

In 1976 a much more dangerous, more insidious form of neo-Nazi revisionism appeared, in the form of *The Hoax of the Twentieth Century* by Dr Arthur Butz, for this book attempts to represent itself as a serious work of scholarship, complete with the academic apparatus of footnotes, bibliography, and references to respected historians of the Holocaust, such as Lucy Dawidowicz and Gerald Reitlinger. The pretence of objectivity is sustained partly by the technique of conceding that *some* of the Nuremberg evidence did prove that war crimes were committed by the Nazis. Butz also concedes that as many as a million Jews may have died in the War, and that SS units serving in Russia may have murdered civilians. By such tactics Butz tries to 'soften up' his reader for accepting his main case, i.e. that the conventionally accepted historians' account of the Holocaust is a gigantic hoax. Any serious historical scholar would not be fooled for more than a moment. The author's virulent anti-Semitism and specious arguments crowd every page. But what is worrying is that some general readers might be gravely misled by the veneer of scholarly respectability into accepting the book as a work of history. Some other historians have begun to peddle this kind of 'revisionism', including David Irving, author of *Hitler's War* and many other widely-read books.

The Institute for Historical Review, based in California, which held its first international conference at Los Angeles in 1979, has become a major propaganda base for this more 'subtle' approach to neo-Nazi revisionism. They go out of their way to sponsor works by neo-Nazis with *bona fide* academic degrees or some sort of formal position in higher education. It also runs a publishing outlet in Britain, the

Historical Review Press, and an institute journal – all trappings of a conventional research institute. But the blatantly neo-Nazi aims of the outfit are not always very carefully camouflaged. For example, they decided to offer a prize of fifty thousand dollars to anyone who could provide proof that the Nazis gassed Jews, and two recent papers given to the Institute's first international conference were entitled 'Auschwitz in Slides' and 'The Holocaust in Perspective'.

The following piece is an excellent summary of some of the tactics used by the revisionist Nazi historians:

'The more accomplished authors of the genre maintain they were exterminationist believers, and experienced terrible soul-searching and anguish in their conversion to the revisionist school. They constantly claim the stamina needed, and the intensity and seriousness of their research in the quest for truth, whatever it might be. An attempt is made to secure the respect and admiration of readers by relating the text to footnotes, references and other technical procedures. Concentration on a number of restrained objectives is the aim; once the objective is delimited, the problem is attacked repeatedly in all possible ways. The systematic denunciation of exterminationist writers who use similar methods must be made to render the impression that the reader is faced by two schools of thought, the more scientific of which is the revisionist school. To call into question one point of normally accepted history is to subvert the whole, thereby creating an intellectual environment casting doubt on every page of opposition writing.' (Barnes, 1981)

These techniques are of course all too familiar to the readers of Marxist–Leninist revisionist historians. It is less widely appreciated that they are being used by historians of the extreme right.

The greatest danger from all this revisionist output is the constant drip effect on the values and attitudes of the general public. By sowing considerable confusion about the facts of the Holocaust, the more subtle neo-Nazi propagandists may provide a way of escape for those who feel guilty that so-called

Christian countries did so little to help the Jews. Perhaps more likely and hence more dangerous is the possibility that in a period of economic crisis and growing insecurity the revisionists' allegations concerning Jewish 'conspiracies' and 'machinations' will help once again to make the Jews scapegoats and targets for fresh waves of persecution.

At the end of the decade a powerful and effective counterblast, reaching a huge audience throughout the western world, stopped the bandwagon of neo-Nazi revisionist propaganda in its tracks. It came from a somewhat surprising source – the commercial television companies of Hollywood – and it took the form of a controversial 'soap-opera' style dramatised series entitled *Holocaust*, screened in the USA and throughout western Europe in 1979–80.

It is difficult to imagine a more sensitive, or more important theme from contemporary history to treat in this medium. As a Council of Europe report on racism and fascism put it: 'the series touched a raw nerve throughout Europe.' One can imagine the intense interest it aroused among German and Austrian audiences, particularly among the generations who cannot remember the Second World War. A survey of the West German television audience for the final episode discovered that 41 per cent of the potential television audience saw it, three-quarters of them were born after Hitler's coming to power. There was an enormous effort by the West German media and educational authorities to prepare the public for viewing the series. Additional programmes were made and special teaching aids and historical background literature disseminated. That the whole experience was a valuable contribution to public education on Nazism is borne out by the response. The survey found that no less than 81 per cent of those who viewed the final episode discussed the film with others, and 65 per cent admitted that they had been deeply moved by the programme. After the showing of each episode there were thousands of telephone calls and letters from viewers. The Austrian Chancellor Bruno Kreisky commented, after the screening of the first episode, that calm and reasoned discussion of the period was the best way to ensure that it never happened again. An exercise in mass education of this kind was certainly long overdue.

Needless to say, the showing of *Holocaust* provoked outburst from the neo-Nazi groups. *Deutsche Stimme*, the NPD journal, published a piece by Martin Mussgnug, its leader, claiming that American Jewish profiteers had used atrocity stories to ensure 'for all time, the existence of the state of Israel by way of payment of billions.' Another extremist newspaper denounced the series in similar terms: *Deutsche National-Zeitung* described *Holocaust* as a confidence trick perpetrated by American networks dominated by Zionists. Other Nazi organs raged that the series was a plot to indoctrinate future generations of Germans into feelings of guilt and helplessness and to frustrate the Statute of Limitation. Many of the Nazi activists did not leave things there: more cases of Swastika daubings and acts of provocation occurred, apparently in direct response to the series, and threats were made against television stations. In January 1979 two television antennas were destroyed by neo-Nazi bombs.

There was a passionate debate in France about whether the series should be shown at all. In the end it was only shown after leading figures like Simone Weil had come out strongly in favour, and as a result of public demand. An estimated 25 million French viewers saw *Holocaust*, and inevitably it touched the sensitivities and guilt feelings of the millions of French people who had passively accepted or collaborated with the Vichy regime. A similarly impassioned debate followed the 1979 showing of the television film *Les Guichets du Louvre*, which dealt with the rounding-up of the Jews in Paris thirty-seven years earlier.

In Switzerland the publication of Max Schmid's *Shalom, Wir werden euch toten*, a history of anti-Semitism in Switzerland, combined with the showing of *Holocaust*, stimulated a lively debate in the Swiss media about the causes and consequences of Nazism. It also coincided with a spate of threats and bomb attacks against synagogues and other Jewish targets in Geneva, Basle and elsewhere. Again guilt complexes were aroused, this time about the war-time sealing of the Swiss frontiers and the activities of the pre-War fascist organisation, the Swiss National Front. All in all most observers agree that the showing of *Holocaust* had a tremendously positive effect on public opinion throughout Europe, especially among the young. The irony is that it should have been achieved so late in the day, not by any effort of governments or political parties, but by commercial television networks.

In France the new right campaign to permeate the intellectual establishment with fascistic ideas and attitudes has proved far more subtle and sophisticated than the efforts of the historical revisionists, though in a sense it is complementary to them. The major organisation master-minding this 'cultural' strategy is Groupement de Recherche et d'Etudes pour la Civilisation Européene (which has the rather contrived acronym GRECE). The leading figures involved are the writers Alain de Benoist, Louis Pauwels and Professor Faurisson, whose right to express his eccentric opinions on the Holocaust has recently been defended by Noam Chomsky. In a major propaganda coup the new right were able to gain control of *Figaro-Magazine* (the colour supplement to *Figaro*), owned by Robert Hersant, a right-wing businessman. Through *Figaro-Magazine*, GRECE's own publishing-house Copernic, and their other magazines *Nouvelle Ecole* and *Elements*, the new right in France has been able to reach the kind of mass reading public only accessible to the left in the 1960s. The highly articulate peddlers of the new right began to enjoy a certain fashionable respectability by 1978–9, carefully distancing themselves from the violence and crudity of the traditional French extreme right. Recruits began to flow in from the universities and even from the *lycées*. But let us make no mistake about the sinister nature of the doctrines that have been disseminated by this grouping. Their doctrine is based on a theory of eugenics and of the desirability of rule by an elite of the new right: it is diametrically opposed to the humane values of the Judaeo-Christian tradition, and to the principles of political democracy. There is disturbing evidence that the surprising ease with which the new right have permeated many of France's leading institutions, such as the top civil service (through *Club de l'Horloge*), the media and the professions, has led to the creation of an intellectual climate far more conducive to racism. GRECE has adapted the theories of Eysenck and Jensen to support its arguments against miscegenation and to back its claims for the cultural and intellectual superiority of the Indo-European over the Semitic and other races. (Note their careful use of euphemisms to differentiate themselves from explicitly fascist doctrines – e.g. they use 'Indo-European' instead of 'Aryan'.) Thus they preach doctrines of racial superiority, exclusivity, and the preservation of a racial elite, and they exhibit a profound contempt for doctrines of democracy and equality.

What is different about their strategy is that it aims to win a battle of ideas, to influence public opinion by changing peoples' views and ultimately by altering their structure of values. (Again note the close parallel to the strategy of the extreme left in seeking to create a 'revolutionary consciousness'. The new right is constantly seeking to learn from the tactical and strategic success of its adversaries on the extreme left.) That their ideas have enjoyed a certain vogue in France, and in the Francophone world, is indisputable, and they have certainly led to a revival of interest among the literary minority in the literature of fascistic attitudes and doctrines. At the popular level their influence is more difficult to gauge, but it is disturbing that opinion poll evidence in France in 1979–80 showed that minorities such as Jews, Corsicans, Africans, Turks and others were increasingly the targets of racist attitudes.

One of the ironies of the intensification of fascist violence at the end of the decade, particularly the terrorist attacks throughout western Europe, is that it will probably do much to crack the smooth facade of neo-fascism and reveal its true nature to the public. Leaders of the new right in France and the MSI in Italy, who have set such store on winning acceptance among the traditional legitimate right, realised this danger at once when the bombing outrages of 1980 occurred. But the fact is that overwhelming evidence of fascism's propensity for violence against the innocent was available throughout the decade 1969–79. That this was not generally emphasised or taken notice of reflects the unbalanced attitudes prevalent in western governments and the media. With a few distinguished exceptions, they refused to recognise that fascism was a threat. Instead they constantly emphasised the threat from the revolutionary left and failed to monitor fascist developments thoroughly. In some European countries like Italy and Spain governments and police forces seem often to have turned a blind eye or even connived to shelter fascists from the law.

Nevertheless, it would be a mistake to see fascist terrorism as a sign of growing *political* strength. On the contrary, its emergence and growth was really evidence of the increasing weakness and desperation of fascist movements, as one after another they failed to make any headway in winning any substantial base of mass support or in destabilising even the most trouble-prone of the democratic systems. The sheer indiscriminateness and barbaric cruelty of their acts of violence should, however, have warned the democratic governments to have recognised them long ago as a serious threat to innocent life and to peaceful community relations, and stronger counter-measures should have been taken to deal with them.

The Bologna and Munich bombings were only the most obvious manifestations of this move into terrorism by the far right as the 1970s came to an end. There were other ominous signs. For example, in February 1978 investigations into the seizure of four machine-guns from a Dutch bivouac on a

NATO training ground in lower Saxony revealed that a neo-Nazi group was responsible. The same group was also suspected of involvement in a bank raid at Hamburg and had activists in the Nuremberg, Cologne and Schleswig-Holstein regions. The Federal Ministry of the Interior estimated at the time that there were over 17,000 neo-Nazi activists and sympathisers in Germany.

In 1978 neo-fascist violence re-emerged as a major problem in Italy. Some of it was prompted by left-wing attacks on the extreme right. For example, a far left group, Armed Nuclei for Territorial Alternative Power, shot dead two young MSI members in Rome, leading to riots and fighting between extremists of the left and right in the streets of the capital. In January 1979 a fascist group, the MSI-National Right Party's youth movement, claimed responsibility for firebombing five cinemas in Rome. And in the same month, in a typically brutal attack, the fascist terrorist group, Armed Revolutionary Nucleus (NAR), attacked a left-wing radio station in Rome, machine-gunning five housewives taking part in a studio discussion on feminism and then setting fire to the building.

Greece also suffered a campaign of fascist bombings during the late 1970s, with cinemas and shops among the targets. On 22 January 1979 the police arrested members of the neo-Nazi Organisation for National Recovery, alleged to have been responsible for planting 70 bombs in Athens over the previous two years. In nearby Turkey political violence was on a totally different plane of intensity, escalating from an average of three political murders per day in early 1978 to *one per hour* by the end of 1979. The Idealist Hearth Youth Movement groups and the Bozkurtlar (Grey Wolves), under the umbrella of Colonel Alparslan Turkes' Nationalist Action Party (NAP), were the main right-wing groups involved. Again their tendency to retaliate with indiscriminate attacks following an act of terrorism by the other side has led to a virtual civil war in many cities. In typical incidents in August and October 1980, neo-fascist gunmen rained bullets on an Ankara cafe frequented by left-wingers. These right-left killings were even mirrored in the split of the police force into right and left factions. And in December Sunni rightists versus Shi'ite leftists had a shoot-out in Maras which lasted four days, leaving 150 dead and many more wounded. Assassination has become the order of the day in Turkey.

At the same time terrorism of the extreme right has been on the increase in the central American states, Nicaragua, El Salvador and Guatemala. One of the most notorious terrorist groups is Organizacion Democratica Nacional (ORDEN), a force estimated to be around 50,000 strong which has been engaged in almost continuous tactics of intimidation and brutal terror since 1968, nominally 'in support of the El Salvador government'. In the late 1970s, as the threat of takeover by Marxist guerrillas grew more real, ORDEN appeared to be operating outside any governmental or external controls or restraints: human rights groups and reliable foreign press witnesses have related its massacres of civilians in the civil war of 1980–1. It must be admitted that there is no definite evidence to say the aims or beliefs of this vigilante terrorist group are explicitly fascist. It appears to be a hotch-potch of retired military men, authoritarian-minded conservative nationalists and businessmen. Nevertheless it is potentially a vehicle for a Salvadorean-style fascism, and it is quite obviously an enemy of law and democratic politics, a bloody and reactionary obstacle to any future liberalisation and extension of social justice in El Salvador.

Guatemalan right-wing para-military groups have been responsible for numerous murders in the past three years. Many of these groups have only recently come into being: for example, Milicias Obreras Gautemaltecas (Guatemalan Workers' Militias), Fuerza de Acción Armada (Armed Action Force), Organizacion Cero (Organisation Zero) and Organizacion de la Muerte (Order of Death) were all formed in the period 1978–9. These are the principal groups comprising the sinister Escuadron de la Muerte (Death Squad).

In the United States, the main threat of extreme right-wing violence has increasingly come from the Ku Klux Klan rather than from the American Nazi Party. For while the latter was still extremely active in demonstrations, rallies and propaganda, it was the Klan that appeared to be gaining many new activists who seemed prepared to use explosives and weapons to launch a campaign of increased violence. One disturbing fact is that much of the fresh Klan recruitment is being done among the young. A pop radio station in Louisiana, WLCS, ran this Klan commercial 50 times in ten days:

'Today the white majority is enduring the butt of discrimination. We're the ones who pay most of the taxes and enjoy less and less of their benefits . . . come to a huge rally of Ku Klux Klan . . . see the beautiful Cross-lighting ceremony.'

David E. Duke, a full-time Klan organiser who visited Britain in 1980 to start Klan branches here, boasted in a recent interview:

'The Klan is certainly not a dead issue. We're getting more press than ever; we're having more demonstrations and meetings. We're reaching a whole new section of the people . . . not only truck drivers and blue-collar workers and farmers, but also attorneys and college professors . . . we're involved in the political campaigns . . .'

But the 'political' work is only one Klan activity. Other clan members are implicated in increased violence and terror. Recently the latter has been escalating, not only in the north-eastern cities of the USA, but also in Britain and West Germany, where Klan klaverns have been formed. In May 1971 the German news weekly *Stern* claimed that the Klan had gained nearly 1,000 members in West Germany, and that the organisation's so-called 'European' branch held regular meetings at Bruch. There is certainly evidence that Klan groups have been activated by American servicemen in the Moselle region, despite Klan activities being strictly forbidden by the American authorities. The US Air Force admits that there have been two cases of Cross-burning since early 1980, and that Klan graffiti have appeared on the bases. *Stern*'s report names a US Air Force sergeant based at Bitburg as the Klan's organiser, and reports that a recruiting officer using the name Bernde Schäfer advertises in right-wing publications as 'the information officer' for the Ku Klux Klan. Herr Kromschröder, the *Stern* reporter who carried out his own private investigation into Klan activities, was invited to meet West German Klansmen after he had written applying for membership.

The American Nazi Party has also been extremely energetic in initiating international Nazi contacts. (Its former leader, Lincoln Rockwell, funded the World Union of National Socialists, of which Colin Jordan later became 'World *Führer*'.) It has become a major source of propaganda leaflets, posters, books and Nazi militaria, which have been exported in considerable volume to Europe. At home, the American Nazis have recently tried to take advantage of racial tensions and increasing socio-economic stresses, particularly in the major Northern cities, but on each occasion they have appeared in their Nazi outfits and attempted to harangue the public, the reaction and counter-demonstrations by anti-Nazi groups have been so powerful that they have required colossal police protection, their appearances provoking a hail of abuse, jeers and missiles. Like the National Front in Britain and the other European Nazi groups, they go out of their way to provoke trouble. For instance, in May 1981 they chose to protest at Israeli Independence Day celebrations in the USA. Thirty Nazis were guarded by heavily-armed police and kept behind barricades, yet even so the police were forced to end the counter-demonstration after only 10 minutes.

The American Nazis have cultivated very strong links with the Ku Klux Klan in recent years, and when, in April 1980, Klan members were brought to trial accused of participating in the murder of left-wingers at Greensboro, North Carolina, 50 American Nazis joined Klan members in a demonstration, simultaneously celebrating Hitler's birthday.

These overt neo-Nazi organisations are not the only manifestations of fascism in America. As in western Europe, it is also expressed through bodies which cultivate a respectable pressure group image. One example is the Liberty Lobby, a far-right group formed in the 1950s which, in spite of its label, is really engaged in anti-Semitic and racist propaganda, and promotes the hoary myth of a Jewish international banking conspiracy. In 1970 a former head of Liberty Lobby, Curtis Dall, and its former legal adviser (1969–73), Warren Richardson, gave an interview to *True* magazine, in which Dall claimed that Zionism was dedicated to 'political and financial world domination', and that it has a 'one-world plan to destroy the United States', and Richardson referred to 'the international money order' (a coded expression for the Zionist conspiracy theory). The facts about this unsavoury organisation came to light recently when the Senate refused to confirm the appointment of Warren Richardson, nominee for the post of Assistant Secretary for Legislation in the Health and Human Services Department in Mr Reagan's administration. In view of his background, it is remarkable that Mr Richardson should have been nominated for this responsible post. However, the openness of the American government system worked very effectively in exposing the Lobby's anti-Semitic and racist role. Infiltration of responsible posts in major institutions by people with such dangerous beliefs is a problem in all democratic systems, and unfortunately in some European states, such as France, West Germany and Italy, there has been a much longer tradition of this.

Fascists in America have more money and propaganda resources than fascists in many other countries. They make an ugly noise. And they frequently promote racial tension. However, the very nature of the political system, with its checks and balances and traditions of constant media scrutiny, helps to guard against fascists penetrating central positions of power.

Small neo-Nazi and fascist groups also operate in Canada and Australia. These elements have never succeeded in winning any significant electoral support, even at local level, but they do remain as a source of racist propaganda, provoking violent confrontation on the streets and maintaining links with fascist centres and personnel in Europe. In Canada, the larger of the two main groups is the National Party. This has recruited both from young racist Canadians and from veteran Nazi sympathisers, some of whom carried their Nazi ideas with them from Germany, France, Italy or other parts of Europe on emigrating to Canada. During the War a significant number of French Canadian recruits to the movement were attracted because of their violent anti-English or anti-British feelings, and their sympathies for Vichy or fascist groupings in France. The other Canadian group is Western Guard, a xenophobic para-military organisation which has only a tiny following.

The main Australian groups are the Australian National Front (ANF) and the Australian League of Rights. The former is very much a replica of the British NF in terms of policies and methods; while the Australian League of Rights, founded by Eric D. Butler, is a more subtle propaganda front, which has tried to influence opinion-leaders and key figures in the Australian establishment, including the Australian Liberal Party. In 1967 they founded a British League of Rights group and attempted to apply similar methods in Britain to those used in Australia. But beneath a veneer of 'common sense' and crude patriotism, the League of Rights preaches anti-Semitism and a Nazi-style conspiracy.

Moving still further afield, it is interesting to note, in the light of developments discussed earlier in this chapter, that there is still evidence of activity by right-wing extremist groups in Japan. The Japanese police estimated in 1978 that there were about 40 tiny fanatical groups of this type, with a total of around 3,500 members. A few years ago armed supporters of the royal family prevented a performance of a play in which Emperor Hirohito was displayed as a weak and tragic figure. The group involved was the Showa Restoration League, which still deifies the Emperor despite his renunciation of divinity six months after the surrender of Japan in 1945. The performance was cancelled after fighting broke out. On 28 July 1978 a demonstration by 1,000 rightists outside the Foreign Ministry protested against the impending peace treaty with China, and in December of that year a former member of the fascist-style Defence Youth League tried to stab Prime Minister Ohira outside his official residence, injuring two bodyguards. The attacker, Sumio Hirose, claimed to have been inspired by the ideals of Yukio Mishima.

What are we to make of the diverse manifestations of the extreme right? Even in Europe, where the majority of explicitly fascist or Nazi groups are concentrated and where there are strong memories of fascist rule and fascist 'traditions', these movements remain tiny and politically marginal. Nevertheless, during the late 1970s they have managed to intensify their racist propaganda and attacks on immigrant communities, and have become increasingly bold in both physical intimidation and terrorist acts against immigrant, Jewish and left-wing targets. Just how serious is the threat they pose to individual democracies and to the international community at large? And what is the most appropriate response for the democracies to use, collectively and individually, in order to combat fascism? Some countries, such as the United Kingdom, have not really developed a concerted policy to deal with fascist racism, other than simply to preserve law and order as best they can. They apparently hope that if fascism is ignored it will wither away. Other societies have made more strenuous efforts to find effective legal and educational measures to protect democracy against fascism. For example, the West

German government has acted on former Chancellor Brandt's warning, in 1977, that action should be taken against Nazi elements. All the *Land* governments were called upon to render reports to the Justice Ministry on neo-Nazism in their regions. And in 1978–9 over 50 neo-Nazi publications were either banned, or their sale to minors was prohibited. A number of youth organisations which had been involved in disseminating race-hatred and violence were raided by the police. Michael Kuhnen, leader of the neo-Nazi Aktionsfront der Nationalisten, was arrested and gaoled for five years (though he later escaped). To back up this tough line the Bundestag agreed to extend the Statute of Limitations.

On March 24 1981 West German police raided nearly 1,000 Nazi homes in the largest-ever swoop on the extremists of the far right. A police spokesman explained that they were particularly anxious to track down individuals responsible for disseminating Nazi propaganda. They confiscated a great deal of material imported from the USA and Canada, with titles such as 'The Nazi Call to Battle' and 'The Auschwitz Swindle'; as well as revolvers, rifles and ammunition. In addition proceedings were commenced against George Dietz and Garry Lauck (German-Americans) and Ernst Zundel (a German Canadian), who were accused of smuggling banned Nazi propaganda into West Germany. Lauck, from Lincoln, Nebraska, was sentenced to four years' imprisonment in 1976 for spreading Nazi propaganda. He was later expelled from West Germany, but was then allowed to return in 1979 to testify in a trial of a neo-Nazi. Lauck stated in court that he was struggling 'for the restitution of the Nazi party'.

In April 1981 the Federal government announced it was planning tougher new laws to prevent the distribution of books such as Hitler's *Mein Kampf* and other anti-Semitic propaganda and emblems. It remains to be seen whether this crackdown by the West German government against Nazism will be successful.

5 FASCISM NOW

The Pope has become a symbol of peaceful resistance to oppression, terror and injustice. In his walkabouts in places like central America, where violence is endemic, he has often walked literally through the valley of death. He has consistently condemned terrorism and state terror alike, fearless for his own safety. The May 1981 attempt on his life, following so soon after the shooting of President Reagan, and followed by a deranged attack on the Queen, provokes examination of some persistent myths about assassination.

First there is nothing new about the use of assassination for political or religious motives. It was in fact pioneered by the Assassin Sect, who launched a campaign of international terrorism in the eleventh century. One of their victims was Conrad, King of the Latin Kingdom of Jerusalem, who was stabbed to death by assassins disguised as Christian monks. A better-known example is Thomas à Becket. But systematic assassination as a weapon of terror has been enormously facilitated by the development of more lethal and portable small arms since the nineteenth century.

Another myth is that contemporary assassinations are usually carried out by lone criminals and madmen. There is, it is true, something of a tradition of this in the United States. Few believe that the killers of President Kennedy, his brother Robert, or Martin Luther King, were working for an organised movement with defineable political aims. President Reagan's assailant had been a member of the American Nazi Party, but apparently even they believed he was too rabid and obsessed with committing violence. All the evidence so far suggests he was acting out some disordered obsession with the film actress, Jody Foster, in his attack on the President. In most European countries though, extremist groups are commoner than lone killers. Numerous extremist groups, fascists, Marxists, separatists, and fanatical exile factions, have strong traditions of political assassination. For these hard-core groups, such as the IRA, ETA, the Red Brigades and the Red Army Faction, killing is a way of life.

In every movement and country the political context of the conflict and the ideology of the extremists dictate a different role for assassination. The OAS, for example, became obsessed with assassinating General de Gaulle, because of his role in conceding independence to Algeria. De Gaulle survived over 30 attempts, including a long burst of sub-machine gun fire into his official car. In Italy, the Red Brigades have specialised in assassinating middle- and high-ranking officials, policemen, lawyers and businessmen. Their highest-ranking political victim was the former Italian president Aldo Moro, murdered three years ago. When his body was discovered in a stolen car in the centre of Rome, it was found that the Red Brigades had inflicted pistol wounds deliberately designed to produce a slow death.

The roll-call of innocent victims of these small murderous sects is ever-lengthening. No one is safe. They have killed not only public figures but also thousands of members of the general public, including women and children, and ordinary policemen and soldiers carrying out their daily tasks in democratic societies. One of the most pathetic aspects of modern terrorism is the large number of innocent victims who are killed in cases of mistaken identity. There are signs of the willingness of terrorists to go beyond individual assassination to mass slaughter, as at Lydda Airport and Munich in 1972, in the Birmingham pub bombings in 1974, and in the bombings at Bologna, Munich and Paris last year. Significantly, the most recent atrocities were all carried out by groups on the extreme right.

Modern assassination is one part of a much larger problem of our democractic societies. Can we prevent fanatics from exploiting the rights and freedoms democracies enjoy to destroy the rights of their fellow-citizens? Public figures who need to be visible and who meet with crowds as part of their job are particularly vulnerable against the lone maniac or the *kamikaze* terrorist. But we must not fall for another dangerous myth, that there is nothing democratic governments can do to improve protection of the innocent, and to lessen the risk of terrorist attack.

It is ironic that the outrage against the Pope should have occurred in Italy, where the anti-terrorist squad, under General dalla Chíesa, had made real progress in putting Red Brigade and Front Line terrorists behind bars. West Germany has achieved spectacular results by using computer technology in rounding up the Red Army Faction. And, though it has been largely overlooked because of all the IRA propaganda over the hunger-strikes, the security forces in Northern Ireland have also been enormously successful over the last 5 years in capturing both Republican and Protestant terrorists, and in strengthening cross-border security co-operation with the Irish Republic.

Police and judicial action by the democracies against philo-terrorist fascist and neo-Nazi movements, on the other hand, has all too often been half-hearted and ineffective. In Italy, France, Turkey, Greece and Spain, and in many other countries as well, there is evidence that fascist groups and parties have been sheltered by sympathisers in high places – senior army officers, heads of intelligence services, even top policemen and government lawyers. Overall, the forces entrusted with upholding the rule of law in many of our western democracies have not pursued the terrorists, subversives and peddlers of racism of the extreme right with anything approaching the energy or efficiency they have shown in cracking down on the extreme left. The rule of law in, for example, Spain, Italy and France, has been blind in the right eye.

The assassination attempt on the Pope by a Turkish fascist, convicted of murder and on the run from the Turkish authorities, dramatised this failure as no other terrorist crime could. It revealed that modern Italy, and indeed the other countries who failed to pursue the repeated warnings about Agca from the Turkish authorities, is no longer able to provide security for even its most distinguished resident. It was, after all, the first attempt on the life of a Pope by a political fanatic for over 1,000 years, and a testimony to the climate of increasing anarchy in which fascism, even more than terrorism of the left, thrives. The Pope's recovery is miraculous, after three bullets entered his body. But terrorism around the world has already succeeded in taking thousands of other innocent lives.

There has been an obvious increase in public disorder since the late 1960s. In the 1970s governments and the media were primarily preoccupied with the terrorist threat from the far left – the Bäader-Meinhof gang, the Japanese Red Army, the Red Brigades, the Weathermen, and their numerous imitators. But only those ignorant of twentieth-century history could have believed that Black terror, the threat of violence from the fascist right, could be forgotten or ignored. After all, the fascist seizures of power in Italy, Germany, Hungary, Romania, Austria, and elsewhere in Europe were in large part achieved by terrorism and intimidation on the streets, and by the brutal suppression of all democratic and working-class organisations. And once in power, the fascists used mass terror as a routine method of control.

Moreover, it was already clear in the 1950s and 1960s that in some countries, particularly in the Mediterranean region, strong native fascist traditions still existed. This was as true of Italy and Spain as it was of Turkey and Greece. While other countries were pre-occupied with the left, all *these* countries, already burdened with the problems of economic backwardness and the stresses of modernisation, were experiencing considerable internal fascist violence. The countless victims of the Colonels' regime in Greece, and of the National Action Party and other fascist groups in Turkey, will not need reminding of this point. But political violence in Turkey and Greece has never been very thoroughly reported in the USA or Britain. The political history of these countries is even now as little understood by the majority of Anglo-Americans as the politics of Latin America.

However, this can be no excuse for the failure by the western community to appreciate the threat from the neo-fascist right in Italy, a member state of Nato and a founder member of the European Economic Community. From the late 1960s it has been evident the fascist talent for violence has already been put to work, mastering the techniques of the new-style terrorism, gaining tactical ideas and practical help from anywhere it can (even 'revolutionary' Libya at one stage), and hitting at Italian working-class, trade union and communist targets indiscriminately. Activists in the neo-fascist party MSI, for all its attempts to present itself as a respectable electoral force of the 'New Right', have been hand-in-glove with the small fascist terrorist groups such as the Mussolini Action Squads, Year Zero and Black Order. A sequence of bombings and shootings against trade union offices, left-wing co-operatives, left-wing organisers and publications, have proved that the old guard of Italian fascists have spawned a new generation equally uninhibited about mass slaughter.

It may be that some of this violence is part of a rationally conceived 'strategy of tension' designed to provoke maximum disruption of democratic institutions and to polarise the political situation with the aim of staging a coup to 'save the country' from a communist dictatorship. There is ample evidence of collusion and conspiracy in the upper echelons of the security and intelligence services and the military, in planning coup attempts such as 'Compass Rose' (see pages 72, 103, and 130). But there is also circumstantial evidence to show that many of the small, autonomous fascist terror groups have been engaged in brutal violence for its own sake, and in what they claim are acts of 'vengeance' against the left, settling historic scores.

The first major wave of post-War Italian fascist terrorism reached its peak with the bomb attack on an anti-fascist rally in the Piazza della Loggia, Brescia, on 28 May 1974. Six people were killed and 79 injured, 36 seriously. The meeting, organised jointly by the Democratic Socialist, Christian Democratic and communist trade union organisations, was the climax of a four-hour general strike called to protest against increasing neo-fascist violence in Brescia. The terrorists placed the high-explosive bomb in a wastepaper box in an arcade. It went off just as a procession of workers was arriving in the piazza to join workers already assembled there. The carnage was described by the trade union leader who happened to be addressing the meeting when the bomb exploded:

'Screaming people ran for safety in all directions. When they fled there was blood everywhere. Cries for help could be heard and mutilated bodies lay scattered on the ground.'

Later Brescia police and two newspapers received typewritten letters claiming credit for the bombing, signed 'Black Order', and listing persons 'sentenced to death' and places 'that will be destroyed'. This bombing was followed a few months later by the bomb attack on an express-train in a tunnel outside Bologna, killing 12 people and injuring 48.

After 1974 the pendulum swung back to the violence of the extreme left, but it would have been a mistake to assume that this temporary eclipse of fascist violence meant that its source had disappeared. Fascists regrouped and recruited just as eagerly, even infiltrating secondary schools in the urban areas, and winning bored adolescents to their cause with blatantly Nazi propaganda. Spasmodically fascism erupted into street violence and occasional bombings and shootings in the mid – and late – 1970s, though the threat of a 'save the country' coup attempt seemed to have receded.

The Bologna railway-station bombing on 1 August 1980 was the worst single attack in Europe in the whole history of

European terrorism. It is clear that the bomb was designed to cause the maximum carnage. It was placed in a second-class waiting-room and devastated the left-hand side of the station, killing 85 people and injuring over 260. The terrorists chose the station's busiest time on the first holiday Saturday in August for their attack, which came on the eve of the anniversary of the bombing of the express-train in 1974. On the very morning of the bombing a Bologna magistrate had sent a neo-fascist, Mario Tuti, and three accomplices, for trial accused of that same express-train outrage.

The Armed Revolutionary Nuclei (NAR), the neo-fascist group responsible for murdering Judge Amato while he was investigating fascist terrorism, quickly claimed responsibility for the Bologna massacre. Amato, who was denied adequate police protection despite repeated requests, had observed that the fascist terrorists he had arrested:

' . . . are 18 years old at most, with very few ideas in their heads except some confused Nazi myths and a cult of violence.'

The NAR is simply one of many such groups, obsessed with Hitler and Mussolini and all the symbols and paraphernalia of their regimes.

On 26 September 1980, just as the Italian police were beginning to blow the dust off their files on Italian fascists, and getting their investigations underway way with the usual delays and procrastination, the world was stunned by news of another terrorist attack which bore the hallmark of neo-Nazi terror, this time in West Germany. The 24 lb bomb, placed at the entrance to Munich's popular beer festival, killed 13 people and injured 312. Strong suspects in the initial investigations were the Wehrsportgruppe (Military Sports Group), led by self-styled *Führer* Karl-Heinz Hoffmann.

The following week, on 3 October 1980, a bomb exploded outside the entrance to a large synagogue in the Rue Copernic, Paris. This time the bomb was placed in a car, and was timed to go off just as evening worshippers were about to leave. It was only the fact that there had been an unusually long service that prevented greater casualties. Four people were killed outright and 20 injured, 7 seriously. Once again the attack bore the stamp of new-wave fascist terrorism: it was deliberately planned to cause maximum casualties.

Police investigation into these attacks is still proceeding and hence there remains some doubt about the precise groups responsible. Nevertheless it is generally accepted that fascist and neo-Nazi groups were responsible in two cases, and in the Bologna and Paris attacks fascist groups rushed out claims of responsibility immediately after the bombings. In none of these cases is there any likely nationalist or separatist terrorist motive, and the attacks show none of the normal patterns of extreme left terrorism. Moreover, in each case the bombings were preceded by an intensification of fascist activity in the region concerned (see chapters 3 and 4).

These events, and the many lesser cases of bombings, arson and shootings by fascist groups, are a sharp reminder of the need for vigilance towards the whole spectrum of potential terrorist threats, not just those from the left. It is true that, since the Munich massacre of Israeli athletes by Black September terrorists in 1972, the west European democracies have considerably strengthened their own security arrangements for dealing with all kinds of domestic terrorism. For example, they have developed crack hostage-rescue commando squads, such as the German GSG-9, the British SAS, the Spanish GEO, the French 'intervention force' and the Dutch Marine commandos: all these units have been successfully tested in real mass-hostage situations. They learn from each other and pool expertise in tactics, techniques and weaponry, as was illustrated by the SAS contribution of 'stun' grenades to the GSG-9 operation to rescue hostages from a Lufthansa 747 at Mogadishu. Moreover, the political systems with the most severe internal terrorist problems – Italy, Spain, West Germany and Great Britain (in Northern

Ireland) – have all developed special anti-terrorist legislation, covering such matters as detention for questioning of terrorist suspects, definition of terrorist offences, and sentences for convicted terrorists. Much of this legislation has been highly controversial, but there are no indications in mid-1981 that any of the western governments concerned are planning to rescind these laws. Also as well as the hostage-rescue squads, specialist anti-terrorist squads have been formed in each country to meet the increasing challenge from terrorism.

In parallel with these domestic responses, the Council of Europe, Nato and the European Economic Community have taken action to improve international intelligence, police and judicial co-operation. Certain other states, such as Switzerland, Austria and Sweden, have also joined with EEC states in aspects of anti-terrorist co-operation. And despite the fact that its constitution officially precludes dealing with politically-motivated offences, Interpol has often been valuable in relaying intelligence on convicted terrorists and the issuing of warrants for arrest.

What impact has all this firm national and international response in western Europe had on the terrorist potential of the fascist groups? Although it undoubtedly makes the apprehension and ultimate conviction and imprisonment of fascist terrorists more feasible, it must be admitted that there is no one-hundred per cent security against terrorism in a democracy. Extremists will inevitably exploit our democractic freedoms and they will be attracted too by the one prize they can be sure of in a free society – worldwide publicity in the media for their atrocities. But for a number of reasons western governments are likely to find this new wave of *fascist* terrorists a more difficult quarry. First, fascist terrorist groups have a far greater tendency to fragment into a multitude of tiny autonomous groups: there is no Black terror equivalent of the centrally directed and disciplined 'columns' of the Red Brigade, or the Provisional IRA structure. This obviously makes the task of the police infinitely more difficult, for where only a few individuals, or perhaps just one individual fascist, carries out a terrorist attack independently, it is usually impossible to learn of the plan by means of interrogating the front men or self-professed leaders of their organisations. Cracking one part of the cell structure does not automatically uncover the sources of the conspiracy. Secondly, the personalities of many fascist terrorists tend to be very close to the suicidal-schizophrenic. Thus they are prepared to take much greater risks. Normal security precautions – like police bodyguarding or crowd surveillance – will never be sufficient against the terrorist prepared to lose his life, or at least his liberty, in order to kill his victim. Von Saloman, the fascist who was an accessory to the 1922 murder of German foreign minister Walter Rathenau, says in his autobiographical novel:

'. . . I died for the nation. So everything lives in me only for the nation. How could I bear it if it were different! I do what I have to do, because I die every day. Since what I do is given only to one power everything I do is rooted in this power. *This power wants destruction and I destroy* . . . I know that I shall be ground to nothing, that I shall fall when this power releases me.' (Italics added)

This passage reveals an intense masochism typical of fascist killers. It seems that in many such cases the individual's whole world has been smashed, socially and morally. Hate and bitterness are combined with a worship of destruction, for which the terrorist is prepared to give even his own life. He is obsessed with the fact that the very foundation of his strongest values – nationalism, hierarchy elitist authority and national or racial purity, for example – have been shattered by the defeat or humiliation of his country, or the downfall of his beloved fascist regime. The world of social or liberal democracy is meaningless to him: he feels uprooted. His obsession with taking revenge on the whole social and political order is born out of this desperation. The contempt shown by the German extreme right for the Federal Republic – when they dream of a re-unified 'Greater Germany' – is just one example of such feelings.

Another factor that tends to make the prevention and punishment of fascist terrorism very difficult is the presence of fascists or potential fascist-sympathisers in ranks of the armed forces, the military reserves, and the police and prison services. At the practical level this means, of course, that many of them can obtain up-to-date weapons training free of charge. In Britain, for example, the para-military fascist groups Column 88 and SS Wotan have been able to obtain military training from their links within the Territorial Army and the Army Cadet Force. Particularly disturbing is the fact that the National Front has cells among prison officers in four British prisons – Dartmoor, Strangeways, Wormwood Scrubs and Pentonville. Some of these are at a senior level – for example, Brian Baldwin, Chairman of the Prison Officers' Association in Manchester, has been a member of the Council of the British Movement and the National Front. The implications of this for the welfare of black, Jewish and Moslem prisoners in the care of these officers are worrying enough. But we must also consider the possible effects of National Front propaganda and recruitment efforts on the minds of prisoners generally, bearing in mind that the prisons contain many who are ill-educated and racially prejudiced.

A more immediate threat is that, through their reservist military contacts, some fascist groups have been able to steal weapons from Nato arms dumps. This was revealed recently when Norwegian chiefs became aware that considerable quantities of arms were disappearing from the special, un-guarded but theoretically secret, arms dumps dotted around Norway. It is reported that 120 automatic weapons, 1,000 rounds of ammunition and scores of hand-grenades were stolen in 1978. And more than a ton of weapons and explosives were stolen in May 1979. Over the past three years it is estimated that over 700 AG-3 automatic rifles have disappeared from Nato arsenals in Norway. Even though many of these weapons may simply have been stolen for disposal on the illegal arms market, there is evidence that at least some have been stolen by Norwegian neo-fascists, probably to attack rival movements and to murder suspected traitors in their own ranks. For example, one such raid took place at Nesodden, near Oslo, in February 1981. Seventy-three automatic weapons, explosives, and uniforms were stolen from an unguarded arms store. The group effected the break-in by blowing open the armoury door with explosives stolen by members when they were on Home Guard training.

Some days later, Oslo police investigating the theft kept watch on the home of a Norwegian regular army sergeant, Espen Lund, on leave from his job as a weapons training instructor. They followed four men who left the house and drove deep into the hilly countryside before stopping. Shots rang out and two dead bodies were left behind in the road. The car raced off, crashing through a police road-block *en route* to Oslo. Some shots were fired from the car at the police, who searched Lund's home and found neo-Nazi pamphlets and weapons stolen from Nesodden. More weapons stolen from another arsenal have also been discovered in the home of another army sergeant connected with the group.

As well as in Norway, extreme right terrorists in many other western countries have exploited their links with sympathisers within the armed forces to obtain weapons and explosives supplies. Sometimes they are prepared to trade these weapons for cash, even to terrorist groups of the far left. For example, the weapons – a Beretta and 250 rounds of ammunition – used by Ulrike Meinhof and her Red Army faction accomplices to spring Andreas Bäader from gaol were obtained from one Gunter Voigt, acting on behalf of the para-military wing of the neo-Nazi NPD.

Substantial help and protection has also been given to fascists in several European countries by sympathisers in the police service. Typical evidence of this came in August 1980, with the announcement that a French police inspector, Paul Durand, had been suspended from his duties because of his role as one of the leaders of the French fascist movements, the Fédération d'Action Nationale Européene (FANE). Apparently Durand, as a fluent Italian speaker, had been made responsible by the leader of FANE, Marc Frederiksen, for liaison with Italian neo-Nazi groups. But though he visited Bologna in mid-July, a fortnight before the Bologna massacre, there is no evidence to suggest that he was implicated in the attack itself.

Further disturbing developments came in early October 1980, when two French police union leaders publicly alleged that the names of 30 serving police-officers were on a list of 152 members of the by-now-outlawed FANE. This was of course denied hotly by the minister of the interior, Christian Bonnet. However, the minister, conscious of the passionate concern of the French Jewish community and sensitive to accusations that the police had failed to do its duty in protecting Jewish targets from terrorist attacks and threats, promised that if seized records listing 3,400 sympathisers of FANE revealed the names of any policemen, the officers concerned would be arraigned before a disciplinary tribunal. Meanwhile, the French police union officials have stepped up their campaign against racism and fascism within the French police, and have also participated in a London rally of the Anti-Nazi League in December 1980. (The French union's insistence on contributing a speaker to this rally caused a furious row in the European Police Federation; the British hinting that they might leave the Federation 'if it looks like becoming partisan and political.')

The challenge of contemporary fascism to democracy, particularly, but not only, in the form of terror, is made far more difficult to counter by the growth of something approaching a Black International of fascist groups. Some have called this phenomenon 'Euro-Fascism' or 'Euro-Nazism' –

misnomers, to some extent, since the USA is the major centre of neo-Nazi propaganda and fund-raising. A recent find by West German police has disclosed an international network of right-wing terrorist contacts of even more byzantine complexity than that of the extreme left. The diary of a leading West German neo-Nazi, Manfred Roeder, revealed that neo-Nazis in Germany were in contact with extremist groups in Spain, Italy and France. The diary also highlighted the key part played by the Canadian, Ernst Zundel, and two American contacts, Gary Lauck and Georg Dietz, who together are responsible for supplying large quantities of neo-Nazi literature to European fascist groups. According to the diary, Roeder had his greatest fund-raising success in the USA. Among the more bizarre schemes of the West German neo-Nazis revealed by the diary were their attempt to get arms and cash from Iran and the Palestine Liberation Organization (PLO), and their leader Karl-Heinz Hoffmann's activities in selling second-hand military vehicles to Lebanon!

In fact, there have been recurring rumours of clandestine co-operation between the PLO and neo-Nazi groups in Europe. In 1969 Jean Tireault, a Belgian who was secretary of the neo-Nazi La Nation Européene, served as an adviser to the Palestinian organisation, Al-Fatah, and another Belgian neo-Nazi, Karl Van de Put, was engaged in recruitment for him.

The Belgian neo-Nazi publication *Alliance* has claimed that in August 1969 a secret meeting of former Nazi leaders was held in Madrid, at which it was decided to give fullest possible support to Fatah and other PLO groups – including instructors and propaganda. At this period also, the Popular Front for the Liberation of Palestine (PFLP) acquired a former Nazi commander for their training-camp at Basra, in South Iraq.

The PLO, which is anyway a loose cluster of factions with a wide variety of weird ideologies, seems to have no rooted objection to occasional clandestine links with the Nazi groups, when it believes them to be useful. No doubt the neo-Nazis have emphasised their *radical* right positions and their fierce commitment to anti-Semitism (and hence anti-Zionism), which undoubtedly appeal to the PLO. Of course, the PLO do not want these *ad hoc* links revealed. They are proud of their recognition by the Soviets, and they boast of their intimacy with the communist world as a whole, but their contacts with the neo-Nazis are distinctly *sub rosa*.

Despite this, some scraps of evidence indicating that there has been substantial mutual assistance have come to light. In January 1970, at a trial of 3 captured PFLP terrorists in Winterhur, Switzerland, evidence was produced of close links between the Swiss Nazi Party, particularly one of its founders, Françoise Geroude, and Al-Fatah. The neo-Nazi magazine *Deutsche National Und Soldaten Zeitung* has carried an advertisement urging movement members to join the PLO. In late 1975 3 members of the Wehrsportgruppe – Guenther Brahburgh, Gunnar Fahl and Eckhardt Will, sought by Interpol for automobile and document thefts – were apprehended and put on trial in Yugoslavia. It was revealed that, at one stage, the 3 had been *en route* to a PLO training camp, and that they had attended an Al Fatah camp at Bir Hassan, south of Beirut. Later, the *Yediot Aharonot* correspondent in Bonn reported that in January 1978 4 members of the Free Corps – Saudi Arabia and Free Corps – Adolf Hitler groups had been arrested on suspicion of smuggling arms from Arab states to members of the PLO in Germany. They were caught red-handed, and at least one neo-Nazi was in possession of a PLO membership card.

On the links between neo-Nazi and fascist movements in different western countries we have far more substantial evidence. The nearest approach to an annual international 'festival' of Nazism is the memorial march held at Diksmuide, Belgium, where most of the European groups and the American Nazis are always represented, parading in black uniforms. The 'hosts' at this event are the Flemish Nazis, Vlammse Militante Orde (VMO), who also organise para-military 'fieldgames' and occasional exchanges of 'troops' with other neo-Nazi organisations such as Wehrsportgruppe.

However, there does not seem to be any central masterminding Euro-fascist organisation which controls all the activities of the national movements and concerts their campaigns. The most probable explanation for the Munich bombing outrage following so rapidly in the wake of the Bologna massacre is that the German neo-Nazi (who as it happens also blew himself up in the explosion) was simply copying Bologna. This contagion effect is familiar to students of terrorism.

A major obstacle to any close co-ordination of European Nazi groups is their personal jealousies and rivalries. Another is the language barrier. When Thies Christophersen, one of the leading German neo-Nazis, went on a propaganda tour of North America, he could only address his audiences in German. At international gatherings such as the annual rally at Diksmuide, where black-shirted fascists bearing flags march to cemetery and there lay wreaths to commemorate slain members of the SS, most of the national groups keep themselves to themselves. Indeed these groups have an intrinsic ideological bias for this national separateness. Groups which constantly preen their national identities, and claim racial or ethnic superiority over everybody else are not exactly programmed for fraternal international co-operation. In June 1981, fighting broke out between British, Flemish and German fascist youths following the Diksmuide rally. Twenty-three Britons were arrested on various charges, including possessing knives and truncheons, and were then ordered to leave the country. A Flemish fascist stated: 'We didn't ask the British to come, and they caused nothing but trouble. We do not want to be associated with that sort of hooliganism.' So much for international fascist solidarity!

A far more significant aspect of the 'internationalisation' of fascist activity is the trend towards establishment of exile fascist communities. After the defeat of the Axis powers Franco's Spain became a centre for fascist self-help groups such as Odessa, aiding former Nazis on the run, and for the funding and organisation of fascist activities in Spain and elsewhere.

In the 1960s a fascist exile community was established, this time in West Germany, where thousands of Turkish migrant workers found work and settled in the 1960s and 1970s. It is among this community that Mehmet Ali Agca, the man who shot the Pope, found shelter, assistance and political collaborators. Agca belonged to Colonel Alparslan Turkes' fascist National Action Party. A former economics student at Istanbul University, Agca came into the party through the Idealist Hearth Movement, the Party's youth section.

The NAP's youth 'Idealists' association, otherwise known as the 'Grey Wolves', has close links with the West German neo-Nazis. It employed a team of professional assassins, among whom was Agca. According to the indictment of the military prosecutor for the 1981 trial of Colonel Turkes and 219 supporters, the Grey Wolves were responsible for organising or carrying out 694 murders in the years 1974–80, including, for example, those of Kemal Turkler (head of Disk, the militant labour federation), Bedri Karafakioglu (a university professor), Cevat Yuurdakul (an Adana police chief), and Bedrettin Comert (an Ankara art historian). In Turkey most of the NAP's victims were left-wing students, union leaders and politicians. One of them was Abdi Ipekci, the liberal newspaper editor: Agca was convicted of his murder in 1979.

The Grey Wolves have an important west European dimension: their underground network is well-established in the Turkish community in West Germany, with an estimated 87 branches and 26,000 members. This makes it one of the largest fascist terrorist organisations in Europe. Bonn experts believe there are a further 42 branches in other major European centres, based among the Turkish immigrant community. In West Germany the NAP established intimate links with the extreme right Turkish Federation in Germany, and with neo-Nazi groups. Turkes' contact-man for building up these links was an Azerbaijani called Mehmet Kengerli, believed to have served with the SS in the Second World War.

It is this active Turkish fascist movement that provides help to NAP activists and plots to seize power in Turkey one day. The Grey Wolves have a reputation for being a tight-knit secret brotherhood that will always look after its own: it even paid its activists employed in the Idealist Hearth Movement a salary, probably the equivalent of thirty pounds sterling per month. But Agca also seems to have been given more generous financial help which enabled him to travel further afield, to Spain and Italy. He did not know any German. Since his name and description had been relayed to the West German authorities by the Turkish government, it is remarkable that he was not picked up, at least when he was leaving or entering western Europe on a false passport. Where did he get the effective backing to enable him to do this, and to float around Europe without being captured for 18 months?

The Grey Wolves are a particularly dangerous example of an exile fascist movement with a built-in propensity for terrorism. The movement propagates a fanatical Turkish nationalism and suppresses any leftist tendencies among Turks working abroad. (Feuding between right and left Turkish extremists in West Germany has led to the recorded deaths of 5 Turks, and serious injury to 30 more over the past three years.) There are up to 3,000 hard-core activists. Much of the movement's energy is expended on indoctrinating Turkish children, in classes held early in the morning before these children proceed to their local schools. They are taught 3 basic rules:

1. behind the mask of every German teacher is a Christian missionary or a Jewish agent

2. there must be no friendships with German children, as they are Christians and eat pork
3. whoever disobeys will be killed

The teachers dress in black and use a cane to punish inattentive pupils.

This kind of fascist movement presents a far more substantial threat of violence and intercommunal hatred and conflict than the tiny fringe groups that congregate at Diksmuide, for it represents the attempt to carry a native fascist tradition across frontiers on a most ambitious and determined scale. It is a common mistake to assume that exile and international terrorism is always of an extreme left orientation. One should not overlook the many examples of violent movements of the extreme right that have originated in emigré communities. The most notable example in the 1930s was the Croatian Ustasha. In the 1960s it was the OAS movement of former white settlers in Algeria, most of whom moved back to France. It is primarily in this mode that terrorism of the fascistic right is likely to become internationalised over the coming decade. And this presents yet more headaches for the western governments and the international community.

If terrorism is the most ubiquitous form of challenge posed by fascist movements, then the second mode of threat, the fascist or fascist-supported *coup d'état* is the one most clearly confined to certain coup-prone states; Spain, Portugal, Italy, Greece, Turkey and Argentina. Other Latin American states are excluded from this category because, although nearly all of them have a fascistic party on the extreme right, it is only in Argentina that there is a tradition of a fascist-style movement – the Peronists – actually attempting a coup of their own and enjoying the fruits of power. Italy is included because although it has succeeded in maintaining its republican democratic system since the Second World War, it has been the scene of a series of coup attempts from the extreme right in the fairly recent past. Lieutenant-General Giovanni De Corenzo tried to organise his own coup in 1964; there was Prince Borghese's attempt, code-named 'Tora Tora', started on 7 December 1970 and then called off; in January 1974 the army and police were mobilised and ministries and other key buildings in Rome were put under special armed guard; and there were further scares in August 1974, when Andrea Piaggio, a financial backer of the 'Compass Rose' coup attempt, was arrested. In October 1974 the most dramatic arrest of all occurred: that of General Vitor Miceli, who had been head of the secret service, and who was accused of involvement both in the Borghese coup attempt and also in a bizarre plot to steal radioactive material from a nuclear plant in the north, and to poison Rome's water supply by infecting the aqueducts. The plotter evidently believed this would stimulate a left-wing backlash, which would in turn force the military to intervene. The coup leaders planned to seize power jointly with the military, offering themselves as 'saviours' of the nation. As more details trickled out in 1974–5, it became clear how serious these attempts were, even if they did not succeed. Most worrying of all was the evidence of Fascist sympathizers, even among the highest ranks of the secret services and the military. General Maletti former head of the defence section of the Servizio Informazioni Difensa (SID), the military counter-intelligence service, was sentenced in 1979 to 4 years imprisonment for obtaining a false passport for the escape of Guido Giannettini, sentenced to life for his part in the 1969 Milan bomb attack. And following the escape of Franco Freda and Giovanni Ventura, also sentenced to life for their part in the Milan bombing, the National Police chief was dismissed.

One of the most disturbing aspects of the succession of plots in this period was the disclosure that the United States Government, in the shape of their Ambassador in Rome, Graham A. Martin, had been making large payments to

General Miceli in 1972 to carry out a secret propaganda project. The sum involved was $800,000. Intriguingly, the CIA, which had certainly plenty of experience at backing undemocratic forces in its interventions abroad, was apparently strongly opposed to the Miceli deal.

The Italian case demonstrates a number of important features of the fascist threat to similar coup-prone states. These countries are vulnerable, because on the one hand of the lack of any deep-rooted tradition of democratic government, and on the other their concomitant strongly-entrenched anti-democratic groups. But they are made more susceptible because of the superior resources of the fascist plotters, and the fact that they tend to have friends and collaborators in strategic positions to undermine governments from within. A conspiracy that includes the head of the secret service has a great deal going for it! If you add the large financial backing available from wealthy fascist industrialists and entrepreneurs, and the fact that the left lacks any equivalent advantages to counterbalance the extreme right, it becomes clear why the fascist coup poses a more serious threat to the survival of democracy in these Mediterranean countries, and why, historically, the *coup d'état* with the collaboration of key elements in the military, is the classic fascist route to power. We have seen how Mussolini's fascist groups beat up leftists, forcibly took over town councils, broke strikes and occupied Fiume, as a preparation for the October March on Rome. As conservative Italian politician Antonio Salandra admitted, it was 'the first time in Italy since the establishment of the constitutional monarchy, that the transfer of political power came about by an act of force, before which the King, and later Parliament had to surrender unconditionally.' Thus, although the March on Rome was not a military attack in the strict sense of the word, it was the culmination of a whole sequence of fascist acts of violence and intimidation in other cities. Since then, every fascist movement that has come to power has depended to a large extent on force.

Of course, to those who have lived all their lives under democratic political systems the idea of such coups seems to have a comic opera quality. But if there is an element of farce in 'Tora Tora' or 'Compass Rose', it is worth recalling that Mussolini achieved power only 60 years ago, and there have been plenty of post-War examples to encourage emulators – in Greece, Turkey, and in every country in the Middle East, in South America, and much of Africa. But it is Spain, with its traditional weakness for coups – *el golpismo* – that provides the most dramatic example of how close the Falangist generals and others on the extreme right have come to actually seizing power and dismantling parliamentary democracy.

At 6 in the evening of Monday 23 February 1981 350 deputies were assembled to give their formal approval to the appointment of Senor Leopoldo Calvo Sotelo as prime minister in succession to Adolfo Suárez. After twenty minutes the proceedings were brought to a sudden halt when Colonel Antonio Tejero and his colleagues of the Civil Guard burst into the Chamber. With his tricorne hat and drooping moustache Tejero looked faintly ridiculous to the worldwide audience who witnessed these events on television, but his armed followers' automatic fire at the ceiling, showering the deputies with plaster, quickly showed that he was in earnest. The conservative leader Manuel Fraga recalled later that 'about a pound of crystal from a chandelier fell on my head'. Several of the socialists admitted they thought they were about to be executed, especially when their leader, Felipe Gonzalez, was taken by the conspirators into a small side room and kept facing the wall with a pistol to his back. In effect the whole Cortes had been taken hostage by a group of Civil Guards, long known to be angry and embittered about the government's policies on the Basque question. Tejero was already known to the authorities as an anti-democratic plotter (in November 1978 he had been among the conspirators who had planned to kidnap Prime Minister Suárez and his whole cabinet while the King was in America). This time the conspirators had got well beyond the discussion stage. Tejero telephoned his fellow-conspirator, General Milans del Bosch, a Falangist who had served Hitler with fellow Blue Division officers on the Russian front, at 7 p.m., giving him the pre-arranged signal to declare a 'state of emergency' and move his tanks onto the streets of Valencia. Meanwhile General Lid Torres Rojas, military governor of La Corunna but formerly commander of the Brunete units outside Madrid, returned to those troops, and at 7.45 p.m. one of his contingents seized the major government television and radio station in Madrid and replaced all the scheduled programmes with a tape of Prussian marching songs.

In the parliament building the frightened deputies were now told by Tejero that Milans del Bosch's troops were moving in on Madrid. Tejero also announced that the military in other regions – Aragon, Seville, Barcelona – were rising in support of the coup. The *golpistas* seemed to be carrying the day. It was widely assumed that General Alfonso Armada was to be the new Franco, the man to 'pull Spain out of chaos'. The deputies realised that the conspirators' claims were exaggerated when news bulletins, picked up by deputy Fernando Abril on his small transistor radio, were relayed in whispers around the chamber. The armed forces had not risen to join the coup. It was only in Valencia that the tanks were on the streets. Most crucial of all, they learnt that the King had spoken and acted firmly in defence of democracy, and the plotters were becoming isolated.

The King had an intimation that a Falangist and military conspiracy was in the offing when General Armada had visited him at the Zarzuela Palace and warned him that the army, police and civil guard were restless and fed up with the civilian politicians, and that the Turkish generals' coup was widely admired among their ranks. Fortunately the King had already prepared with his ministers a contingency plan to cope with a coup attempt of this kind, and the plan – Operation Diana – worked effectively to protect the legal authority. But it was the King's own firmness in effecting it, his crisp instructions to the Captains-General of the various regions and his cool and dignified appeal to the people on television that ensured the defeat of the coup. As one socialist politician remarked: 'one trembles to think what would have happened if the King had been out of the country.' Juan Tomas de Salas, the experienced and astute editor of *Cambio 16*, commented: 'without the King we would today once again be plunged back in the night of shame, stupidity and hatred.'

It is indeed food for thought that only the King prevented a relapse into Falangist-style dictatorship. Meanwhile two things are certain. There are still many Falangist and Franco-ist officers and powerful civilians capable of staging further coup attempts, and many who are not actively plotting will hold back from any active defence of democracy. Secondly, next time the conspirators will certainly aim to get rid of the King.

What has also been too easily overlooked by commentators on the Spanish-Tejero coup attempt, is the evidence that Tejero, and certainly others were sheltered by people in high places. Tejero had already been caught red-handed in plotting against the government in 1980. Yet instead of being court-martialled or dimissed he was simply transferred to the less sensitive post of commanding the motor transport pool. It is difficult to escape the conclusion that there were those in high places whose private sympathies lay with Tejero and Bosch and who were unwilling or psychologically unable to deal with the danger that such men might initiate a fascist mutiny, even though they must have been fully aware that such a conspiracy was being cooked up.

It is in the light of this that one must consider the complications of the bank siege organized by right-wing extremists at Barcelona on 23 May 1981. Gunmen held 269 hostages, demanding the release of Tejero and his co-conspirators in the 23 February plot. The siege was ended by a commando assault by Spain's special 'GEO' force, but later discoveries by the police reveal that this siege was only the precursor of a far more dangerous concerted attack during Armed Forces Week in Barcelona. On 27 May the police announced that they had found the beginnings of a tunnel dug beneath a ground floor apartment in Barcelona, only 30 yards from where the King was due to pass in the celebrations on Sunday 31 May. Not only the King, but his entire Cabinet, were due to be in Barcelona on that date, and the implication was that an assassination attempt was planned. Police found out about the tunnel as a result of interrogations of gunmen involved in the bank siege. The apartment had been rented since early April by one of their number who was killed in the rescue assault. Handguns, ammunition, and over 30 national identity cards, were found in the flat.

Following this, the Spanish police arrested 8 well-known fascists, including José Antonio Assiego, leader of a breakaway group from Fuerza Nueva called the National Syndicalist Trade Union. Assiego had been expelled from Pinar's Fuerza Nueva on the grounds of his continued 'excessive violence'. Another leading fascist arrested was Jorge Mota, head of CEDADE. A third leading suspect was José Antonio Girón, a former Franco minister with strong Falange connections, who is President of the Federation of Ex-combatants, the Francoist body of civil war veterans. Far from being isolated or eccentric incidents as some foreign observers implied, the events of February and May 1981 are part of a much wider plot by the extreme right to destabilise or overthrow Spanish democracy.

Prime minister Calvo Sotelo expressed the growing concern about threats from right-wing extremists when he told the Cortes that Spain's democracy was under attack. The major internal threats come from two directions. Hard-core militant ETA military terrorists have been doing their best to undermine the Madrid government's Statute of Autonomy solution to the Basque problem. By a campaign of murders of Spanish army officers, police and civil guards, and other acts of terrorism, they have been seeking to provoke a backlash so

The annual international fascist gathering at Diksmuide, Belgium, hosted by the Vlaamse
Militante Orde, where participants march through the town and lay wreaths on SS graves

The Vlaamse Militante Orde marched through Antwerp on 4 October 1980 to protest against
immigrant workers' right to vote. Note the salute from the passer-by

Inside a National Front meeting in Ilford, Essex

opposite: The National Front and the British Movement have both canvassed vigorously for support among young people, particularly among 'skinheads' and 'punks'

The National Front marched through Lewisham, a predominantly black area in South London, on 13 August 1977. Their march attracted counter-demonstrations from local youths and the Anti-Nazi League

B. P. PUBLICATIONS catalogue 1980

95A Chester Road East,
Shotton, Clwyd, N.Wales.

TELEPHONE DEESIDE

BRITISH PATRIOT PUBLICATIONS ⊕

3 FRIARS CLOSE, BEBINGTON, MERSEYSIDE, L63 3HY.

051-645 9955

British Movement propaganda. On the left is a catalogue of British Movement publications; on the right a catalogue of their tapes – all songs and marches from the Third Reich

A CEDADE book-stall selling neo-Nazi propaganda in Madrid, May 1981

6 p.m. on 23 February 1981. Antonio Tejero addresses the Spanish *Cortes*, surrounded by armed accomplices. Note also startled deputies crouching to the right of the picture

200,000 supporters of the extreme right, including delegates from all over Europe, met on 20 November 1980 in Madrid to celebrate the 5th anniversary of General Franco's death

A bomb planted by right-wing extremists exploded in Bologna Station on 2 August 1980. This was Europe's worst ever terrorist outrage, killing 84 people and injuring over 250

Weapons, including bomb-making materials, found by police in a Rome garage after a police crackdown on right-wing terrorists in April 1981

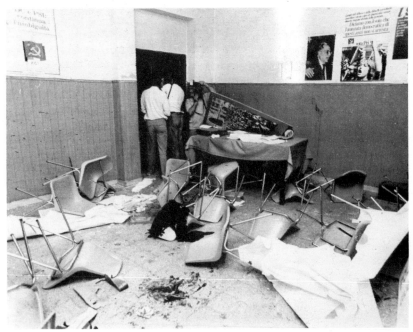

An Italian Communist Party (PCI) office after an attack by the right-wing Armed Revolutionary
Squad in June 1979. 23 of the 50 PCI members meeting at the time were wounded

Outside the synagogue in the Rue Copernic, Paris, after a bomb-attack on 3 October 1980
which left 4 dead and 12 wounded. FNE, the fascist anti-Semitic group, claimed responsibility

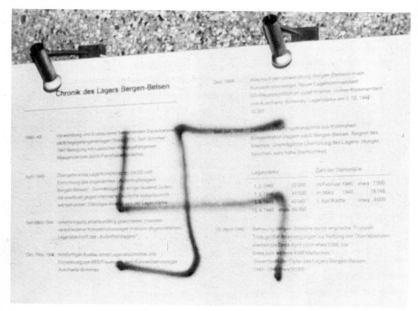

Nazi graffiti at the Belsen concentration camp

Jewish graves at Bagneux, Paris, desecrated by right-wing anti-Semitic groups. Many of the graves desecrated contain the bodies of those who died in Nazi concentration camps

The European Convention of the Extreme Right held in Hamburg on 8 August 1976. On the right is Martin Mussgnug, leader of the German neo-Nazi party, the NPD

Welkommen zum Oktoberfest. A neo-Nazi group has claimed responsibility for the bombing during the Munich Beer Festival on 26 September 1980, killing 12 people and injuring 312

Members of the American Nazi Party and the Ku Klux Klan pose together for photographers in Benson, North Carolina, on 19 April 1980

Nazis protesting against Israeli Independence Day in Southfield, Michigan, on 10 May 1981

above left: Indoctrination starts young: children dressed in the uniform of the American Nazi Party

above right: Nazi activist Frank Collin being interviewed after a rally in Chicago during 1977

Collin suffers missiles and taunts from the crowd at a rally in Berwyn, Illinois

Japanese writer and Nobel prize-winner Yukio Mishima tries to stir jeering soldiers into armed rebellion on 25 November 1970. Minutes after this photo was taken he committed *hara-kiri*

strong that it would suspend or undermine the democratic government and with it the centrist 'solution' to the Basque problem – the automomy arrangement negotiated and in principle accepted by the majority of the moderate Basque National Party (BNP) supporters. The worsening terrorism in the Basque region has certainly polarised the situation dangerously. Given the strong tradition of military *golpistas* (a tradition established decades before Franco's seizure of power) and the relatively deep-rooted indigenous fascism from groups like Ledesma de Rivera and JONS, right down to Pinar's contemporary Fuerza Nueva and its para-military-style youth movement, the dangers of a fascist-supported coup are considerable. What makes the Spanish government's task in preventing this much more difficult is the fact that the armed forces, always the last defence in an attack on the constitution, cannot really be seen as a reliable institution. It is a serious indictment of the Spanish military intelligence network that it failed either to predict the coup attempt in February 1981 or to perform effectively while the conspiracy was being launched. According to statements by Tejero under interrogation, leaked to the Spanish press in April, Major José Cortina, the officer in charge of the Defence Ministry's own intelligence agency (CESID), was one of the plotters. He was later charged with rebellion, as was his former chief, Colonel José San Martin, head of the Brunete Armoured Division's general staff. The two of them had worked together in Admiral Carrero Blanco's intelligence service under Franco. It is all very well for the Spanish left to talk of 'purging' the Army of unreliable elements: the fact is that over sixty per cent of the officers of staff rank are men who were schooled into hard-line Francoism. They cannot all be dismissed without denuding the forces of their ablest professional officers, but they need to be kept under firm and effective civilian control.

Closely linked with proneness to fascist coups is the apparent facility with which fascists have been able to penetrate the power-centres of certain European societies and to engage in corruption on a considerable scale, establishing secret networks of fascist mutual assistance, peddling political influence in return for bribes, and feathering their nests through financial corruption. Spain, Greece, Italy and Argentina have all experienced this kind of political corruption over a long period, and we have seen in chapter 3 how industrialists and financiers deeply implicated in sustaining Hitler's Germany's economy and reaping profits of slave labour, were able to edge back into positions of influence in the post-War West German economy.

The most startling recent instance of this is the *scandalo* of Propaganda Due (P-2) in Italy, which broke in May 1981 and brought down the government of Signor Arnoldo Forlani. P-2 was a masonic lodge, and its founder, Grand Master, and *eminence grise* was Licio Gelli, a fascist extremist who had volunteered to fight with the Italian forces sent by Mussolini to aid Franco in the Spanish Civil War, and then became a devoted servant of the Mussolini regime during the Second World War. He is alleged to have tortured partisans in the Pistola region. He emigrated to Argentina after the War and during his 20-year stay there he became closely identified with the Peronists. When he returned to Italy he became a freemason, and set about securing the readmission of extreme right-wingers who had been formerly excluded because of their links with fascism. Gelli also cultivated contacts with British and American masons.

While police were searching Gelli's villa in Arezzo in connection with allegations that he was involved in the Sindona fraud scandal, they discovered the now notorious lists of 963 P-2 members. These revealed that Gelli had managed to use his lodge to set up a network in every key sector of the Italian establishment. It included 3 cabinet ministers, 30 generals, 8 admirals (including Admiral Giovanni Torrisi, head of the armed forces), the heads of the 2 counter-intelligence services, the civilian co-ordinator of intelligence, 43 MPs, the police chiefs of 4 cities (Cagliari, Salerno, Palermo and Treviso), the prefects of Brescia and Pavia, and the editor of the distinguished Milan newspaper *Corriere della Sera*. It has also been suggested that members of the P-2 lodge may have been linked to an oil tax fraud in which a journalist was murdered. Yet by June 1981 the only 2 members of P-2 accused of criminal activity were Gelli himself and a former colonel of the secret service, accused in connection with Gelli's possession of secret state papers about bribes paid to buy oil from Saudia Arabia. Most sinister of all are the suggestions that P-2 members may have been implicated in acts of terrorism.

But corruption is as Italian as macaroni, and it is not yet clear whether Gelli and his colleagues had any concerted *political* aims, whether fascist or otherwise. What Gelli was clearly engaged in was exploiting the access he had to secret service files to blackmail persons in high places. The motives were probably greed, a desire to maintain the power of his network, and anxiety to protect himself. Perhaps the most worrying element in this scandal is the light it throws on the extent to which Italy's secret services and armed forces have been compromised for over a decade. It is interesting that General Vitor Miceli, the head of the secret service refered to earlier, was also listed as a P-2 member.

Financial and political corruption is, of course, only one form of disorder debilitating to the democratic political system. It is by no means the most destructive, especially in a country hardened to political scandals. As has been shown in our comparative study of fascist movements in earlier chapters, there are two far graver threats posed by fascism to the survival of democracy. The first is the pollution of intellectual life by fascistic ideas in general such as racism, anti-Semitism, and the glorification of violence and war. It is important to remember that fascist attitudes and doctrines can infiltrate the general climate of thought in an insidious and piecemeal fashion. Thus the increased influence of the fascist *mentality* is not necessarily signalled by any significant growth in the formal membership of fascist and racist organisations. For instance, in West Germany the neo-Nazi party, the NPD, has never attained the 5 per cent of the vote required to get seats in the Federal parliament. Yet recently, in a study of West German public opinion carried out by the Sinus Research Institute, it was revealed that 13.3 per cent of the electorate ($5\frac{1}{2}$ million people) saw history and politics very much through National Socialist lenses. This large minority hates democracy, pluralism and all foreign minorities, and firmly believes in absolute loyalty to the Fatherland. Most worrying of all, the researchers found that this group was unshaken in its belief that violence is not only inevitable and necessary, but also that it is a cathartic and cleansing force. A more hopeful finding was that those below the age of 40 are largely immune to these extreme right-wing views; the highest concentration is, not surprisingly, among the over-50s who fought in the War.

Recent evidence of the way in which extreme right-wing sentiment can still be aroused to protect Nazi criminals from justice was provided by the Kappler case. Herbert Kappler is a former SS colonel who was sentenced to death by the Italian courts for his part in the massacre of 335 hostages, many of them Jews, in a cave near Rome in 1944. According to the report of Kappler's part in the massacre published with great courage by *Die Welt*, Kappler gave cognac to the executioners 'who were wading in blood' and shot some of the hostages himself 'to set an example'. This same man became a hero to the German public when a Nazi underground group called 'Gaeta' (after the name of the Italian resort where Kappler was imprisoned) managed to spirit him out of a prison hospital where he was having treatment for cancer, and smuggle him over the border and into Germany.

It is indicative of the attitude of many Germans to the SS and the War as a whole that Kappler was feted as a hero, and showered with floral tributes and telegrams. Even more worrying is the fact that the West German government flatly refused to hand Kappler back to the Italians. The commitment of the new democratic republic to the pursuit of war criminals is more cosmetic than real. This does not mean that the West German government is brim-full with currently active Nazis, or that there is some sort of official conspiracy in league with neo-Nazi movements. But it shows that there are whole sectors of German opinion who have no real regrets, no feelings of guilt, about the past. It is as if they have simply developed a mental block about the crimes committed under the Nazi regime. Hence they are psychologically wide-open to the restoration of creeping Nazism. The outcry in West Germany over Mr Begin's May 1981 speech on German Nazism partly reflected their resentment at the notion of war guilt.

In the United States, the dissemination of racist ideas has gone hand-in-hand with the resurgence of violent groups such as the Ku Klux Klan, the neo-Nazis, and the many new organisations that constitute the extreme of the American new right. Although the Klan claims to be on the march again in many states, the fact is that few of these extremists would think of dressing up in bedsheets and pointed hats. Nevertheless they do share many of the basic ideas of the Klan: anti-Semitism, anti-desegregation, anti-communist, anti-welfare, anti-gun controls, anti-abortion, anti-racial intermarriage, anti-equal opportunities, and pro-'white supremacy'.

The Klan is now making a considerable effort to set up 'Klaverns' in Britain, Canada, Australia and even West Germany (see page 106). The self-styled Imperial Wizard, Bill Wilkinson, claimed in 1979 that they had already recruited 500 members in Britain. In 1981 it was reported that Ku Klux Klan petrol-soaked Crosses have been burned in London, and that a Klan group in Hackney, claimed to be 200 strong, had been given instructions on bomb manufacture. The Klan has already increased its links with fascist movements internationally, especially through contacts with the National Front and the VMO rally in Belgium.

The best known Klan propagandist to visit Britain to date has been David Duke, who runs the Patriot Bookstore at Baton Rouge, Louisiana, a major distribution centre for fascist and anti-Semitic propaganda. The passage of Klan literature Duke describes as his 'favourite' conveys the crude neo-Nazi character of its message:

'The Negro masses are biologically inferior and easily manipulated (by Jews). But the Jews can't as easily manipulate white men, so they are doing everything possible to destroy the idea that there is any such thing as "race" .... The continued existence of white civilization and the white race depends on white civilization and the white race depends on whether enough Americans are concerned about imminent catastrophe to do something professional and revolutionary about it .... ONLY AN ATTACK CAN DO THESE THINGS – and no half-hearted, Vietnam-styled 'attack' either, but the old-fashioned kind in which our purpose is simple and direct: to ANNIHILATE the enemy – to smash him, beat him down and exterminate him.'

In France the 'intellectual' new right has recently begun to put forward doctrines on biology, race, heredity, and cultural roots reminiscent of fascist theorists in the inter-War period. Possibly their most influential 'intellectual' spokesman is Alain de Benoist, who claims to have a following of 10,000 fellow-intellectuals. De Benoist puts forward his ideas in a quiet and 'respectable' fashion. He claims they are the ideas of an intellectual 'school' rather than a political movement or party, and that he and his colleagues are against violence and racism. Yet the implications of de Benoist's views would strike a chord in the mind of any fascist. He believes that heredity is more important than environment in human development; that those born with superior qualities should lead; that egalitarianism is bad because it undermines the best (i.e.

elite) elements in the human race; that the Indo-European cultural heritage is superior to that of either super-power; and Marxism and materialism must be resisted. De Benoist claims his ideas are scientifically based, and were just 'abused' and 'discredited' by Hitler. It is sad that these terrible ideas, disguised as a 'new philosophy', have been finding a regular platform in the weekly *Figaro* magazine and elsewhere in the opinion-forming media. It has become fashionable among students to purvey this new right philosophy, just as it was popular to be a neo-Marxist in the late 1960s. The arrogance and aggression of this intellectual tendency was well-illustrated in the bizarre 1981 legal case, in which Professor Faurisson sought to prove that the Holocaust did not happen.

It is but a short step from the moral pollution caused by such ideas to racialist attacks on Jews and other minorities. In France there has been, as we have observed in previous chapters, a resurgence of anti-Semitism, ranging from the desecration of synagogues and Jewish cemetries to bombings and machine-gun attacks on Jewish targets. The warning signals were clear months before the Rue Copernic synagogue bombing. Over 40 fascist attacks of this kind were recorded in France in the period July–October 1980 alone, including a bombing of a printing plant in which 1 man was killed and 17 injured; machine-gun attacks on the Jewish martyrs' memorial; another machine-gun attack on a Jewish nursery; and an incendiary attack on the apartment belonging to the leader of the League of Human Rights, Henri Nogueres. Despite this mounting evidence the French police appear to have done little or nothing to improve protection for the Jewish community: it took the Rue Copernic attack to jolt them out of their complacency, and by then younger and more militant Jews were no longer prepared to trust the French police to carry out the task. Many suspected tolerance of neo-Nazi activities in some quarters within the police.

Yet serious though the danger and apprehension felt by Jewish communities in Europe may be, it hardly compares to the prospect of mass terror and persecution reappearing in the Middle East and elsewhere. In Argentina evidence has come to light of a massive wave of anti-Semitic attacks, apparently tolerated by the dictatorship and actively encouraged by those in charge of internal security. There is, as we have noted, a large body of unreconstructed Nazis living in the country, both those who fled from Europe at the end of the Second World War to escape war crimes prosecution, and the committed fascist members of the armed forces and establishment who had been passionate supporters of the Axis powers throughout the War, and were never purged thereafter. In 1980–1 there has been a campaign of vilification and hatred launched in the Argentinian media against their 400,000-strong Jewish community, one of the largest in the world outside Israel. The testimony of Jacobo Timerman, founder editor of the liberal newspaper *La Prensa*, indicates potential for a pogrom against the Jews on a scale not experienced since the Second World War. Timerman was snatched by government employed gunmen from his home in April 1977 and held without charges for 2½ years before international human rights pressure gained his release. Timerman adds his testimony to those tortured and persecuted earlier by the Argentinian secret police. He confirms that Nazi doctrine is practised wholesale by the repressive apparatus. Timerman recounts how one of his interrogators opened every session of questioning with the words 'Are you a Jew?' He met an old man who had been brutally beaten in the secret prison of Coti Martinez because his interrogator refused to believe that he had been converted to Catholicism from Judaism in his youth. Timerman also tells of hearing a woman captive crying out for mercy and shouting that she was not a Jew. Many victims have described pictures of Hitler, swastikas and other Nazi symbols in their torturers' rooms. General Galtieri, when head of the Army, publicly demanded a new war against what he calls' intellectual subversion'. In view of his record, and the fact that so many of the professional and intellectual classes in Argentina are members of the Jewish community, there is little doubt what he has in mind. At the time of writing (mid-1982), Argentina's government is refraining from officially supporting a campaign of anti-Semitism. But the armed forces and the trade unions with their deep-rooted fascist elements are already engaged in an unofficial campaign of discrimination and persecution, and no one in power is doing anything to stop it.

The re-emergence of fascist movements and intensification of fascist violence are, alas, not confined to a mere handful of European and Latin American countries. One of the most astonishing developments has been the growth of a fascist fringe within Israel. During the election campaign in the summer of 1981 a tiny extremist party, Kach, inserted a full-page advertisement in every major Israeli newspaper, advocating the expulsion of all Arabs from Israel as a 'stage' in the establishment of a 'Greater Israel' (an appalling echo of Hitler's concept of a 'Greater Germany'). The advertisement goes on to declare: 'We shall propose a law which will punish every non-Jew who has sexual relations with a Jewish woman with five years imprisonment' The resemblance to the Nazis' anti-Semitic Nuremberg race-laws are both terrifying and tragic. Kach claims that this is just the beginning: any Arabs who resist expulsion are to be drafted into 'compulsory labour battalions'. Among the methods of violence used by the extreme right in the elections were rolling burning rubbish bins into political meetings and beating up activists of moderate and left-inclined parties. Of course, the overwhelming majority of Israelis reject Kach's ideas and regard both Kach and Rabbi Kahane, its founder, as lunatics. But this cannot disguise the truth of the argument made repeatedly in this book: no culture or political system is immune from the dangers of the fascist mentality, not even the people who have suffered most from the barbarity of fascism.

A corollary of these modern neo-fascist and racist campaigns is that political extremism breeds counter-terror in the name of self-defence. Thus the Provisional IRA claim that violence was forced upon them in Northern Ireland as their only protection against the violence of the armed 'loyalist' or Protestant para-military groups. Colonel Turkes' National Action Party in Turkey claims it was essential to set up a private army of assassins to fight the neo-Marxist gunmen of the Dev-Sol (Revolutionary left) and the Turkish People's Liberation Army (TPLA). Thus, from the early 1970s until the Generals' coup in 1980, gangs of murderous rightists and leftists shot it out in the streets of Turkish cities. One day gunmen would strafe a well-known leftist cafe or party office. the next a similar attack would be launched against rightist targets. A similar syndrome has been observed in the tit-for-tat war between the Red Brigades and neo-fascists in Italy, between the French FNE and Jewish vigilante groups, and (so far only in the form of marching confrontation and street fights) between the National Front and the Socialist Workers' Party (SWP) or Anti-Nazi League (ANL) in Britain. There are countless other examples revealing this particular form of fascist threat. Violent extremism acts as a catalyst, bringing rival gangs, terrorists and vigilantes on to the streets. This enormously strains the constitutional authorities, the police and the judiciary, and, by threatening escalation to civil war, may even put the survival of democracy in peril. That, of course, is often precisely what the extremists on both sides, though for different motives, want to happen.

6 RECENT DEVELOPMENTS

The Scandinavians have managed to avoid the major political conflicts and instability that have characterised other parts of Europe in recent years. Norway's oil boom in the North Sea has given her small population (under four million) an unprecedented prosperity. Sweden, which managed to remain neutral in the Second World War, has gained a world-wide reputation both for political stability and for the comprehensive and generous provisions of her welfare state system. Even so, both countries have been by no means immune from the contagion of neo-nazism. We have noted earlier the case of Norwegian fascist terrorists involved in a major arms theft, and murders. Since 1981 the extreme right-wing groups have continued to recruit and spread neo-Nazi propaganda. In particular they have sought to incite hatred against immigrants, many of whom went to Norway to work in the oil or oil-related industries.

Recently Sweden has been experiencing a similar phenomenon. In August 1982 police in central Stockholm were faced with an outbreak of particularly ugly racial clashes. Gangs of skinhead youths armed with iron bars, knives and karate batons fought with gangs of immigrant youths, and thirty were arrested. In one incident a fourteen-year-old boy was shot in the stomach during a fight with a gang of Turkish immigrants in Kulma, a Stockholm suburb. Immigrant homes, businesses and organisations have been attacked and have been the targets of numerous telephone threats. Anti-immigrant graffiti have proliferated and there have been a number of Swedish press reports of Ku Klux Klan crosses being burnt in front of immigrants' homes.

The Swedish government has become gravely concerned at

these trends and the department of immigration has mounted a special educational programme in schools to combat racial prejudice and to reduce tension. (They have made a more concerted effort in this field over the past eighteen months than many other European countries, including those with far worse racial tensions.) The Swedes have also gone a stage further than the United Kingdom in police response to the problem: they have now established a special police squad to deal with threats and attacks against immigrants.

One of the Swedish extremist groups which has sought to capitalise on the growing racial tension is the blatantly neo-Nazi Nordiska Rikspartiet founded by Göran A. Oredsson. The party, which seeks to spread its Swedish variant of Nazi ideology, tried to gain votes in the autumn 1979 elections, hoping to benefit from the growing disillusion of the right with the Conservative Party and the growing anti-immigrant feeling. It has been a total failure in electoral terms. However, like other European fascist parties it has managed to secure propaganda outlets to young people and to attract some fanatical new young members. This has been done largely through meetings, street-corner propaganda and infiltration of schools and colleges. They have encountered considerable difficulties in publishing propaganda material. The Swedish printers' union boycotted the printing of the Rikspartiet organ, *Nordisk Camp*, and using their legal powers to participate on the board of publishing companies the workers have also refused to allow the printing of Oredsson's national socialist credo 'In Praise to All that Made me Harder'. This shows an exemplary sense of decency and responsibility on the part of the Swedish printing workers, who are clearly well aware of the damaging effect of racist propaganda, especially in the cities where there have been attacks on immigrants.

Throughout 1981–2 the Low Countries continued to experience both indigenous and imported neo-fascism. After a lengthy trial which opened in January 1981 Bert Erikson, leader of the VMO, and 106 other VMO militants were eventually acquitted at the court of appeal in Antwerp in June 1982 of charges of seeking to set up a private army. The organisation therefore could not be banned on those grounds. Yet despite the effects of the growing recession (Belgian unemployment rose to 457,587 in the first half of July, an unprecedented 11 per cent unemployment rate), and the increasing unpopularity of the coalition centre-right government, right-wing extremism totally failed to make any impact on the electorate.

Neo-Nazis from neighbouring countries continue to make use of Belgium and Holland as sanctuaries, though improved European police co-operation is beginning to show results. In October 1981 four West Germans alleged to have been members of a unit of the neo-Nazi Peoples Socialist Movement of Germany (VSBD) which was involved in a shoot-out with Munich police in which two members of the group were killed were arrested. They were extradited to West Germany in January 1982. And another West German neo-Nazi, Karl Leroy, was arrested in Brussels in May 1982.

One of the worst terrorist attacks ever experienced in Belgium occurred on 20 October 1981, when a bomb exploded outside an Antwerp synagogue about twenty minutes before the ceremony for the end of the Feast of the Tabernacles was due to begin there. The casualties were passers-by, most of them early-morning shoppers. Two women were killed, and nearly 100 injured, 16 of them seriously. The identity of the group or individuals responsible is still unknown. The Israeli Embassy accused the Palestinians of the attack, but the PLO spokesman in Brussels condemned the attack as being 'on innocent victims'. The fact that the main target was clearly intended to be the Jewish community also raises the possibility that the attack was carried out by an extreme right anti-Semitic organisation.

Nazis and other anti-Semitic groups in France suffered a considerable setback in July 1981 when a Paris court found Professor Robert Faurisson, who became notorious for his writings denying the existence of gas chambers in German death camps, guilty of incitement to racial hatred and violence. In his summing up the public prosecutor stated: 'To deny the existence of gas chambers is to kill for a second time those who died . . . and to add to the suffering of the survivors and their families.' Faurisson was given a three months suspended sentence and fined 5,000 francs. In addition he was ordered to pay 4,000 francs in damages to the League against Racism, and 6,000 francs each to the Movement against Racism and the association of former Auschwitz concentration camp victims, Faurisson and the publisher of his book, *Memoir in defence against those who accuse me of falsifying history*, were fined an additional 2,000 francs for libelling Professor Leon Poliakov, a leading authority on the Nazi treatment of the Jews.

In July 1981 Gaston Defferre, minister of the interior, assured the powerful French Federation of Police Unions that he would be more zealous than the previous government in acting against extreme right-wing organisations. A few days later (25 July) the secretary-general of a mysterious Gaullist strong-arm organisation, Service d'Action Civique (SAC), Pierre Debizet, was charged as an accessory before the fact in connection with the murder of Jacques Massie, a junior police inspector who was until recently the head of the organisation in the Provence region, and five members of his family. The scandal deepened as Bernard Deleplace of the Federation of Police Unions alleged that many senior police officers had close links with the SAC. The Gaullist party headquarters denied any connection with the SAC. *La Marseillaise*, the Communist newspaper, linked the murdered Inspector Massie with an arms-smuggling operation involved with the Italian P-2 Masonic lodge. On 30 July four members of the SAC commando in Provence confessed to killing the Massies.

Originally set up in 1958 to 'protect' Gaullist political meetings, the SAC grew into a kind of private parallel police force and it was frequently used to carry out illegal operations. The judicial investigation into the massacre of the Massie family at Auriol, near Marseilles, revealed that the crime was probably motivated by revenge, the desire of some members of the SAC to settle old scores and their fear that Inspector Massie knew too much about the organisation and would not part with compromising documents in his possession. The whole judicial and political establishment was shaken by the revelations and wider ramifications which came to light in the Auriol Massacre inquiry. People were dismayed to discover how a clandestine police squad specialising in dirty tricks had been able to shelter for years behind the authority of the state and the entrée provided by its tricolour identity card. The concern voiced by police union officials the previous year about close links between the extreme right and highly placed police officers was again shown to have been entirely justified. And few were convinced by the hasty denials by leading Gaullist party members and officials of any connexion with SAC.

Another intriguing manifestation of the extreme right occurred in December 1981 when a small ultra-right-wing group based in Brazil, Sociedade Brasileira de Defesa da Tradiçao, Familia e Propriedade (Society for the Defence of Tradition, Family and Property), launched a million-dollar advertising campaign in western newspapers attacking French socialism. Advertisements placed in the *Washington Post*, *New York Times*, *Los Angeles Times*, *Frankfurter Allgemeine Zeitung*, *Le Figaro* and the *Observer* warned that President Mitterrand's brand of 'self-managing socialism represents a grave threat not only to France but also to the whole world'. The group was apparently founded in Brazil in 1960 by Plinio Corrêa de Oliveira, a lawyer now in his seventies, from São Paulo. It is quite small with only 2,000 permanent members working as full-time lobbyists and propagandists, supported by roughly 6,000 donors, including some very wealthy businessmen. Accusations that the society is a fascist organiza-tion have been angrily denied, and certainly the message of

Plinio's propaganda more closely resembles arch-traditionalism, and preaches a return to the authoritarian Catholic doctrines enunciated by Pius X. All manifestations of secularisation, socialism and progressivism are totally rejected, including divorce, equal rights for women, and trade unionism. However, their street demonstrations and marches in Brazil have occasionally led to street fighting, and they are extremely secretive about their sources of funds. Little has been heard of the group outside Brazil since its advertisements appeared.

In July 1982 extreme right-wing terrorism again surfaced in Paris with numerous arson, bombing and shooting attacks on Jewish premises, swastika daubing, threats against French Jews and attacks and threats against immigrant families. A new fascist group emerged, calling itself the French Revolutionary Brigades, and claimed responsibility for the 21 July bombing of a flat that had been used by Regis Debray, now one of President Mitterrand's advisers, and warned of further attacks.

Fascist terrorism, however, has not been the primary concern in French government circles. The main motivation for the new package of anti-terrorist measures announced on 18 August 1982 was fear of the increasingly bloody spill-over of international terrorism in Paris, such as the car bomb attack in the Champs-Élysées in which the Syrians were believed to have been implicated, and the terrorist attacks by Action Directe, an extreme left-wing group. The government proscribed Action Directe, established a new post of Secretary of State for Public Security to oversee the combating of terrorism, appointed a senior officer in the Gendarmerie to co-ordinate the work of the security agencies involved in countering terrorism, tightened frontier and visa controls, centralised the collection of anti-terrorist data, and promised closer co-operation with other European governments and police forces against terrorism. Many observers believed that these measures were long overdue, but they are tangible evidence of the government's will to tackle this problem and they do not constitute any threat to civil liberties. It remains to be seen how effective they will be in deterring, preventing and punishing extremist violence.

Meanwhile fascist terrorism in Italy has continued, though fortunately on a far smaller scale than in 1980. On 31 July 1981 Giuseppe de Luca, a neo-fascist activist, was killed by rival fascists, and in Rome on 21 October 1981 an Italian special branch police officer, Captain Ranco Straullu, an expert in the investigation of right-wing terrorism, and his assistant were killed with automatic weapons firing bursts of armour-piercing bullets. In a telephone call to several daily newspapers responsibility for the killings was claimed by the NAR. The same fascist terror group also claimed responsibility for shooting a Rome policeman, Romano Radici, in December 1981, in revenge for the shooting by police of a neo-fascist, Alessandro Alibrandi, a terrorist wanted in connection with the 1980 Bologna railway station bombing. This pattern was repeated in May 1982 when Rome police killed Giorgio Vale, an NAR activist, in a shoot-out. Two days later NAR shot dead a policeman, Giuseppe Rapesta, in reprisal for Vale's death. In June a weird Nazi-Maoist group, Third Position, made an arson attack on Christian Democrat offices in Rome. A previously unknown neo-Nazi group, Ludwig, murdered two priests at Vicenza in July 1982, and the following month an imprisoned right-wing extremist strangled a fellow-terrorist in gaol at Novara. In Milan on the same day a bomb, obviously intended to strike Jewish community targets, exploded in the commercial quarter of Milan.

Three other major developments in the affairs of the ultra-right groups in Italy during 1981–2 should be highlighted. First, a number of arrests were made in connection with the Bologna railway station bombing of August 1980. Nine Italians were taken in for questioning by London police in September 1981. Seven of them (six men and one woman) were wanted by Italian police in connection with armed robbery and subversion. Five of the suspects were said to be wanted on warrants issued by magistrates in Rome and Bologna for questioning in connection with the Bologna massacre. Extradition proceedings were started against the group. It is known that the Metropolitan Police were acting on information received from Interpol and from the anti-terrorist police in Rome. However, it was not until September 1982 that the Italian judicial authorities felt confident that they had sufficient evidence to bring charges in connection with the Bologna bombing. The group's leader is said to be Stefano Della Chiaie, founder of the National Advance Guard, a neo-fascist terrorist group, who has been living in Latin America. In October 1982 police in Bolivia arrested one of the main suspects, Pierluigi Pagliai, after a shoot-out, and he was flown back to Rome in a requisitioned airliner under armed guard. But Della Chiaie got away. The other members of the group are a German, a Frenchman and two Italians, all right-wing extremists. It is believed that the police are basing their confident claims on evidence from several witnesses, including the confessions of Elio Ciolini, a former employee of the Italian Post Office with links with the French secret service, currently serving a gaol sentence in Switzerland for extortion. Ciolini is said to have given evidence to the Italian police about a meeting of the P-2 Masonic lodge (now banned) in Monte Carlo at which he alleges plans for the Bologna bombing attack were discussed, and several members of the bombing group and Licio Gelli, P-2's grand master, were present. On 13 September 1982 Gelli was arrested when he attempted to draw money from a Geneva bank account. Following inves-tigations by the Swiss judicial authorities into the transfer to Switzerland of sums paid out by Latin American subsidiaries of Banco Ambrosiano, the public prosecutor's office in Lugano sequestrated the funds in the account (L5.7m). Italian authorities issued a warrant for Gelli's arrest on a number of serious charges, including extortion, fraud, drugs and arms peddling, political blackmail and plotting to overthrow the legal government and establish an authoritarian regime. These last charges indicate that the police have accumulated more substantial evidence on the links between the P-2 lodge and fascist terrorism. It remains to be seen whether the suspicions of the police and the many claims made in the Italian left-wing press regarding P-2 involvement in the Bologna station bombing will be substantiated.

The P-2 scandal not only brought down Signor Forlani's coalition government in May 1981 and wrecked the public careers of many leading Italian politicians, senior officers, government officials and other leading figures; it also initiated a major investigation into possible links between the powerful secret society and neo-fascist terrorism, with international ramifications. Gelli used his base in Uruguay, where he lived in an expensive villa in Montevideo, to promote a huge network of business interests, property deals and banking ventures. Gelli and his main Latin American associate, Umberto Ortolani, helped Robert Calvi of the Rome-based Banco Ambrosiano to expand his business and purchase subsidiaries in Peru, Nicaragua, Paraguay and Argentina. It is believed that the Uruguayan secret police (DN11) have in their possession 500 files on Gelli's contacts in Italy and abroad, which they seized from Gelli's home in Montevideo.

Responding to the grave concern throughout Italy at the corruption revealed by the P-2 affair, Signor Spandolini, the Italian prime minister, promised in July 1981 to take action to ban secret societies, including what he termed 'the aberrant parallel organisations' (P-2). A Bill outlawing and dissolving all secret societies was approved by the Italian government on 24 July 1981.

A third major focus of attention among observers of right-wing terrorism in Italy has been the case of Mehmet Ali Agca, the Turk sentenced to life imprisonment for the attempted murder of the Pope in 1981. Initial police investigations into the crime were hampered by Agca's unwillingness to cooperate with his interrogators. Agca tried to get his trial shifted from an Italian court to the Vatican. When this was refused he virtually boycotted the trial proceedings. At that time Agca insisted that he had been acting alone. No mention was made in the brief trial of a 'Bulgarian connection'. Nevertheless some major questions remained. What about the rumours of an accomplice seen running away from the scene of the shooting? How did Agca finance his expensive journeyings around Europe prior to the assassination attempt? And what was his motive?

It has always been clear that the Soviet Union had a powerful motive for plotting to murder Pope John Paul. The Polish Pontiff has been widely recognised as an inspiring force behind Solidarity and the whole struggle for human rights in Poland, in which the Polish Catholic Church has played such a courageous part. Indeed in December 1982 the Soviet news agency TASS carried a strongly worded attack on Pope John Paul. TASS accused the Catholic Church of giving birth to the 'notorious Solidarity', and subversive activities in other socialist countries in Eastern Europe.

It is also known that the Pope promised help and support to Solidarity leader Lech Walesa, and the Soviets would have been particularly alarmed at reports that the Pope had promised Lech Walesa that he would return immediately to Poland in the event of any Soviet military intervention.

The first real clue to a Bulgarian connection was the discovery by a respected Turkish journalist, Ugur Mumcu, that Agca had stayed for a time at the Vitosha Hotel in Sofia in early 1981, where Bulgarian agents and a Turkish arms smuggler were also staying. However, terrorists of all kinds have used Bulgaria as a channel for arms and drug trafficking, and a visit to Sofia and a clear Warsaw Pact motive do not constitute adequate proof of Bulgarian complicity in the attempt on the Pope.

The study of terrorism has been bedevilled by simplistic theories that the KGB is behind every act. I shared the doubts of many observers when theories of Warsaw Pact complicity were first voiced. Nor was this simply the habit of academic scepticism. My researches had convinced me of Agca's fascist affiliations. Moreover, two Turks who have been arrested abroad in connection with the inquiries into the assassination attempt, Musa Celibi and Omar Bagci, have also been members of Turkish fascist organisations. And it is well known that fascists do not normally collaborate closely with communist regimes. Another reason for scepticism was the fact that the KGB and other Warsaw Pact secret services have generally held back from assassination attempts on major Western leaders and heads of state. Not only would an attempt on the life of the Pope be a radical departure from Soviet practice, it would also be extremely reckless. There would always be the danger of the Warsaw Pact link being revealed through subsequent investigations or leaks.

The choice of Agca as assassin is also baffling. Why select a person who has escaped from a Turkish gaol and whose description would inevitably be passed by the Turks to the governments of other European countries where Agca was sighted? And was it not particularly reckless to pick someone who had already (in 1979) publicly proclaimed his desire to murder the Pope? Was this fact alone not enough to stimulate even the most comatose West European police force into hunting for Agca? One can only assume that the choice of assassin and the operational planning were left almost entirely to the Bulgarians. It has been claimed that they bought Agca's services for roughly £700,000. Such a large sum of money would certainly have been tempting to a man on the run who was desperate to buy a fresh identity and live in comfort. The Bulgarians may also have been impressed by two other factors: (i) Agca's powerful motivation to murder the Pope and, (ii) the choice of a known fascist would throw the Italian police off the scent if the scheme misfired.

By December 1982 the Italian authorities were confident that they had obtained conclusive proof of Bulgarian, and implicitly Soviet, complicity in the attempted assassination.

The information given by Agca since he first decided to talk to the Italian authorities in December 1981 had been dramatically corroborated. Agca was able to guide Signor Martella, the investigating magistrate in the case, to the correct Rome addresses of the Bulgarian agents named in his confession. He was able to describe the furnishings of the apartment belonging to Antonov, a Bulgarian airlines official arrested and charged by the Italians for active complicity in the plot. A man bearing an uncanny resemblance to Antonov appears in a picture taken at the time of the shooting. Meanwhile, in a separate case Luigi Scricciolo, a left-wing trade union official, who has admitted spying for the Bulgarians, identified the same Bulgarians named by Agca when they were separately shown an album of photographs of foreigners 'suspected of activities hostile to the Italian state'.

Trusted diplomatic staff and the senior Bulgarian airline official in Rome must have been acting on instructions from the Bulgarian secret service. But it does not end there. We know enough about the domination of the Warsaw Pact secret services by the KGB to be sure that such a dangerous and unprecedented operation could have been authorised only by the Kremlin. Brezhnev would certainly have consulted closely with Andropov, now Soviet leader but formerly KGB head. It is likely that the Bulgarian secret service was given some scope in detailed planning. The Soviets are always careful to act through proxies in such matters in case the scheme backfires. From what we know already we can surmise that the Soviet leadership did instigate this dastardly attack. By a strange twist of fate Bulgarians made use of a gunman initiated into terrorism as a Turkish fascist.

The trial of Colonel Alpaslan Turkes and 586 other right-wing extremists was the most important event in the development of the ultra-right in Turkey in 1981. Most of the defendants at the military law tribunal were members of Turkes' National Action Party, and the prosecutors demanded the death sentence for 220 of the defendants. Turkes and his

NAP were accused of seeking to overthrow the constitutional order and to seize power and of the murder of at least 594 people. The 945-page indictment described the ruthless terror groups run by Turkes and his NAP throughout the country. It signified the new military regime's apparent determination to eliminate terrorism of both extreme left and extreme right. The trial resulted in the conviction of the NAP members, but only after weeks of interruptions, courtroom scenes and frequent disruption. In October two of the military judges on the tribunal resigned after a series of clashes between the defence and the military prosecutor. Colonel Turkes totally rejected the charges against him and fresh charges were brought against him of insulting the court in his fiery speeches. Throughout 1981–2 the level of political violence from all quarters fell dramatically as the Turkish generals established their grip on the country and restored order throughout the provinces. Nevertheless, despite the tough measures that have been taken and the deterrent effect of the mass trial of NAP members, there is still a considerable following for right-wing extremist ideas which will again express itself in political violence when the opportunity arises.

Fascism in Spain continued to pose a worrying problem to the democratic government, increasingly beset with economic problems and the weakening of centrist support behind Prime Minister Calvo Sotelo. A sign of the latent mass sympathy for fascist ideas, or at least for a return to *caudillo* rule by a military man on the Franco model, was the elevation of Antonio Tejero, the civil guard officer who held the Spanish *Cortes* hostage at gunpoint, into something of a folk-hero. His picture appeared on mock bank-notes, souvenirs and trinkets of every kind. At his comfortable and easy-going army 'prison' at the military garrison of Castillo de la Parma, near El Ferrol, he was virtually allowed to hold court to his admirers and friends, including many ardent members of Fuerza Nueva, the fascist party. In interviews with journalists, Tejero was cocky and defiant, vowing that he would make another *coup* attempt and risk imprisonment again. Tejero voiced popular fascist demands for law and order and the restoration of traditional family morality. He blamed democratic parties and universal suffrage for Spain's ills, and called for the restoration of dictatorship. One of the journalists who interviewed him at Castillo de la Parma, David Gollob of the *Sunday Times*, reported being told by one of Tejero's ardent supporters that he had been 'sitting beside the next *caudillo* of Spain'. Did Tejero share that view? asked Gollob. 'Of course not. He's terribly modest. But we will lift him up to that height. He's the man we've been waiting for,' he was told by a woman with burning eyes. The faith of the extreme right in *golpismo*, the tradition of the *coup d'état*, is still very much alive.

Further evidence of danger from this direction came in July 1981 when *Cambio 16*, Spain's major news magazine, disclosed that there had been an ultra-right conspiracy to seize King Juan Carlos on 24 June and either force him to leave Spain or shoot him. According to the report, which has been authenticated by senior security sources in the government, there was a plot to attack the Oriente Palace, Madrid, during a major diplomatic reception and to kidnap the king. This was to have been preceded by a bombing attack at a Barcelona football stadium, where 100,000 Catalans were due to celebrate their national day, in order to create a crisis atmosphere. The plot was forestalled by pre-dawn police swoops on the conspirators in Madrid. Although no one has yet been charged in connection with this conspiracy, there has been no official denial that such a plot existed.

Other incidents involving the extreme right in July 1981 were the burning of the King's portrait by a fascist rally in Seville on 11 July, and a fascist attack in Madrid three days later against buses carrying children from the Basque region. Then on 18 July, Blas Pinar, leader of Fuerza Nueva, at the last minute called off his attempt to hold a mass rally in Madrid to celebrate Franco's military rising of forty-five years ago, even though he had earlier called on his supporters to defy the ban. However, five people were hurt when a fascist bomb exploded in the city.

The following October two court-martial verdicts again underlined the strong bias towards the ultra-right in the highest military echelons. In one case Captain Juan Milans del Bosch, the cavalry officer son of one of the generals charged with rebellion for his part in the February coup attempt, was sentenced to one month and a day for calling the King a 'useless pig'. In the other case Colonel Alvaro Graino, with thirty-eight years' service, was given a sentence twice as long for simply having written a letter to the editor of *Diario 16* magazine in which he denounced the existence of extreme right-wing elements in the armed forces. Well-known fascists gave Captain Juan del Bosch a hero's welcome at the court martial, while the colonel was practically sent to Coventry by his fellow officers. Realising the ominous implications of these verdicts for the court martial of the coup plotters, the cabinet decided to file appeals against the verdicts. At the same time they tried to counter a growing whispering campaign accompanied by leaflets among the army and right-wing circles trying to claim that the King knew beforehand of the February coup and was implicated in it. Doubts about the ruling Centre Democratic Union (UCD) party's unity and its ability to control the army were deepened by an incident which led to the dismissal of General Fernando Ortiz by the defence minister. Ortiz, who had been in command of a unit of the Brunete armoured division destined to play a major role in the February coup, had been moved to a post at army headquarters in charge of promotions and decorations. Ortiz had decided to approve the award of a decoration to General del Bosch for 'sacrifices to the fatherland', a singularly obvious act of defiance and a way of causing embarrassment to the government.

Meanwhile the delays, divisions and hesitations of the centre government – so understandable and natural given the challenges of regional autonomism, Basque terrorism and economic crisis – have increased the confidence of the extreme right and disaffected army officers that democracy is leading Spain into a chaos from which only they will be able to rescue their country's national honour and 'order'. The weakness of Spain's democratic forces has unfortunately been aggravated by the lack of success in negotiations for Spanish entry to the EEC in the face of French obstruction and opposition. It was anticipated that Spain's low-cost agriculture sector would pose special problems, but it is surely reasonable to suppose that if similar problems in Greece could be surmounted then some special effort could be made to bring in Spain from the cold. Spain badly needs the benefits of access to EEC markets if her democracy and her economy are to survive.

However, despite the more propitious circumstances for increasing their support the Spanish fascists were disappointed that they achieved an estimated turnout of below 100,000 at their 22 November rally in the Plaza del Oriente, Madrid, marking the sixth anniversary of Franco's death. Main speakers were Blas Pinar of Fuerza Nueva and Raimundo Fernandez Cuesta of the Falangist Youth Movement. After the rally the young fascists, many of whom were dressed in paramilitary blue uniforms, were involved in fights with the police. Street violence continued until four o'clock the following morning, and there were twenty-six arrests.

In December a group of 100 junior army officers and NCOs issued a manifesto attacking government interference in the armed forces, condemning the free press, and expressing total sympathy with the leaders of the February coup attempt. The signatories of the manifesto were 25 captains, 22 lieutenants, 15 sergeant-majors and 38 sergeants. All signatories were placed under fourteen days' house arrest in their barracks. It was yet another symptom of the strength of ultra-right sympathies at all levels of the Spanish Army. It is also significant that all the dissident officers were serving in the first military region, centred on Madrid, the most crucial area in the event of any coup attempt. Another worrying aspect is that the army's intelligence services, though they knew of the plan to publish the manifesto, failed to inform the defence minister and the commander of Madrid military district. There was a half-hearted and indeed somewhat ambiguous 'condemnation' of the manifesto of 100 issued by the joint chiefs of staff. It mainly concentrated on the fact that the officers had not gone through the correct military procedures for airing complaints, and glossed over the manifesto's praise for the officers awaiting trial for their part in the February coup.

The court martial of officers involved in the coup (3 generals, 29 other officers and one civilian) opened at Madrid four days before the first anniversary of the coup attempt. In his pre-trial testimony read out in court, General Alfonso Armada totally denied the substantial prosecution evidence that he had organised the coup with two fellow ringleaders, General Milans and Lt Col. Tejero. He denied having met Milans and Tejero in Valencia and Madrid to plan the operation. Milans and Tejero, with support of other officers on trial, testified that Armada had informed them that the King supported the idea of a new government to be headed by Armada. Clearly either Armada or Milans was lying. Tejero claimed that he was acting under orders from Armada and Milans. He also tried to involve the Queen, and claimed he had been told the King had tried to bring about a Turkish-style coup in Autumn 1980 but had failed. The prosecution asked for thirty years' imprisonment each for the three main defendants and lesser terms for the others accused. The government was clearly worried at the constant attempts to besmirch the reputation of the King, and the centre and left parties and press clearly all hoped for firm sentences against the plotters.

In the event the military court's sentences reflected a compromise which angered both the government and the extreme right. Tejero and Milans were each sentenced to thirty years' imprisonment, the maximum sentences possible in such cases. But General Armada, who was accused of telling the rebels that they were acting with the King's approval, got only a six-year sentence instead of the thirty years requested by the prosecution. General Torres, commander of the crack armoured division during the coup attempt, was sentenced to six years rather than the fifteen demanded, and Colonel Jose San Martin, the former chief of staff of the division, received three years and one day instead of the fifteen years demanded. These light sentences and the twelve acquittals caused considerable anger and concern in government circles. The prime minister commented:

'Everything seems to indicate that the responsibilities have been concentrated on the two leading figures and the principle of responsibility has, by contrast, not been applied in the case of those involved to a lesser degree.'

The Spanish military court, not surprisingly, showed itself blind to the real seriousness of the challenge to democracy from the extreme right. Calvo Sotelo also reflected a widespread disillusion with the 3½-month-long trial when he observed:

'As a Member of Parliament I must say it is very difficult for me to contemplate the acquittal of officers who commanded the forces which kept us sequestrated in Parliament for more than seventeen hours.'

On 3 October 1982 the Spanish authorities revealed that they had foiled a far more serious Colonels' conspiracy to stage a coup on the eve of the 28 October general elections. The plot, code-named Operation Cervantes, allegedly involved over 100 officers who planned to capture key government buildings, hold the King prisoner, cut vital communications and start a rebellion manned by junior officers throughout Spain. The government announced the arrest of three colonels alleged to have been at the centre of the plot: Luis Munoz Gutierrez, Jesus Crespo Caspinera and his brother, José Crespo Caspinera.

Among the many sympathetic and warm reviews of the first edition of *The New Fascists* it was disconcerting to find two apparently serious critics in the *New Statesman* and the *Economist* writing as though the National Front was the only contemporary manifestation of fascism worth bothering about. It is to be hoped that anyone who reads my survey carefully will be aware that there are *many* countries where fascism is a much more powerful tradition and a potentially far more dangerous political force. It is the height of parochialism to assume that, because of the National Front's electoral débâcle in England in 1979 and the splits that have occurred in the party, the dangers of fascism can be safely dismissed. Have they never heard of mass fascist parties in Italy and Spain? Or the onward march of the ultra-right in South Africa, El Salvador and elsewhere?

Nor does the demise of the National Front in electoral terms mean that fascist extremism in Britain is a spent force. In a brilliant recent analysis of the social bases of the National Front, Dr Christopher Husbands observes:

'the NF was not merely an ephemeral and transient political and social phenomenon. Instead, it drew upon sensitivities and susceptibilities that are deeply entrenched in English culture, perhaps especially so in parts of English working-class culture. It seems incontrovertible that such sensitivities persist, and particularly among white populations in locations with certain distinctive social and political histories.' (Husbands, 1981)

Dr Husbands and other investigators have focused on the phenomenon of racial exclusionism among certain sections of the urban working class as the main source of National Front voting support. Their studies suggest that this support could very easily be mobilised by some successor organisation to the

National Front. It is clear that the May 1981 county council election results were a total disaster for the NF. They fought 41 of the 92 GLC constituencies but succeeded in averaging only 2.3 per cent of the votes cast. The New National Front (the faction identified with John Tyndall) fought 18 GLC seats and averaged only 1.2 per cent of votes cast in its 18 contests. And the Constitutional Movement (a faction identified with Paul Kavanagh and Andrew Fountaine) gained only 0.8 per cent of votes cast in the 25 GLC constituencies it fought. The total vote for extreme right-wing candidates, including four for the 'Enoch Powell is Right' campaign, totalled roughly a third of those gained by the National Front and the National Party in the 1977 GLC elections. The National Front seems to have kept the allegiance of branches in the East End and inner London south of the river, while the New National Front seems to have its main base in SW London and its suburbs. In areas such as Harrow, Hounslow, Hillingdon and Brent, the National Front support seems to have shifted more towards the Constitutional Movement.

In the rest of the country the elections showed the National Front in even greater disarray with no candidates in many areas where they had previously had candidates. Splinter parties on the extreme right, such as the Constitutional Movement, the British Movement and the British Democratic Party (BDP) tried to capitalise on traditional National Front sympathy in specific areas, but all made a pitiful showing and none of them could be identified as a clear national successor to the original National Front as the party of the extreme right.

As argued in chapter 5, however, electoral showing is by no means the only significant indication of continuing fascist activity. In Britain much of this has been channeled into street-corner violence and racial attacks by skinhead gangs often incited by neo-Nazi supporters of the British Movement. In his vivid pen-portrait of British Movement skinheads, David Robins explains how one such youngster became fed up with the 'respectable racism' of the National Front and their poor electoral showing and their splits. He describes how this teenage boy became attracted to the British Movement by its aggression and the excitement of action on the streets. Robins points to the worrying fact that in Britain:

'neo-fascists and overt Nazi sympathisers have *politically* mobilised a significant section of youth ignored by the major parties as too stupid or apathetic ... The extreme right have been helped not only by massive youth unemployment, but also because fascism is fashionable in contemporary youth culture.' (Robins, 1982)

The dangers to race relations and to the safety of the innocent posed by this sinister sub-culture of violence in Britain's multiracial cities became increasingly apparent in 1981–2 in the form of racial attacks, street fights, confrontations with the police and the danger of further major disorders on the scale of Brixton and Toxteth.

In Coventry alone in the five months between February and June 1981 the Community Relations Council recorded fifty-five racial attacks. One of the most dreadful cases occurred in June 1981 when a general practitioner of Indian origin, Dr Amal Dharry, died after being stabbed outside a fish-and-chip shop. Nearly every city in Britain with substantial black and Asian communities can provide a catalogue of tragic cases of this kind. A Home Office inquiry into racial incidents between mid-May and mid-July 1981 covered 2,700 incidents, and the ethnic minority organisations claimed that the volume of attacks had doubled over the previous year. It is true that the Home Office team did not find that the majority of racial attacks were the direct result of conspiracy by neo-fascist groups. However, the House of Commons all-party Joint Committee Against Racialism and the Home Office have received ample evidence that attacks are encouraged by the general atmosphere of racial hatred and aggression generated by extremist propaganda. Many attacks have been not only incited but also perpetrated by neo-Nazi groups, and they have left their graffiti as a signature for the crime. For

example when the home of an Asian councillor and magistrate, near Maidenhead, was attacked with a heavy iron pipe
hurled through the windows, slogans reading 'Race traitor
lives here' and 'wogs out' signed by WDF (White Defence
Force), a Croydon-based néo-Nazi group, were sprayed on the
walls. Shreela Flather was comparatively fortunate: neither
she nor her family suffered any physical injury. Some people
have died as a result of racially motivated petrol-bomb attacks
on their homes. According to the Home Office study of
racialist attacks published in November 1981, the incidence of
attacks on members of the Asian community is fifty times
greater than attacks on white people. It is thirty-six times
greater for members of the Afro-Caribbean community.
These facts cry out for urgent action by police, judiciary and
local authorities.

A significant achievement in the struggle against racialism
during the year was the successful prosecution of the editor of
Bulldog, the youth paper of the National Front, for inciting
racial hatred. Joseph Pearce pleaded not guilty, but was
convicted following a retrial after the jury failed to agree on a
verdict at the first trial in August 1981. The prosecution's case
was that the magazine approved of and encouraged racial
violence and was openly provocative and wholly against the
public interest. One *Bulldog* article cited in the trial was headed
'Coloured Immigration can Damage Your Health' and
claimed that immigrant doctors were killing, injuring and
raping patients. The successful prosecution of Pearce may
serve as a deterrent against others who peddle such vile racist
rubbish.

It would, of course, be a mistake to assume that all the racist
activities of the extreme right were now directed solely against
the Asian and Afro-Caribbean communities in Britain. Anti-
Semitism remains right at the centre of the fascists' obsessions.
For example, the National Front always places its anti-Black
racialist propaganda within the context of a Jewish conspiracy
to destroy what they call the 'free nations' by a combination of

economic, political and racial contamination. British Movement and National Front sympathisers have maintained harassment and attacks of Jewish community members, synagogues, cemeteries and business premises. A British Movement publication recently described the notorious anti-Semitic tract, *Protocols of the Elders of Zion*, as 'more relevant than ever before' and the New National Front booklist in 1981 described it as 'the world-famous report of a Jewish meeting at which a blueprint was laid to control the world'. Nor should one underestimate the insidious effect of the neo-Nazi revisionism presented in the pseudo-academic guise of publications of the Institute for Historical Review denying that the Holocaust ever happened. A curious English activist on the intellectual 'new right' is the historian David Irving who has written a work which whitewashes Hitler, suggesting that Hitler was unaware of the extermination of the Jews. Irving has been attempting to establish new right groups under sponsorship of Focus, which made an unsuccessful venture into British politics in 1982.

We have seen in earlier chapters how right-wing criminal groups in West Germany have been increasingly resorting to terrorism over the past few years. Herr Heinrich Sippel of the Federal Office for the Protection of the Constitution has suggested that neo-Nazi terrorists' activities and their techniques of acquiring weapons and explosives, using bank robberies to finance their crimes, maintaining safe houses and forging links with foreign terrorists, are copied from left-wing terrorists. It certainly seems likely that the Nazis have tried to adapt some terrorist methods pioneered by other groups to their own purposes. But, as I have argued in chapters 4 and 5, the Nazi groups' potential for terror violence is inherent in their ideology and fanatical hatreds.

In 1981–2 this trend of increasing terrorist activity by the extreme right in the Federal Republic continued and caused deepening concern to the government. In May 1981 five members of the National Socialist Action Front were arrested at Lubeck on charges of murdering a homosexual. The following month Karl-Heinz Hoffmann, leader of the banned Wehrsportgruppe Hoffmann, was arrested and charged with establishing a criminal organisation. (His group, with an estimated 400 members in several *Länder*, had long been under police surveillance and was suspected of involvement in the 1980 Oktoberfest bombing. Evidence also emerged that Hoffmann's group had been involved in terrorist links with Middle Eastern groups, including sending neo-Nazis on training courses and trading in used vehicles.) Then in August came the issue of warrants for the arrest of Hoffmann and his friend Franziska Birkmann on charges of murdering a Jewish publisher, Shlomo Levin, and his companion Freda Poeschke.

Five members of another neo-Nazi terrorist group, the Volkssozialistische Bewegung Deutschlands (VSBD) or People's Socialist Movement of Germany, led by Friedhelm Busse, were involved in a shoot-out with plainclothes police in Munich on 21 October 1981. Two of the neo-Nazis were killed, one injured and two arrested; two policemen were injured. The VSBD is based in Munich and has attracted support from fanatical neo-Nazis both in Bavaria and across the rest of the country. In his fortnightly newspaper *Der Bayerische Löwe* (*The Bavarian Lion*) Busse argues for the replacement of West Germany's democratic form of government by a Nazi-style regime, and the expulsion of all 'foreigners'. One of his pamphlets has the Goebbels title *Der Angriff* (*The Attack*). Busse also formed a youth branch Junge Front which holds paramilitary exercises and sings Nazi songs. In April 1981 Busse and ten members of Junge Front were sent back to West Germany having tried to cross the Austrian border. (Busse has been banned from entering Austria since 1976 when he staged a demonstration outside the house where Hitler was born at Braunau.) In December 1980 one of Busse's young followers, Frank Schubert, was involved in a gun-fight with Swiss customs officers who caught him trying to smuggle arms across the Rhine. Two Swiss officials were killed, and Schubert took his own life. Busse and the VSBD now claim Schubert as a martyr. The Federal Republic authorities estimate that the VSBD has around 1,000 hard-core activists and many more sympathisers, as well as a branch of foreign Nazi supporters. In August 1981 forty neo-Nazis who planned to set up a branch of VSBD in Hanover were arrested after fighting in Hanover city centre. Among those arrested were a Frenchman and six British soldiers from BAOR, though this was hardly noticed by the British media at the time. There is certainly no doubt that Busse's movement is one of the most potentially violent and hence dangerous Nazi formations of recent experience in West Germany. This is a group which blatantly glorifies Hitler as the greatest figure in history, openly endorses Hitler's message in *Mein Kampf*, and denies that the Nazis were responsible for the Second World War or for the Holocaust. No one suggests that the VSBD and the many other neo-Nazi terrorist groups in the Federal Republic have any significant following among the electorate. Nevertheless, the very existence of such militant groups, with their capacity for terrorist attacks on the innocent and for spreading the poison of racialism thirty-seven years after the defeat of Hitler, is deeply disturbing.

One important breakthrough by the authorities came in June 1982 when two neo-Nazis of the German Action Group were sentenced to life imprisonment by a Stuttgart court for carrying out seven bombing and arson attacks in 1980, including those in which two Vietnamese were killed and two Ethiopians injured. If the West Germans are to curb the neo-Nazi terrorist groups, which between them killed nineteen people and injured over 220 in the three years 1979–81, there will need to be a far better record of successful apprehension and conviction, and realistic sentencing of those responsible for such crimes. Data published by the Bonn interior ministry in August 1982 shows that the number of offences committed by ultra-right extremists in 1981 reached the highest level since the end of the Second World War. The number of crimes committed rose to 1,824, an 11 per cent increase on 1980. Two thirds of these were directly linked to neo-Nazi groups, and over 300 were anti-Semitic. Nor should we assume that there has been any stemming of the flow of weapons to Nazi terror groups. The authorities were astonished to discover over twenty arms and ammunition caches at the end of October 1981 in the Luneburg heath area alone. All had been hidden by neo-Nazi groups. They included anti-tank weapons, pistols, rifles, 13,000 rounds of ammunition, one kilo of potassium cyanide and a large store of hand grenades. If neo-Nazis in just one region were able to accumulate such an armoury we can be confident that groups elsewhere in West Germany have also been able to lay hands on weapons and explosives with relative impunity. Manfred Roeder and his Deutsche Aktionsgruppen, the neo-Nazi group found guilty of carrying out seven bombing and arson attacks, clearly had no difficulty in acquiring weapons and explosives.

It would be a mistake, however, to assume that Nazi ideas are confined to small groups of terrorists and young thugs. As Professor Martin Broszat of the Institute of Contemporary History, Munich, pointed out at a 1981 SPD conference on right-wing extremism, it is also very important to look into the 'grey zone', the prevalence of Nazi attitudes and beliefs among wider sections of the population. For example, in a recent study Professor Alphons Silbermann found that 20 per cent of West Germans have 'distinctly' anti-Semitic views, and that there is anti-Jewish prejudice latent in a further 30 per cent of the population. This is all the more astonishing when one considers that the total size of the Jewish community in West Germany is only around 30,000 in a total population of over 61 million. Much of this prejudice, Professor Silbermann concludes, is handed down unconsciously from generation to generation. General xenophobia and prejudice against foreigners has also undoubtedly intensified in the past few years with growing resentment against the 4½ million strong population of guest-workers and their families at a time of deepening recession and worsening unemployment. Inevitably the extreme right has tried to capitalise on anti-immigrant feeling.

There has also been a growth in armchair fascism in certain intellectual circles. This often takes the form of small discussion groups and magazines trying to present themselves as the respectable new right in Germany. For example, in 1981 a group of university professors calling themselves the Heidelberg Circle drew up a manifesto which demanded the establishment of an independent association for the preservation of the German people and its spiritual identity. In pseudo-scientific language they warned against 'the ethnic catastrophe' of a polycultural society. The race doctrine of the Nazi era is only thinly disguised:

'Every people, including the German people, has a natural right to its own identity and characteristics in its own territory ... only vibrant and intact German families can preserve our people for the future.'

The manifesto called for a policy to repatriate the Federal Republic's 4½ million foreign residents. The draft of the Heidelberg Circle document was apparently not intended for publication, but was leaked to the press by left-wingers who discovered a copy of the manifesto in a Bonn telephone box. It is to say the least shocking to learn that such ideas are held by individuals occupying responsible positions in West Germany's academic life.

The ultra-right beyond Europe

Nothing could more clearly reflect the ethnocentrism of many European observers than their ignorance and lack of concern about the powerful regimes and movements of the extreme right in other continents. Historians and social scientists are also partly to blame because they have been so anxious to preserve the term 'fascism' for European variants of Italian fascism and German Nazism that they have not even been prepared to explore the possibility of new non-European variants. This attitude is also very convenient for those who wish to believe that in any case all the serious threats to democracy and human rights derive from the Soviet Union and its communist allies. After the events of 1982, when a British dependency fell victim to unprovoked aggression by the extreme right-wing military dictatorship of Argentina, and the Lebanon suffered aggression, occupation and savagery following invasion by the right-wing expansionist government of Menachem Begin in alliance with Phalangist militias, this is hardly a tenable position.

Historically in any case the thesis that fascism had an exclusively European appeal simply does not bear careful scrutiny. We have earlier noted that imitators and admirers of fascism established movements in countries as diverse as the United States, Japan, Argentina, Brazil and South Africa. Even Australia had its 'Iron Guard'.

Fascism also attracted many admirers in the Middle East in the 1930s. Not only did they find an enthusiastic affinity with Hitler's anti-Semitism, which they wished to mobilise to eliminate the Jewish presence in Palestine. There were also many attracted by the militaristic and authoritarian features of the fascist party model as an instrument of national mobilisation and modernisation. An example of this is the Phalangist Party and paramilitary force in Lebanon (Arabic name Hizb al-Kata'ib) founded by Pierre Gemayel in 1936. The name means the party of 'brigades'; in French, Phalanges Libanaises. Gemayel was an ardent admirer of Hitler who attended the Berlin Olympics in 1936 and was wined and dined by European fascist leaders.

It is true that in 1949 the movement tried to drop the name 'Phalangist', but the label stuck and the movement is to this day known as the Kata'ib in Lebanon. It is also the case that the

Maronite Christians who identified with the Phalangists as *their* movement did attempt, until 1975, to work within the Lebanese constitutional and parliamentary framework. They did not become a totalitarian party. But neither were they a normal democratic party. From the very beginning they were also an armed paramilitary movement, a typical feature of the European fascist movements, and from the beginning they adopted similar uniforms and symbolism. Their other major fascist characteristic was their extreme nationalism coupled with a total belief in their racial superiority over the Muslim Arab population in Lebanon.

These two fascist characteristics of paramilitarism and fanatical ethnic supremacism became more brutally evident when Pierre Gemayel and his son Bashir unleashed the Phalangist militia in a direct contest for power against the Palestinian leftists and the Muslim militias in the bloody civil war of 1975–6. In this war Bashir Gemayel and the militia acquired a reputation for ruthlessness which made them feared and hated by their Palestinian and Lebanese leftist rivals in the struggle for power and mistrusted even by their allies. In the course of the civil war the Phalangists established what was virtually a state within a state. The Gemayel clan became virtual dictators of this fiefdom.

It was to this right-wing paramilitary movement that Begin's government turned for alliance in the 1982 Israeli invasion of Lebanon to rid the Lebanon of the PLO and Syrian presence. After the long and bloody Israeli siege of west Beirut and the evacuation of PLO fighters from the city, the Israelis hoped to get a new and acquiescent government installed in the Lebanon. The man they naturally set their hopes on was the Phalangist militia leader, Bashir Gemayel. Under the very shadow of Israeli tanks Gemayel was elected President of Lebanon on 23 August. There was no other candidate. It does appear that Gemayel had recognised the need for a long-term national reconciliation and sincerely desired a strong, united and independent Lebanon. Whether he could have delivered these goals, or whether he could have succeeded even in carrying the bulk of the Maronite Christian community and the Lebanese Muslims behind such policies, we shall never know, for Bashir Gemayel was assassinated in a bomb attack in Beirut before he could take up his office.

What did become very clear in the weeks following his assassination was that the Phalangist militia's capacity for savage violence, which Gemayel had himself promoted and exploited, had not in any way declined in the wake of the military victories by their Israeli allies. On the contrary, they seemed determined to use their forces to settle old scores and to extend their own grip on those parts of the country vacated by the PLO and other factions. The so-called Christian Militia showed the depths of barbarity they could still descend to in the massacres of Palestinian civilians in the refugee camps. Every objective student of Middle Eastern affairs knew full well the danger of atrocities by the Phalangists and Haddad's Christian Militia. For years they had been taught by their leaders to hate and despise the Palestinians, to treat them as sub-humans. The terrible atrocities of September 1982 occurred because of the extent to which these armed groups were in the grip of racial hatred and blind vengeance, and because the Israeli forces at the very gates of the refugee camps stood by and allowed them to happen. In the light of the recent tragic history of Lebanon the very idea that such a single blood-stained faction, whether the Phalangists or anyone else, should be allowed a free hand to impose its rule on the country should be opposed by all responsible international opinion. There is a real danger of further massacres. In November 1982 the Israeli commission of inquiry investigating the September massacre warned Prime Minister Begin, Defence Minister Sharon, Foreign Minister Shamir, and six army commanders and intelligence chiefs that they might be harmed by its findings.

*

As anticipated in chapter 5, the extreme right in South Africa has continued to gain strength, and by 1982 has split irrevocably the traditionally monolithic structure of Afrikaner nationalism. In addition to the neo-Nazi-style Wit Kommando, responsible for a number of bomb attacks, there is the Afrikaner Weerstandsbewegining (AWB) which has set up 'storm commandos' and is rumoured to have planned kidnappings of members of parliament who reject its demands to stop the government's alleged capitulation to blacks. The leader of AWB is Eugene Terre Blanche. They wear swastika-like badges and want a military dictatorship in South Africa.

The Botha government has been increasingly forced on to the defensive since 1981, retreating from its earlier commitments to ease the apartheid laws. The retreat began in earnest after the April 1981 elections when the extreme right-wing Herstigte Nasionale Party (HNP) made an unexpectedly large advance. Another danger sign was the reported decision of the Broederbond secret society, in September 1981, to lift its ban on members of the HNP joining its ranks. In view of the influence the Broederbond wields in the Afrikaner establishment this is a very significant blow to the Verligte (liberal) segment of the ruling party.

A major power-base and focus for the extreme right in South Africa has been Namibia, where they have mobilised hard-line white opposition to independence under the UN plan. The HNP, led by Jacques Marais, and the National Conservative Party led by Dr Connie Mulder have been the major activists in this strident campaign. The extremists paint independence as a deadly threat to the survival of white supremacy in South Africa itself. They, and the Afrikaner Resistance Movement which is also heavily involved, preach against a 'sell-out' of white interests. Their message is 'resist, resist' and they have demanded a white referendum on the issue. At their rallies the ultra-right extremists have sold copies of *Mein Kampf* and the magazine *South African Patriot* carrying a story describing what it called 'the collapse of

Britain's multi-racial experiment' and saying that British and other immigrants would only be welcome in South Africa if 'their gene pool matches our north-west European make-up'. By November 1981 Marais and his HNP followers had gone so far as to call on white civilian members of commando units in Namibia to refuse to hand over their weapons as required under the independence settlement. As most whites in the region belong to the commando units and would be likely to respond to Marais' call, this would constitute a grave embarrassment to the South African government. Marais and the HNP are capitalising on the hard-line Afrikaner supremacist ideology preached for years by the Broederbond and others.

A further important development in the South African extreme right occurred in March 1982 when Dr Andries Treurnicht, leader of the Verkrampte (hard-line) group in the National Party, broke away from Prime Minister Botha on the issue of some very limited degree of power-sharing for coloureds and Indians. Treurnicht and his supporters are deeply opposed to any kind of reforms in the apartheid system. After being expelled from the ruling party, Treurnicht and seventeen other rebel MPs launched their new Conservative Party of South Africa at a rally of 7,000 fervent supporters. They denounced power-sharing and demanded a return to the pure ideology of the Verwoerd period. The only consolation for Botha was that the HNP failed to make an alliance or merger with the new group, so that the extreme right remains split; but Dr Connie Mulder's National Conservative Party has allied with the new party of Dr Treurnicht, as have the tiny South Africa First Campaign (an English-speaking extreme right group) and Aksie Eie Toekoms (Action Own Future). Many members of the Afrikaner Resistance Movement also backed the launching of the new party.

At a by-election in the Germiston constituency on the outskirts of Johannesburg in August 1982 the government National Party candidate got back by only a narrow 308 majority. The combined strength of the new Conservative

Party and HNP candidates was 1,330 votes greater than that of the government party. This was seen as a considerable shock to the government, and indicates a real danger of any future merger on the extreme right. Such a party might stand a chance of winning power at national level. The traditional Transvaal power base of the ruling party is seriously at risk. Liberals in America and Western Europe who have little liking for Botha or his policies nevertheless realise that a swing to the extreme right Conservative Party in South Africa would make the situation infinitely more difficult.

In Central America the extreme right continues to play its grisly part in the civil strife and terrorism which have plagued the region throughout 1981–2. As indicated in chapter 4, some of the worst intimidation and acts of terror have occurred in El Salvador's civil war. Right-wing paramilitary groups in El Salvador even participated with government forces in attacks on refugees fleeing the turmoil, and there are eyewitness accounts of how on several occasions they even attacked refugee camps across the border in Honduras.

One of the most powerful ultra-right-wing groups to emerge in the past two years has been the Nationalist Republican Alliance (ARENA) under its fanatical and aggressive leader Major Robert D'Aubuisson. D'Aubuisson is a former member of the national guard, notorious for its excesses against the civilian population. From ARENA's foundation he has worked tirelessly for its cause, which he sees as saving El Salvador from communism. D'Aubuisson has succeeded in building up a powerful coalition of supporters, especially among landowners and the business class, and he enjoys enthusiastic support of many military officers (traditionally a key group in El Salvador's power structure). It is known that for some time he enjoyed the protection and support of the minister of defence under the Duarte junta. A flamboyant political campaigner, he was practically the only party leader to go electioneering in the remote rural areas in the campaign for the March 1982 elections. He undoubtedly showed personal courage in taking his jeep through guerrilla-held country with no protection other than a personal body-guard and his own weapon: several attempts were made to assassinate him.

The United States ambassador to El Salvador under the Carter administration was under no illusions about D'Aubuisson's own role as an instigator of extreme right-wing violence. He publicly accused him of complicity in the assassination of Archbishop Romero in 1980. D'Aubuisson's message to his supporters was that he alone could purge Salvador of the Marxist guerrillas, and he constantly accused the mildly reformist Christian Democrat Party of former President Duarte of betraying the country, describing its programme as indistinguishable from communism! On two occasions in 1981–2 he was accused of plotting to overthrow the constitution, and in view of the fact that the right-wing death squads were among his most ardent supporters his threat in March 1982 that he would not 'allow the election to result in a "communist constitution"' was not an idle one. ARENA is clearly not a normal democratic party, but is rather a Central American variant of Fascism prepared to exploit both the ballot box and the gun to achieve power. The fact that El Salvador's March 1982 election took place at all, in the middle of a guerrilla war, is something of a miracle. But both the circumstances and the results provided an embarrassing and bizarre twist in the United States' relations with El Salvador. As the left had refused to take part, Washington clearly anticipated that President Duarte's Christian Democrats would be returned to office. It was felt that the legitimising effect of proving themselves at the hustings would give the party a badly needed boost. Contrary to expectations the parties of the extreme right achieved a larger combined vote than the Christian Democrats, and won 36 of the 60 seats in the constituent assembly. It is true that Duarte's party won the largest individual share of seats with 24, but they were completely isolated because the three key extreme right-wing parties –

ARENA (almost 30 per cent of the votes cast), the National Conciliation Party (16 per cent) and Acion Democratica (9.4 per cent) – decided to work closely together. It was these three major extreme right parties, together with two smaller groups, which combined to form a 'government of national unity'. Undoubtedly Major D'Aubuisson is the most powerful individual in the new government. The choice of a moderate figure, Alvaro Magaña, as interim President, was in deference to heavy pressure by the US state department. Even so, the right used its majority in the assembly to ensure that it received all ten key parliamentary offices. The post of president of the assembly was awarded to D'Aubuisson who won thirty-five of sixty votes cast in the ballot. This is a key position of power, as it is this body which will shape the regime which replaces the junta. Although the US government clearly hoped to pressure D'Aubuisson and his colleagues into being more conciliatory and improving their human rights record in deference to Congress, it was clear by June 1982 that the new government of Salvador was defying this advice. 'Death squad' murders of civilians, including leading Christian Democratic mayors and politicians, continued unabated. Also the constituent assembly coolly defied US wishes by voting to suspend part of the agrarian reform programme. There are also signs that Salvadorean commanders, impatient at delays, have rejected US advice, and are planning fresh anti-guerrilla sweeps in the countryside. Not for the first time the United States finds itself allied with a truculent extreme right-wing regime whose actions it cannot control. But this one is farther to the right than even the US is used to in Latin American terms. What is new and particularly dangerous about a party like ARENA is its capacity for mobilising mass support and its fanatical dedication to violence and an avenging crusade against the left. More worrying still is the fact that crises in Guatemala and other neighbouring countries are producing similarly ugly mutations of the ultra-right such as the avowedly fascist National

Liberation Movement (MLN), the most powerful civilian political organisation in Guatemala.

It is characteristic of extreme right-wing regimes to exploit nationalist feelings and to create foreign adventures and threats to divert the attention of the masses away from domestic economic hardships. For instance, Kemal Ataturk played on Turkish xenophobia and hostility to Greece in the 1920s; Mussolini used his crack-brained schemes for building a 'new Roman Empire' in Abyssinia and North Africa; military dictatorships in Central America harp on the threat from Cuba; and the South Korean and Taiwanese regimes keep their populations in a constant state of readiness for the communist invasion.

Argentina displayed this phenomenon in spring 1982, but this time the external diversion was directed at annexing the British dependency of the Falkland Islands. Ever since the creation of an independent Argentinian state in the nineteenth century, successive governments in Buenos Aires have claimed that the Falklands, which they call the Malvinas, are an integral part of their territory. However, despite the fact that a long series of abortive attempts at a negotiated solution of the dispute with Britain through the 1960s and '70s were frequently accompanied by Argentinian threats to invade the islands, the British government was militarily unprepared when General Leopoldo Galtieri, head of the Argentinian military junta, launched his invasion of the Falklands in April 1982. Leaving aside for a moment the matter of how much early intelligence concerning Argentinian military preparations London received and how far British signals of lack of will to resist (such as the withdrawal of the patrol ship *Endurance*) were responsible for the failure to prevent the assault — and these are among the matters to be considered by Lord Franks' Inquiry — there was undoubtedly an appalling political misjudgement, at the highest level, in London. This was the failure to understand that the severity of Argentina's economic crisis and intensifying popular discontent, far from being obstacles to an invasion, actually made the seizure of 'the Malvinas' the only guaranteed method of sublimating the growing internal opposition and rallying public opinion behind the regime in a haze of national pride and military glory. British policymakers had failed to take sufficient account of the instability and potential for aggression of ultra-right regimes.

On the eve of the 1982 invasion of the Falklands, Argentina's inflation was raging at about 140 per cent, and the peso showed no signs of recovering against the dollar. Though official estimates put unemployment at around 10 per cent, the real figure was probably double this amount. The average wage was equivalent to £70 per month, and it was common for people to do two or three jobs simply in order to survive. Roberto Alemann, the economy minister, promised severe medicine to bring recovery, but things were getting worse week by week.

Popular frustration and anger against the regime flared up in major street disturbances in the capital on Tuesday 30 March. The Peronists' traditional power base, the trade unions, and the suppressed opposition political parties organised a major demonstration which then tried to march on the central plaza calling for an end to military rule and the removal of Alemann, minister for the economy. The crowd became locked in bloody battles with police and troops, and there were over 1,500 arrested before the demonstration was ended. Faced with the very real threat of being swept away in a tide of popular revolt, it is easy to see how attractive the Malvinas card was to Galtieri and his colleagues.

The cost of Galtieri's ultra-nationalist adventurism and Britain's unpreparedness was huge in terms of both British and Argentinian lives and resources, and damage to diplomatic and economic relations. Without entering into the

detailed history of the war or the reasons for and consequences of Britain's impressive military achievement in lib-
erating the islands, we may observe that the war brought home
to the British public, and probably to the other western
democracies to some extent, the ugly face of ultra-right dictatorship. Suddenly many people became aware that although
the Argentinian junta was by no means systematically following a fascist programme or using fascist labels and party
organisation, it was clearly a brutally repressive regime following fascistic policies. The suppression of democracy and of
even the most basic legal rights and protection, the fate of the
thousands of 'disappeared ones' (those who had been abduc-
ted, tortured and murdered by the regime), the arbitrary
violence and cruelty of the secret police, and the dictatorship's
clumsy and lying propaganda and crude attempts to keep the
truth about the war from the people vividly taught younger
Britons of the post-war generations what it must be like to live
in a vicious dictatorship of the ultra-right. British people
inevitably and naturally identified with their kinsmen and
women in the Falklands who were suddenly faced with being
ruled by such a regime. Had they not been liberated by the
task force the Falkland Islanders would still be living under
the heel of an Argentinian governor and military regime
whose hands were stained by years of bloody repression. Now
that they are free, any thought of appeasing the Buenos Aires
regime, or of doing a 'deal' which would result in the restoration of their sinister regime's brief control of the islands, is
unthinkable to the British people. It is to be hoped that future
British governments will realise this and face up to their
long-term responsibilities for the security and economic welfare of this tiny, remote and peaceable community.

Trends in the ultra-right in the United States have been
described in earlier chapters. There is an intensifying and
fascinating debate on the identification of an 'American fas-

cism', and in particular on the possibilities of a 'left-wing fascism', which has been engaging the interest of a growing number of historians and social scientists. I shall be discussing this debate in the next chapter. However, it is useful to conclude our survey of recent trends in the ultra-right beyond Europe with a brief look at a law case which indicates that blatantly fascist and racist movements, though very small in relation to the whole political system, are still very much alive in the United States.

The case in question is the Greensboro murders trial. As mentioned on page 108, when six members of the Ku Klux Klan and the Nazi Party were put on trial for the 1979 murder of five Communist Party members at a rally in Greensboro, North Carolina, American Nazi Party members demonstrated in their support. The outcome of the trial outraged civil libertarians and shocked the American public. An all-white jury acquitted all the accused. It seems incredible, but the jury actually had access to videotapes provided by local TV stations covering the rally on 3 November 1979. The tape shows clearly adults and children singing freedom songs in a peaceful rally. A nine-car convoy of Klansmen and Nazis then appears. A Klansman in the first car then fires what looks like a signal into the air. From the rear a clearly identifiable group of Klansmen then take their weapons from the trunk of the car and advance up the street, shooting. Two minutes later the attackers withdraw leaving bodies in the street, and someone yelling for a doctor. One of the Klansmen admitted firing the first shot, but one of the jurors said after the verdict that he had decided to find the Klansmen not guilty because it 'was the Communist Workers' Party which began the violence by striking one of the Klan cars'.

This outrageous verdict came at a time of growing Klan activity in Southern states. And when, in 1980, Harold Covington, a former head of the Nazi Party, ran for the post of state attorney-general in a Republican primary, he won an astounding 43 per cent of the vote (56,000 votes). This clearly indicates that there is a wider sympathy for fascist and racist ideas than could be guessed by the membership of the Klan and the Nazi Party. The jury foreman at the Greensboro trial was a refugee from Castro's Cuba. Before the trial he told the court he thought the Klan was 'patriotic'.

Anti-Nazi groups in the USA are understandably very alarmed at the Greensboro trial outcome. Lyn Wells, director of the national anti-Klan network, summed up these fears: 'If they go free after all this, it will just be a green light for all their activities.'

7 THE FASCIST MENTALITY

'It would be dangerous, even foolish, to suppose that a set of psychological variables or political positions determines disposition towards fascism. However, appeals to authority, to tradition, to the mystique of nation, blood, or race are necessary preconditions. Ideological denunciation of appeals to evidence, discourse, rationality, individual conscience, decision reversals, or consensus for specific policies is also characteristic.' (Horowitz, 1981)

In the opening chapter of this book it was argued that we must be strict and consistent in our use of the term 'fascism' to designate movements, parties and regimes. It is all too tempting to use it as a 'boo' word for any political groups we dislike. We should not confuse and mislead by promiscuous use of a term which has a specific and complex historical context and political meaning. For example, it is plainly an abuse of the term to apply it to Conservative and Christian Democrat parties in western countries. The conservative is an admirer and upholder of traditions, he is patriotic and a believer in the values of authority, discipline and order. But this does not make him a fascist. Fascists want to change society radically and are prepared to destroy the existing order by force to impose their own dictatorship and programme: it is a crucial distinction that the modern conservatives in the western democracies are totally committed to the principles and procedures of parliamentary democracy. Fascist parties have in many cases sought to gain power through means of the ballot box, but they generally seek every chance to coerce the electorate, and if this does not work they are always (as they will admit privately if not publicly) prepared to seize power by *coup d'état* or by waging civil war.

Clearly many of the parties and groups mentioned in our survey do not contain all the defining characteristics of fascism. The Peronists, the Afrikaner Broederbond and the Ku Klux Klan are examples of this. Yet I would strongly defend their inclusion in this study because in each case these groups not only showed strongly developed aspects of the fascist mentality and doctrines in their attitudes, policies and organisations; they have also been very intimately connected with, and allied to, fascist organisations and regimes. We have found that a good rule of thumb is that the fascist organisation explicitly boasts the formal ideology, language and symbolic trappings of the fascist tradition. All the contemporary new fascist movements I have studied to a great extent identify themselves by their infatuation with Hitler and Nazi ideas and history. Yet we must beware of equating the membership of explicitly fascist parties and groupings with the reservoir of potential support for fascism in society, or with the diffusion and strength of the fascist mentality. This would be to fall into the trap of reification. A key factor to be recognised is the very considerable degree of overlap in beliefs, attitudes and doctrines between the explicitly fascist groups and the many other parties of the right. And should this really surprise us? Is there not a similar untidiness and overlap between the movements and parties of the left?

Let us take some examples on the ultra-right. General Franco was a believer in the value of tradition and the mystique of the Spanish nation, dedicated to the maintenance of order, military organisation and discipline. But was he a true fascist? He gained power in the civil war, it is true, only because of the military support of Hitler and Mussolini. And a part of his 'national movement' regime coalition was the Spanish Falangist party (described in an earlier chapter). But as soon as the Allies appeared likely to defeat Hitler, Franco cooled his enthusiasms and reverted to being a traditional military *caudillo*. Leaders such as Begin and de Gaulle have from time to time been labelled fascist. Again let us consider what is the basis for such allegations? Both de Gaulle and Begin are believers in guardians of the mystique of nation, posing as the saviours of national honour. Both implicitly practised a belief in the superiority, if not the supremacy, of their own nations. But does this make them fascist in any true sense? It must be remembered that both of them proved to be passionately devoted to the parliamentary democratic system. Both ultimately were prepared to place themselves before the judgement of the electorate. Fascist leaders would never be prepared to accept the democratic will of the people, as expressed in the ballot box, unless they could be sure in advance that the result would be favourable to them. Being a stubborn romantic ultra-nationalist does not make you a fascist, though it undoubtedly means you have something in common with them.

However, there is an unintended but significant consequence of the success of ultra-nationalist leaders in the democracies. If they appear strong on the use of force to defend national honour against attack, whether from within or without, if they develop a charismatic status which elevates their power and influence far above that of other politicians in their own countries, then they will inevitably tend to attract supporters and admirers from among full-fledged fascist groups. For instance, despite de Gaulle's role as a leader of the French Liberation forces, many ex-Vichy people flocked to his Rassemblement banner in post-war French rallies. Another example of this effect concerns Enoch Powell, the British MP. Because of Powell's reputation for making blood-and-thunder speeches advocating an end to black immigration into Britain and a 'voluntary repatriation' scheme for 'New Commonwealth' immigrants, he began to attract positive support from the farthest fringe of British ultra-right politics. Indeed, in the May 1981 local elections in Britain a new fascist electoral campaign emerged to fight a small percentage of local government seats, calling itself 'Enoch Powell was Right'. De Gaulle again attracted bedfellows from the wild extremes of the right in the period 1958–60 when they still thought de Gaulle would remain committed to the idea of Algérie

Française. When de Gaulle, in their view, betrayed them by making peace with the FLN at Evian, the OAS and the generals in Algiers mobilised the extreme right backlash. Given a more successful pursuit of fascist-supported goals a major leader could unwittingly become a vehicle for the partial fascistisation of society. Another danger in democracies is the powerful elected leader who assumes the role of national saviour or guardian of national honour and destiny; such leaders and their closest advisers may become so mesmerised by the pursuit of national Absolutes that they are prepared to use unconstitutional methods, fraud, or even terrorism in order to obtain or retain power, or to pursue their policy goals. For example, Richard Nixon was prepared to use spying on opponents, burglary and other dirty tricks in order to hold on to the Presidency. The climate of secrecy and elitism and temptations of the colossal power of modern government provide conditions in which democracy can become eroded if not completely undermined. Right-wing politicians and parties, far from being immune to this trend, are inherently susceptible: businessmen and retired military figures who so often occupy leadership roles in right-wing parties tend to be inherently impatient about the delays and uncertainties of the democratic process and contemptuous of mass opinion and participation. Embryonic fascist attitudes and policies can be found in these circles as well as at the level of working class racial exclusionism and prejudice.

National leaders and other powerful political figures can encourage racism, extreme nationalism and expansionism. A clear recent example is Israel, where Begin and Sharon and their hardline supporters are actually using foreign and domestic policy to establish a Greater Israel *imperium* on the West Bank and in Gaza. But there is also the grave danger of secret 'entryism' by the extreme right into the political institutions and decision-making processes. The British Conservative Party in some of its constituency and student branches has occasionally fallen victim to such methods. Meanwhile Harvey Proctor, the Conservative MP, and certain others are apparently happy to go on appearing on National Front-style platforms with known members of fascist groups and blocking legislative and other progress towards improving race relations.

It is not only the more obviously fascistic doctrines of rascism, extreme nationalism and expansionism that can have such a destructive and corrupting effect on democracies. There are also attitudes and policies which have a more insidious and long-term effect on democratic values. For example, we have earlier noted the concerted attack on historical truth by the Nazi revisionist historians trying with varying degrees of subtlety to suggest to the young, the ignorant and the gullible that the Holocaust never really happened. There is also a growing flood of more traditional anti-Semitic literature pouring into western countries. Revolting propaganda, such as the notorious *Protocols of the Elders of Zion*, has been reprinted again, some financed by Arab regimes.

Perhaps the most dramatic and saddest illustration of the relationship between the ultra-right politics of nationalism and expansionism has occurred in Israel, where the internal political system is far and away the most democratic in the region. Yet if we look at Begin's foreign policy it is perfectly clear that he has pursued aims, and used means, incompatible with basic moral principles, in the Lebanon conflict. These have rebounded strongly against Israel, leaving her feared but hated in the Middle East, but also increasingly isolated from her traditional ally and backer, the United States. Indeed, with Begin's defiant rejection of President Reagan's peace proposals for the Middle East, it looks as if the allies are heading for a collision. From the earliest weeks of Begin's coming to power in Israel close observers became aware that his long period in the political wilderness had by no means dimmed his fanatical and dangerously romantic ultra-nationalism. Interviewing some of his hardline Herut supporters and backbenchers, I became aware that many of them confidently believe in Jabotinsky's dream of re-creating what they claim is the original biblical Greater Israel, including the whole of the area that constituted Transjordan on the East as well as the West Bank. Nor are these ideas confined to Herut. Professor Ne'eman, leader of the small Revival Party, who later joined the coalition government as minister of science and development, is one of many now in positions of power and influence in Israel who passionately believe in the intensive expansion of the settlements on the West Bank. Ne'eman also believes that the Greater Israel, at least in principle, includes southern Lebanon.

Even those unfamiliar with the ideas of Israeli right-wing nationalism have had numerous warning signs of the increasing aggressiveness and assertiveness of Begin's Israel. Israel's military success in the 1973 war made her individually the strongest – though, as Begin is now being reminded, not necessarily the dominant – military actor in the Middle East. In 1978 Israel's forces were able to make a major incursion into southern Lebanon with impunity. And in 1981, with devastating coolness, Israel bombed Iraq's nuclear reactor at Osirak and, in December, annexed the Golan Heights, which had formerly belonged to Syria. These events, combined with Begin's obvious stalling tactics on the Palestinian autonomy phase of the Camp David process, should have prepared US policy-makers of the need to discipline, or at least constrain, their Israeli clients. After all, the struggling Israel economy, with inflation running at 130 per cent, has been propped up by $785 billion a year in economic assistance, and the US has met the cost of roughly a third of Israel's military budget. This gives the US government considerable leverage. Just as it is true that the United States could never morally or politically wash her hands of her Israeli ally, so Israel would suffer severely from any prolonged freeze on US economic support.

Polls show that Israeli public opinion has rallied behind the government through the Lebanon war. A mid-August poll showed only 9 per cent opposed to the war, and only 23 per cent doubtful about carrying the war into Beirut. Prime Minister Begin would win an election tomorrow with considerably increased support. Although the Israel Labour Party has welcomed Ronald Reagan's plan as a basis for discussion, it is deeply divided, with the doves urging a withdrawal from Lebanon and progress towards a Palestinian 'mini-state' on the West Bank and in Gaza, while the majority of the party supports the government's policy. Large demonstrations by Peace Now may be a heartening sign of healthy democracy and debate, but they do not make any significant change in Israeli policy more likely.

The Begin government's first reaction to the Reagan peace plan was hardly encouraging. Foreign Secretary Shamir described it as a departure from Camp David, and reiterated his government's position that they would never relinquish control of the occupied territories. No doubt the hardliners now in a position to dominate Israeli policymaking believe that, after they have disposed of the PLO and 'pacified' Lebanon, they can move on to annexing the West Bank and Gaza. Israeli settlements on the West Bank, far from being 'frozen', will be considerably expanded, and every effort will be made to impose co-opted and pliant Palestinian structures to facilitate civilian and administration absorption. (This is, needless to say, a recipe for bloody and protracted confrontation in the occupied territories.)

In discussing the ways in which the fascist mentality overlaps with parties and movements elsewhere in the political arena it is worth reflecting on the possibility of a new indigenous 'left-wing fascism' in America. A major debate on this thesis was initiated by a 1981 symposium edited by the American scholar Irving Horowitz and published in *Transaction: Social Science and Modern Society*. Certainly Horowitz and A. James Gregor make a powerful case showing that many left-wing groups have the preoccupation with violence, the ruthless authoritarianism, the racism and the dogmatic intolerance which make them at least potentially totalitarian.

The present writer shares the doubts and fears voiced by writers such as A. James Gregor and George Mosse in the *Transaction* symposium. Where are the concrete examples of groups to fit the left-wing fascism label in America? Are Lyndon La Rouche's National Caucus of Labour Committees (NCLC) and a few dotty religious cults really serious evidence of the existence of a left-wing fascism? In America, as A. James Gregor has argued:

'Not a few political pundits note that not the Left, but the "evangelical Right", constitutes the vanguard of a native "fascism". Few of course would deny that the loose coalition of religious groups now identified with the "New Right" is authoritarian in some meaningful sense. Each makes regular appeal to the authority of sacred texts and displays considerable indifference to orthodox science.' (Gregor, 1981)

But Gregor concludes that the 'moral majority' fundamentalist religious groups lack the essential component of socialism which fascism needs, and he argues that the far left groups simply do not have the nationalist component so vital in fascist ideology.

Hugh Seton-Watson, A. James Gregor and many other scholars have performed a very useful task in drawing attention to the considerable overlap in ideas between the potentially totalitarian extremists of left and right: they are anti-liberal/democratic; they are in favour of violence not only as a reluctant final resort, but as an integral part of their struggles; they are strongly authoritarian in leadership and élitist in decision-making.

Yet there are some key differences between them which could be quickly identified. Fascists aim at a totally redesigned world based on principles of racial and national supremacism. Leftists desire social and political equality. Fascists want a world of nation states, with their own as militarily the most powerful. The left speaks of a classless world society of international peace and harmony.

Most important of all for us to understand is that, notwithstanding a handful of *ad hoc* links, the key relationship between extremists of left and right is hatred and strife. The rival groups constantly fight and as they fight their movements feed off each other. In so doing they can (as was seen in Turkey, Spain, Italy and Central America) stay in business for a very long time.

There is one specialised sense in which the left-wing fascism label does fit: it can be applied to those factions or elements in fascist movements which favour a larger element of socialism as a sop to the working class, for example Strasser's group in the Nazi movement. But let us not confuse the issue by trying to classify some fascist movements as genuine movements to the left. The very act of identifying themselves with the fascisms of the past, each fanatically dedicated to the destruction of bolshevism, makes the term 'left-wing fascism' really a self-contradiction.

However, so far as the influence of the fascist mentality is concerned, it is a significant threat to centre and left and moderate right. They threaten institutions with corruption and penetration. In many ways the attempt to corrupt and manipulate major democratic parties is a worse problem. At least when small groups are using terrorism it soon becomes clear who is involved. The most severe long-term threat to western democracies is almost certainly not nuclear war, in any case practically ruled out by the superpower balance: it lies in the increasing desertion of liberal and humane values and international co-operation for the dark corners of nationalist aggression.

8 FASCISM VERSUS DEMOCRACY

A main thesis of this book is that fascism is not confined to any specific era, culture or countries. Far from being a phenomenon limited to the European states which have experienced fascist regimes, movements of this type are to be found in practically every western country, and indeed are growing more strident in those leading democratic societies which have never experienced fascist rule.

A critic might well object that in nearly all the western countries fascist and neo-Nazi parties are electorally insignificant. Even in Italy, where there has been the largest neo-fascist party in Europe, the peak of the Movimento Sociale Italiano representation came after the May 1972 general election when they won 56 of the 629 seats in the Chamber and 26 out of 322 in the Senate, and could boast a membership of 400,000 in a total population of 54 million. Fascist parties are rejected by the overwhelming majority of citizens in every democratic country. It is also true that in one major respect the international prospects of fascism appear to have suffered a setback: the last of the fascist-supported regimes in Europe have been swept away and constitutional democracies are now taking root in Greece, Portugal and Spain. Even the Turkish generals, desperately anxious to avoid their country's permanent exclusion from full membership of the European Community, have now undertaken to arrange elections for the restoration of democratic government.

The significance of this absence of a fascist power-base in the international system becomes clearer if we compare the situation of the communist-sponsored revolutionary and national liberation movements. Ever since the establishment of the Third International (Comintern) in March 1919, these movements have been able to depend on the Soviet Union for substantial financial, military and diplomatic support. In the post-War world this backing has been transformed into the manifold benefits of superpower sponsorship by a Soviet leadership with an enormous nuclear and conventional armoury at its command, a global 'reach' and capacity for intervention at every level. Moreover they now have the additional benefits of a whole bloc of Soviet allies (the Warsaw Pact countries), and client states and proxies (such as Cuba, Vietnam, Libya, South Yemen, Ethiopa and North Korea), which can provide alternative conduits for all kinds of support to client movements. Just as Mussolini funded and trained Croat terrorists to harrass the Jugoslavs, and Hitler established pro-Nazi fifth columns to undermine or soften up his intended victims, so the Soviets and their allies are today engaged in a massive and systematic campaign to subvert and destabilise non-communist governments whenever and wherever they see the opportunity. In contrast fascist groups now have to rely on their own private 'armies', weapons, cash and other resources, with very limited occasional assistance from one or other of the groups that make up what has been termed the Black International. Thus Italian neo-fascists have obtained guns and explosives from their Greek colleagues. American Nazis have provided huge quantities of propaganda for European neo-Nazi groups. And Belgian and Spanish fascists have been particularly active in 'hosting' international fascist rallies and meetings, and in disseminating weapons and propaganda. This does not mean that all fascist movements operate in a uniformly hostile environment. But it does mean that their firepower and other resources are relatively puny compared to those acquired by a big national liberation movement such as the Palestine Liberation Organisation had in Lebanon until 1982, where it had a base area comparable to a mini-state.

The vast differences between communism and fascism in terms of ideology, aims and real political power, are by no

means the whole story. There is no doubt that fascism has to
contend with the enormous (one hopes crippling) disadvantage that it is seen to represent a defeated movement. The total
war of 1939–45 resulted in such devastating defeat of the
leading fascist power that the movement still appears to the
majority of young people today to carry the stink of defeat, as
well as the blood-stained records of its crimes against humanity. However, in earlier chapters we have seen that this defeat
was by no means total. Fascist ideas and leaders survived to
create the post-War nucleus which led to the fascist
movements of today. Nevertheless the military defeat of
fascism was sufficiently complete to ensure the shattering of
the widely-held myth of Nazi invincibility, and to provide a
public opinion in the defeated Axis states willing to discard
dictatorship in favour of the republican parliamentary democracies favoured by the Allies. In political history the myths of
success, and of the inevitability of victory, tend to be self-
fulfilling.

In the wake of the Soviet invasion of Afghanistan and their
intensifying intimidation of the Poles it could hardly be said
that western youth was flocking to the Soviet standard in the
early 1980s. In almost every western country the communist
parties' share of votes and numbers of party members has
been either remaining static or has been in rapid decline. Yet
it would be quite wrong to assume that this dimunition of
support for the anti-democratic left will automatically provide
a swing in support to the totalitarian right. Mainstream
politics in almost every western country is still about the
battle for the centre ground. This fact, combined with the
relatively successful implantation of parliamentary democracy in Italy, West Germany, and now Greece, Portugal and
Spain, may have encouraged some commentators to dismiss
the future prospects of fascism in democracies somewhat
prematurely. A recent report to the Political Affairs Committee of the Council of Europe on 'The Need to Combat
Resurgent Fascist-Propaganda and its Racist Aspects' under-

mines the value of the impressive body of evidence collected on the resurgence of fascist propaganda by concluding that 'it would be foolish, and premature, to say that a major revival of fascist or racist ideology was taking place in Europe today.' If the members of the Political Affairs Committee mean by 'major revival' that something equivalent to the restoration of the Hitler and Mussolini regimes is about to take place, then one would be bound to agree. But in *relative* terms it is extremely disturbing that there has been a tremendous outpouring of fascist and racist propaganda in Europe over the past few years. Most of the movements we have examined show an arrogant confidence in their own power to whip up racism. They are recruiting the young and the very young on a larger scale than anything experienced in the democracies since 1945. When one looks at the propaganda of contemporary fascist organisations it becomes clear that this is where *they* see their great opportunity. For example, a National Front members' newletter in July 1980, describing 'Our Plans for the 1980s', argues as follows:

'If it is true that the National Front has no hope of gaining power under conditions that are stable – economically, socially and politically – we should not be preoccupied with making ourselves more "respectable" under present conditions. We must appreciate that the "image" that we have been given by the media and which may well lose us some potential support *today*, will be a positive asset when the streets are beset by riots, when unemployment soars, and when inflation gets even beyond the present degree of minimal control.'

If one examines the evidence of widespread diffusion in our society of dangerous elements of the fascist mentality, such as racism, belief in violence for its own sake, and a contempt for parliamentary democracy, one is led to challenge the attitudes of complacency and indifference shown by many of our fellow-citizens towards the fascist threat. How often must we be reminded that fascists are not simply waiting politely in the wings until such time as they acquire a democratic mandate? They are in the business of creating the conditions for a successful seizure of power by violence and intimidation. Fascists wish to provoke violence, to polarise the political situation, and, either by a strategy of tension or by an armed conspiracy, to take power. Must not Hitler have seemed a harmless lunatic to many superficial observers in the 1920s? Fascism must be prevented *before* the movement gets powerful enough to pose a direct challenge. What must be understood is that today's fascists are eager to exploit certain critical defects of our present international and democratic systems. If we are to prevent them from growing stronger, democratic governments and their publics urgently need to appreciate the ways in which endemic weaknesses of our system can hasten the fascists' re-emergence.

The problems experienced by the international economy since the dramatic oil price increases of 1973–4 are so major that 'recession' seems an inadequate term to describe them. Traditional economic ideas lead us to expect periodic 'troughs' in economic activity, to optimistically assume that every slump will inevitably be followed by recovery and ultimately by boom, and that all recessions are temporary phenomena. Yet since the early 1970s we have witnessed the international economy as a whole degenerating slowly but surely into chaos. Even before the oil crisis of 1973, the Bretton Woods system which had provided a stable framework for the international monetary order and the growth of international trade and investment had already collapsed. It has not been adequately replaced, and chaos and speculation still reign in the world money-markets. The volume of world trade has declined drastically as Third World states have increasingly found themselves in serious deficit as a result of the oil price rises, and more and more countries have had to apply to the International Monetary Fund for help to deal with balance of payments problems. Many of the non-oil rich developing states, sometimes called the Fourth World, are in such dire straits that they are depending on economic aid to meet their basic needs. They are simply unable to buy the goods they so badly need from the developed countries. Meanwhile the industrialised western states are suffering growing unemployment and falling output while home and foreign sales decline, and more and more firms are forced to lay off staff or to close down.

It should not be necessary to point out that unemployment, particularly among young people, carries serious social as well as individual consequences. Young people who are unemployed for long periods of time become bitter and bored. They are ready to be mobilised into extremism and violence, if only 'for kicks', because it gives them something to do. All their pent-up energy and aggression can be so easily channelled into the thuggery and intolerance of an extremist paramilitary movement. The uniforms and badges make them feel big. By belonging to the brotherhood of the gang or to a violent para-military movement, these young people may find a shelter against the psychosis of fear and insecurity, deepening because of the economic climate of collapse. This syndrome has been particularly evident in British cities. The British Movement has recently recruited very successfully among teenagers, and has now an estimated 2,000–3,000 members. Fascists have set up their own rock groups to play propaganda numbers such as 'Kill the Reds' and 'Master Race'. And 'Oi' music issued an album called 'Strength through Oi', an obvious pun on the Nazi slogan 'Strength through Joy'. The record cover showed a British Movement member dressed as a skinhead who had recently been sentenced to 4 years' imprisonment for a racial attack. Sometimes groups of thugs dressed in neo-Nazi regalia invade other concerts to break them up by chanting abuse and provoking fights. The young skinheads who have adopted the neo-Nazi style now constitute an ugly sub-culture in many depressed inner cities, with their swastika and NF/BM badges.

'Putting the fear in people' has become almost a way of life for some of these bored and hate-filled youngsters. According to a report by the Union of Pakistani Organisations of the UK and Europe, the number of racial attacks in Britain is now averaging between 50 and 60 per week, double the number in 1980. These attacks range from daubing graffiti on immigrants' homes and temples to firebomb attacks and murders. In July 1981, an alarming front-page story in the *Daily Mirror* claimed that Special Branch officers had uncovered a plot by British Nazis to bomb the mainly black Notting Hill Carnival in August. One of the men involved in the conspiracy was said to have been a former soldier who had served in Ulster, now affiliated to Column 88.

Social groups or classes hardest hit by unemployment will always tend to pick on minorities, especially easily identifiable immigrant groups, and blame them for 'stealing their jobs' or for depriving them of other benefits, such as adequate housing, education and welfare services. It is a tragic fact about societies under severe socio-economic strains that minorities become the scapegoats for the failures of the system. As the Council of Europe report mentioned previously observes:

'Very often all that is left to the most deprived is the supposed superiority of their colour, nationality or language. It is among the poorest that the slogans of racial discrimination are likely to find their first followers. A demagogue who tells an ignorant, illiterate white with no work and no hope that he belongs to a superior race is more than likely to be listened to. Being white will be the only thing to be proud of that society has left to the outcast.'

It should be pointed out that left-wing as well as right-wing movements will on occasion stoop to exploiting racial tension for their own ends. The anti-immigrant campaign run by the French Communist Party in the recent presidential elections is just one example of this. The campaign was accompanied by fire bomb attacks by communist activists on immigrant hostels.

There are three important ways in which the democracies can resist the challenge of fascism: through economic development and the achievement of greater social justice, which may at least reduce the conditions in which fascist and racist ideas take root and grow; the strengthening of the rule of law and the protection of human rights by means of appropriate judicial and police measures; and the countering of fascist ideology and propaganda by means of moral and civic education. It is important to stress that all these elements of the strategy of countering fascism are interdependent.

At the international level, there is a great deal that democratic governments could do to reduce the socio-economic conditions conducive to fascism and racism. To some extent they are already engaged in this task. When West Germany pumps generous economic aid into Turkey's hard-hit economy the hope would be that the conditions in which civil strife and extremism of all kinds flourish will be curbed. The negotiations for Greece's entry to the European Community which led to her formal admission in January 1981 inevitably centred on the economic aspects of the transition. But any careful reading of the debate on membership in Greece and among other Community members discloses the profoundly political motivation behind Greek entry. It was widely believed that participation in the Community's institutions, and the potential long-term benefits to both the agricultural and industrial sectors of the Greek economy, would help to consolidate democratic institutions in the country and strengthen it against any renewed movement towards a fascist-supported military dictatorship. Similar thinking will be uppermost in the minds of Community members charged with negotiations for the entry of Spain and Portugal.

More generally, democratic governments should act in concert to condemn governments that follow fascist or racist policies. This can be done through the United Nations and other international organisations, and by a whole range of diplomatic and economic pressures, unilateral, bilateral and multilateral. It is notoriously difficult, as President Carter discovered, to follow a consistent and effective policy on human rights which does not at the same time undermine western security interests. Communist powers and their client movements, the major violators of human rights on a mass scale in the modern world, are all too ready to exploit the turmoil and internal wars which almost invariably erupt when a non-communist dictatorship falls apart. But this does not mean that we should ignore violations of human rights in areas such as South America or South Africa. The struggle for human rights is indivisible, and there are all kinds of ways in which western governments can help to pressure regimes guilty of discrimination against minorities and acts of persecution. For example, they can use the UN Human Rights Commission machinery. Regional organisations can be petitioned and pressure can be exerted through trade and aid negotiations. Western-owned companies and multi-nationals can be informally encouraged to use their leverage on investment, jobs and valuable specialist technologies, to campaign for improvements in the observance of human rights. This method has already been used with some effect by foreign companies operating in South Africa, to force the authorities to relax aspects of their harsh and unjust system of apartheid. The United States has used military and economic aid and agreements as a carrot, and withdrawal of aid or rescinding of agreements as a stick.

Nor should we neglect the important role of moral and political pressure, through public protests in international forums and formal condemnations in official statements. The media can be a valuable weapon, particularly for informing the world about serious or widespread violations of human rights. Governments can give moral support to non-governmental organisations' campaigns for human rights. And if certain governments fail to respond at all, or respond too ineffectually, there are channels for non-governmental organisations, such as the churches, missionary societies, cultural, educational and professional organisations and trade unions, to make their voices heard in defence of human rights. All these organisations should ensure that they oppose the resurgence of fascist policies and practices as determinedly and effectively as they can.

In the field of law enforcement the role of international organisations and the community of western states as a whole is far less significant in dealing with the fascist challenge. The responsibility for upholding and enforcing the criminal law and for preserving public order lies with the sovereign national governments and, where relevant, the regional and local authorities and their police. There is, however, one area in which international judicial, intelligence and police intelligence co-operation has a direct bearing on fascist movements, and this is in cases of terrorism. The western European countries have now developed quite elaborate machinery for anti-terrorist co-operation. These are the Nato, Interpol, and Trevi systems of data exchange on the movements of terrorists, weaponry, tactics and targets. The Council of Europe and the European Community Conventions on the suppression of terrorism are designed to ensure that terrorist suspects are either extradited for trial or prosecuted in the state where they are apprehended. Sadly, implementation of the Council of Europe Convention has been delayed by the snail's pace of ratification, and the community Convention has not been put into operation because of a disagreement between France and the Netherlands.

Despite its obvious weaknesses the European framework for international co-operation in this field is better than the arrangements for any other region of the world. Why has it been so unsuccessful in helping to bring fascist terrorists to justice? One suspects that the main reason is lack of will and determination on the part of national and local police and judicial authorities already under considerable strain in trying to cope with purely domestic crime and terrorism. Sometimes it is because of bureaucratic muddle or failures of communication and co-ordination within a country's security agencies. In a few cases there may have been efforts to shelter fascists or to turn a blind eye to their activities, either because of crypto-fascist sympathisers in the police or judicial organs, or out of the mistaken notion that fascist terrorism is not a serious problem and that only the threat from left-wing terrorists on the run should be taken seriously.

A really appalling instance of this lack of follow-through was the case of Mehmet Agca, the member of the Turkish Grey Wolves movement who escaped from a Turkish gaol following his conviction for the murder of a newspaper editor, moved around Western Europe on a forged passport, and then went to Italy where he tried to assassinate the Pope in Saint Peter's Square. The Turkish authorities repeatedly warned the West German authorities of Agca's presence in Germany, even reporting his latest known whereabouts. Later the Italian Ministry of Justice were told of Agca's shift to Italy, his criminal record, and his earlier threat to murder the Pope. Yet the Italian Ministry of Justice failed to convey this important information to the Italian border police. Consequently there was no alert for him and he was not spotted when he flew into Italy. This is a dramatic illustration of the fact that all the carefully drafted anti-terrorist agreements in the world are of no avail if the national authorities do not follow them up with speed, professionalism and vigour.

National governments must obviously co-operate as closely as possible with their local or regional agencies in dealing with the fascist threat. In the task of economic and social measures to prevent the seed-bed of fascism from developing in the major cities, the cash and other resources controlled by local government is unlikely to suffice to meet the costs of a crash programme of economic development and job creation or the necessary improvements in housing and welfare services. In most western countries, and certainly in Britain, local authorities would in any case have to go to central government for special help.

It should be stressed, however, that establishment of new factories and the general improvement of conditions of life are only part of the preventive measures needed. The most important lesson learned by the American cities that experienced the major race riots of the 1960s and 1970s is that the improvement of community relations in the broadest sense is a vital prerequisite for preventing fresh outbreaks of violence. A police response alone, however tough and efficient, is simply not enough, for it cannot remove the suspicion and hatred which causes the conflict in the first place. And if these underlying social tensions and antagonisms are not dealt with they inevitably tend to be directed against the police, who are seen as the enemy of the community rather than the upholders of law. The urban areas which have been subjected to protracted fascist activity and provocation tend to be those most urgently in need of the healing touch of improved community relations.

How can national and local authorities help achieve this? Again the American experience, supported by the evidence and testimony of numerous commissions and inquiries, shows persuasively that a key need is to represent the major ethnic minority groups at every level of the community's decision-making process. Put bluntly, you cannot have social peace in multi-ethnic communities unless the ethnic communities have some real power over their own future. Only in this way will the moderate mainstream leaders of each community feel they have a stake in the system, and that they live under a legitimate political and social order. Token co-option is simply not good enough. It is often counter-productive because it gives an illusion of greater equality and a say in things, when really the power levers still stay in the hands of those who pulled them in the past. Inevitably any attempt to alter the power structure in this way is inclined to provoke particularly intense opposition from racist and fascist groups.

Nevertheless it is a nettle that must be grasped. Many of the immigrant 'guestworker' communities in Europe, for example, have very few civic rights, and this undoubtedly exacerbates their sense of 'foreigness'.

If efforts to create improved community relations on these lines are to succeed they must be accompanied by a well-planned and intensive programme of civic education on problems of race relations, warning the public of dangers of fascist and racist movements exploiting and fostering prejudice and mistrust. This programme should be carried not only in the schools, colleges and universities, but also in the mass media. Television and radio programmes should be especially devised to assist in fostering better community relations and combatting racism. It is worth noting that it was the commercial television series *Holocaust*, discussed earlier, that has given the most effective education to young people on the consequences of the vile creed of Nazism.

It is in the work of public education that the voluntary organisations come into their own, for by providing skilled counsellors, tutors, visiting speakers, conciliators and spokesmen to the media, these can provide the essential personnel for a successful community relations effort. It would be regrettable if the entire burden for countering fascist and racist propaganda in Britain should fall on the shoulders of organisations such as the Anti-Nazi League (ANL) or the Anti-Apartheid Movement. The ANL, for example, is not really representative of the full spectrum of political opinion: in practice it is very much dominated by Socialist Workers' Party activists. Moreover, because it expends much effort in organising counter-demonstrations and marches to counter the National Front, it has little time or expertise available for the patient educational work in anti-fascism I have described.

Nevertheless the ANL in Britain, which has no real equivalent abroad, has some very positive achievements to its credit. It has awakened young people to the danger of a Nazi revival and it has strengthened the vulnerable and frightened immigrant communities in British cities with the enormous moral and psychological reassurance that *someone* cares enough about resisting racism to do something about it. There is a real sense in which the ANL has defended human dignity by standing up to the arrogant obscenity of Nazism parading itself through our streets and intimidating our citizens. They have provided a focus for political resistance that none of the major political parties or other institutions, by themselves, were prepared to mount.

But there is also a crucially important job to be performed in countering fascist propaganda in the schools. Taking a leaf out of the book of French and Italian fascists in the early 1970s, fascists in Britain have been making a major bid to recruit and disseminate propaganda in the schools. A recent Contemporary Affairs Briefing *Nazis in the Playground* (May 1981) describes some typical incidents in the year beginning May 1980:

May 1980:	Black pupils outside their Camden school attacked by skinhead sympathisers of the National Socialist Party of the United Kingdom.
October 1980:	British Movement recruiting at schools in Dartford, Kent.
October 1980:	Young National Front recruiting at Hammersmith schools.
October 1980:	Young National Front wage campaign against teacher in Dover school.
November 1980:	Both British Movement and National Front actively recruiting in Merseyside schools.
December 1980:	British Movement members actively recruiting in Peterborough school.

January 1981:   Young National Front actively recruiting and campaigning in schools in Fleet, Hampshire.

February 1981:   National Socialist Party of the United Kingdom recruiting in Merseyside schools.

February 1981:   Manchester school daubed with swastikas and National Front symbols.

February 1981:   Jewish boy attacked in London school.

March 1981:   33 pupils, mostly Asian, leave classroom of Birmingham junior school shortly before fire-bomb explosion – racist attacked suspected.

The British Centre for Contemporary Studies strongly advocates a nationally co-ordinated strategy or policy through which to confront or counter the activities of the racists in schools. The Centre is impressed by the evidence that the Department of Education and Science, other relevant government departments, and even many of the local education authorities themselves, have often been unaware of extremist activities. In view of this, the British Home Secretary Mr William Whitelaw's announcement in February 1981 that the Home Office was to initiate research into the organisation of extremist racist groups in Britain is particularly welcome, but still, as a Parliamentary select committee pointed out: 'there is no effective co-ordination for policies impinging on racial disadvantage.' The main recommendations made by the Centre for Contemporary Studies to combat racism in schools are so eminently practical that I will quote them in full:

1. That a permanent structure be implemented, initially at local level, through which to monitor the racist and political activities of the extreme right in the schools. The local authority's education officer should bear responsibility for establishing within his portfolio the capacity for the collection of information and for further investigation or consultation as necessary.

2. That there should exist at national level, a central co-ordination for the monitoring services provided by the local authorities, to which education officers will periodically, or when necessary, report.

3. That due consideration be given to the role which political education might usefully play in the school curriculum, and that the overall concept of multi-cultural approaches to education be re-assessed with a view to a more positive deployment.

4. That existing bodies, including the Commission for Racial Equality and the main teaching unions, apply themselves more directly than hitherto to the confrontation of racism in schools, and to the provision of resources to teachers.

5. That immediate attention be applied to the existing legislation governing the limitations of the incitement laws, with a view to broadening its scope, improving its enforcement and strengthening its prescribed penalties.

As has been shown in earlier chapters, there are many other western countries which have experienced a similar upsurge of racist propaganda and recruitment at school level. The situation in France, Italy and America, for example, is in many respects far worse than in Britain. A positive approach to combatting racism in the education system is urgently needed in those countries as well. In France and Italy there is the problem of endemic bureaucratic inertia and lack of will to tackle these urgent problems. In the USA much has been achieved by certain imaginative and progressive city governments, as in Detroit, but there is still a huge task to be accomplished at Federal level to co-ordinate the monitoring of racist activities in education systems throughout the country, and to provide greater leadership and resources to assist the professional voluntary organisations engaged in combatting racism at local level, especially in the areas where the problem is most acute.

Another factor which works to increase racial tension in our communities is that of institutional racism. This is by no means confined to America and Britain, where there are large Black minorities. In West Germany, Switzerland, Sweden, the Low Countries, and in many areas of France there are large communities of 'guestworkers' and first or second generation immigrants – Turks, Algerians, Greeks, Spaniards, Palestinians and Yugolsavs, to name but a few. And in nearly every 'host' country there is built-in discrimination against the immigrant. Wages and conditions, housing, education and welfare facilities, and, above all civic rights, are usually very much inferior to those of the native-born citizen. What is more this built-in discrimination is actively fostered, or at least condoned, by the major political parties, trade unions and official bodies, mainly because they are unwilling to risk the unpopularity they might incur from championing equal rights for immigrants. Until we learn to resist and ultimately eliminate this institutional racism, it will act as a seed-bed for racial tension and conflict, which racist and fascist political movements will readily exploit. Anti-fascism, like charity, must begin at home.

These long-term economic, social and educational measures are extremely important, yet inevitably controversial and difficult to apply. Still more controversial is the question of identifying and implementing the appropriate response to the fascist challenge against law and order in a democratic society. The problem is immensely complicated by the fact that acts of terrorism, intimidation, thuggery, incitement to racial hatred and provocation, inevitably stimulate direct action by anti-racist and anti-Nazi groups which may itself constitute a breach of the law. The ensuing *mêlée* may get so out of hand that the police are no longer able to contain the violence, and innocent bystanders are injured and property damaged.

Are the inevitable difficulties and costs involved in policing fascist marches and demonstrations to prevent a violent confrontation on the streets part of the price we have to pay for living in a free society? In Britain there is a hallowed tradition of peaceful demonstration. However much you deplore the aims and ideas of the extremists, the argument runs, the rights to free speech and political association demand that fascist and anti-immigration groups be allowed the right to hold peaceful demonstrations and meetings. Organisations like the National Front, which have fought local and parliamentary elections, argue that they have the right to all the usual facilities to air their views to the electors, including public addresses by their local candidates and broadcasting time on radio and television commensurate with their scale of activities as a minority party. Furthermore, they point to the fact that in Britain and other European countries extreme minority parties on the left, which (for different reasons from the fascists, of course) also declare their rooted opposition to the present parliamentary democratic form of government, are allowed to stand for election and to campaign.

West Germany and Italy actually have constitutional provisions forbidding attempts to reconstitute fascist parties, an admirable token of the good intentions of the post-War Christian Democratic leaders that fascist rule in their countries would never happen again. In practice what has happened in both countries is that neo-fascist parties have been set up which carefully avoid the use of the terms 'fascist' or 'national socialist', but which peddle a watered-down version of the old fascist doctrines and policies and appeal deliberately to both the traditional supporters of fascism and to the fascist-minded among the younger generations. Any attempt to proscribe these new parties would probably be counter-productive, because it would lead to more small underground fascist groups being set up, with all their potential for violence and terrorism, and it might lend them a certain persecuted glamour which could enhance their ability to make trouble.

It is therefore, I would argue, both impracticable and counter-productive for democratic societies to try to ban or suppress these movements by means of legislation. On the other hand it is quite misguided to see these fascist and racist groups as being just like other political parties and campaigns. Every western industrial society today is to *some* extent multi-ethnic and multi-religious. Most of our major cities contain minority communities, no matter how small, with some recognisable characteristics that are different from those of the majority of their fellow-citizens. They may be immigrants from as far away as Indonesia or Bangladesh or China, or they may be Turkish guestworkers in West Germany, Algerians working in France, or simply religious, ethnic or linguistic minorities who have remained among us for centuries.

It should be obvious that much of the recent effort at legislation against discrimination of minorities, in all our western countries, is at least a formal recognition of the fact that modern democratic governments realise the need to protect the interests of minorities in our society. Now what makes fascist and racist groups so different from other political movements is that they totally reject the basic assumptions of minority rights. Their very creeds and manifestoes proclaim that minority ethnic groups *should* be discriminated against, that they should be treated not merely as second-class citizens but as a kind of sub-human category, an enemy to be eliminated. Thus their very beliefs and propaganda, as well as their acts of physical intimidation, are a threat to minority communities. When National Front or British Movement supporters try to march through areas heavily populated by immigrants they are not, of course, looking for votes or even for rational debate. They are setting out to instil fear in those communities, and to try to provoke violent confrontation with counter-demonstraters such as the Anti-Nazi League. They hope to deflect all blame for the ensuing violence onto their adversaries and the police, to gain massive publicity from the television and press coverage of the confrontations, and to whip up racial antagonism and conflict, with a view to exploiting it politically.

There is surely no good reason why fascist and racist movements should be allowed to carry out these provocative actions. Is their freedom to associate and to express their ideas or their right to fight elections seriously infringed by the authorities acting to prevent them from incitement of racial hatred in the streets of our multi-ethnic communities? Is society as a whole less free as the result of banning, for example, the British Movement and National Front from provocative marches, especially when the police know that they lack the resources to protect innocent life and property in any ensuing confrontation? And what of the huge costs of policing such marches? Do we not need to balance the rights and needs of the majority against the rights of the fanatical minority? I believe temporary bans on marches to be justifiable in situations where there is a real danger of injury to the police or to members of the general public. It is noteworthy that recent bans by the British police authorities on political marches in racially-sensitive areas have not prevented the National Front and British Movement from continuing to disseminate propaganda and seek recruits. In Britain the Anti-Nazi League, the churches, the democratic political parties and the trade unions must therefore make every effort to counter this poisonous propaganda by means of civic education.

One very important aspect of the task of protecting the ethnic minorities' rights and combatting racism is the improvement of co-operation between the police at all levels and the ethnic community leaders and activists. If these relations had been rather better in Brixton it is probable that the tragic confrontation in April 1981 between youths and the police would not have occurred. There must be much more consultation and liaison at all levels, and it would also help if more police officers could be recruited from the ethnic minority groups and deployed in the areas where there are large concentrations of immigrant population. There should be a greater effort to involve the police in community relations work in these areas, assisting with youth clubs, sports and similar activities, in order to break down the damaging and unnecessary 'us' and 'them' divide between police and public. There should also be far more specialist briefing and instruction on ethnic minorities and community relations in the police colleges and training systems.

At the same time, as so often emphasised in earlier chapters, the authorities in a true democracy must not under-react to the direct attacks made by the fascists against the law. In a true democracy the rule of law must not be blind in the right eye. Fascist groups that perpetrate terror and intimidation must be pursued with the same determination and efficiency that has been shown recently in the crackdown on terrorists of the extreme left. In countries such as France and Italy where there is considerable evidence of fascists or crypto-fascists having penetrated the ranks of the police and intelligence services, there must be a thoroughgoing effort to dismiss such individuals.

We have seen how fascist tendencies in the armed forces can threaten parliamentary democracy. In West Germany, where officially they claim to have expunged Nazism from the armed services, covert sympathisers remain. In December 1982 the Bonn government was gravely embarrassed when Luftwaffe jets swooped low, dipping their wings in apparent salute, at the funeral of Hans-Ulrich Rudel, an ardent neo-Nazi and Second World War air ace. If careful selection procedures and civic education cannot eradicate fascists from the military, it is all the more vital for democracies to keep their military under firm civilian control.

To sum up, all these practical measures – social and economic reforms, education, and more sensitive and effective policing – can, in combination, considerably assist western democratic societies in the unending task of combatting fascism. Underlying all these measures, however, must be the moral awareness and will among the general public to resist the evil of fascism. For as long as democratic publics maintain their belief in democracy and the values of humanity and freedom, we have the best guarantee of all against a relapse into fascist tyranny.

In February 1943, when Hitler's power over Germany and Europe still seemed unshakeable, there was a brave but now almost forgotten revolt by a group of Munich university students led by the brother and sister Scholl, called the Leaves of the White Rose. The Scholls entered the main hall of the university carrying two suitcases, climbed the main staircase and then emptied a snowstorm of leaflets bitterly attacking the Hitler regime. Timid students tried to avoid picking them up, while janitors scurried round trying to sweep up the contaminating literature. The Gestapo arrested the Scholls, and after a summary trial they were executed. In reply to a visitor asking about the likely outcome of her trial Ruth Scholl said 'What can you expect of such people?' Their demonstra- tion was a courageous but hopeless gesture against Nazi tyranny. Yet their literature of protest against Hitler is among the most impassioned and powerful ever written, and deserves to be remembered as a fitting indictment of fascism for all time:

'Every word out of Hitler's mouth is a lie. If he says peace, he means war, and if he calls frivolously on the name of the Almighty, he means the power of evil, the fallen angel, the devil. His mouth is the stinking throat of hell, and his power is fundamentally rotten. Certainly one has to fight against the Nazi terror state with rational weapons, but whoever still doubts the real existence of demoniacal power has not understood the metaphysical background of this war. Behind the concrete and perceptible things, behind all real and logical considerations, there is the irrational, there is the fight against the demon, against the messenger of anti-Christ. Every-where and at all times the demons have lurked in the dark for the hour when man becomes weak, when he arbitrarily abandons his human situation in the world order founded by God for him on freedom. ... After the first voluntary downward step he is compelled to the second and third with rapidly increasing speed, but everywhere, and at all times of the greatest human distress, men and women who have retained their freedom have risen as prophets and saints, and called on men to turn back to God. Certainly man is free, but he is unprotected against evil without the living God, he is like a boat without oars, exposed to the tempest, or like a baby without a mother, or like a cloud which dissolves.'

SELECT BIBLIOGRAPHY

(including works quoted in the text)

Abel, T., *Why Hitler Came to Power* (Englewood Cliffs, N.J.: Prentice–Hall, 1938)

Adorno, T. W., Frenkel-Brunswick, E., Levinson, D. J., & Sanford, R. N., *The Authoritarian Personality* (New York: Harper & Brothers, 1950)

Allen, W. S., *The Nazi Seizure of Power* (London: Quadrangle, 1965)

Allport, G. W., *The Nature of Prejudice* (Reading, Mass.: Addison Wesley, 1954)

Arendt, Hannah, *The Origins of Totalitarianism* (London: Brace and Harcourt, 1951)

— *Eichmann in Jerusalem: a report on the banality of evil* (New York: Viking, 1963)

Aronsfeld, C. C., 'The Britons Publishing Society', *Wiener Library Bulletin 1*, No. 2, pp. 31–5, 1966

Ashkenasi, A., *Modern German Nationalism* (New York: Halsted Press, 1976)

Banton, M., *Racial Minorities* (London: Fontana, 1972)

Barnes, Ian R., 'Other Neo-Fascist Strategies', *Politics 1*, No. 1, pp. 24–9, 1981

Bell, D., 'The Dispossessed', in *The Radical Right* (ed. Bell, D.) (New York: Anchor, 1962)

Benewick, R., *Political Violence and Public Order* (London: Allen Lane, 1969)

Billig, Michael, *Fascists* (London: Harcourt Brace Jovanovich, 1978)

— 'The New Social Psychology and "fascism"', *European Journal of Social Psychology 7*, pp. 393–432, 1977

Boca, Del. A., & Giovana, M., *Fascism Today: a world survey* (London: Heinemann, 1970)

Bower, Tom, *Blind Eye to Murder* (London: André Deutsch, 1981)

Bracher, Karl D., *German Dictatorship: origin, structure and consequences of National Socialism* (Harmondsworth: Penguin, 1973)

Broszat, Martin, *The Hitler State* (London: Longman, 1981)

Bullock, Alan, *Hitler: a study in tyranny* (Harmondsworth: Pelican, 1962)

Select Bibliography

Butz, A. R., *The Hoax of the Twentieth Century* (Richmond: Historical Review Press, 1976)

Carocci, Giampiero, *Italian Fascism* (Harmondsworth: Penguin, 1974)

Dawidowicz, Lucy, *The War against the Jews 1933–45* (Harmondsworth: Pelican, 1977)

Eisenberg, D., *Fascistes et Nazis D'Aujourd-hui* (Paris: Albin Michel, 1963)

Feder, Gottfried, *Hitler's Official Programme* (London: George Allen & Unwin, 1934)

Fergusson, Adam, 'How Britain brought back 400,000 Nazis into Society', *The Times*, 1973

Field, G. G., 'Nordic Racism', *Journal of the History of Ideas 38*, pp. 523–40, 1977

Fink, Willibald, *Die NPD bei der Bayerischen Landtagswahl 1966* (Vienna: Gunter Olzog Verlag Munchen-Wien, 1969)

Fox, John P., 'Japanese Reactions to Nazi Germany's Racial Legislation', *Wiener Library Bulletin 23*, Nos 2 and 3, pp. 46–50, 1969

Fromm, Erich, *The Anatomy of Human Destructiveness* (London: Jonathan Cape, 1974)

— *Fear of Freedom* (London: Routledge and Kegan Paul, 1942)

Gentile, G., 'The Origins and Doctrine of Fascism', in *Italian Fascisms* (ed. A. Lyttleton) (London: Jonathan Cape, 1973)

Germani, G., 'Political Socialization of Youth in Fascist Regimes: Italy and Spain', in *Authoritarian Politics in Modern Societies* (ed. S. P. Huntington & C. H. Moore) (New York: Basic Books, 1970)

Germino, D. L., *The Italian Fascist Party in Power* (Minneapolis: University of Minnesota Press, 1959)

Giovana, Mario, 'Italy's Neo-Fascists—The MSI', *Wiener Library Bulletin 25*, No. 2, pp. 29–32, 1972

Hartshorne, E. Y., *German Youth and the Nazi Dream of Victory* (London: Oxford University Press, 1941)

Hauptmann, Jerzy, 'The Re-emergence of the German Radical Right', in *The Central European Federalist* (New York, 1967)

Hayes, Paul, *Fascism* (London: George Allen & Unwin, 1973)

Hellendall, F., 'Nazi Crime before German Courts', *Wiener Library Bulletin 24* No. 3, pp. 14–20, 1970

Hitler, Adolf, *Mein Kampf* (Transl. Ralph Mannheim) (London: Hutchinson, 1974)

Hofstadter, R., *The Paranoid Style in American Politics and Other Essays* (London: Jonathan Cape, 1966)

Husbands, C. T., 'Racism in Society and the Mass Media: a critical interaction', in *White Media and Black Britain* (ed. C. Husbands) (London: Arrow, 1975)

— 'The National Front: a response to crisis', *New Society 32*, pp. 403–5, 1975

Joes, A. J., 'Fascism: the past and future', *Comparative Political Studies 7*, pp. 107–33, 1974

Kahn, Leo, 'Achievement and Failure at Nuremberg', *Wiener Library Bulletin 25*, Nos 3 and 4, pp. 21–9, 1972

Kedourie, Elie, *Nationalism in Asia and Africa* (New York: World Publishing Company, 1970)

Kevenhorster, Paul, *Zur Ideologie der NPD* (Eichholz, Materialien zur Auseinandersetzung mit der NPD. Herausgegeben vom Wissenschaftlichen Institut und der Politischen Akademie Eichholz der Konrad-Adenauer-Stiftung, 1968)

Kitchen, Martin, *Fascism* (London: Macmillan, 1976)

Kneller, George Frederick, *The Educational Philosophy of National Socialism* (New Haven, Conn.: Yale University Press, 1941)

Konow, Gerhard, *Zur Parlamentarischen Methode der NPD* (Frankfurt/Main: Frankfurter Hefte Nr. 4, 1968)

Laqueur, Walter (ed.), *Fascism* (Harmondsworth: Pelican, 1979)

Lacqueur, Walter (ed.), *Fascism* (Harmondsworth: Pelican, 1979) Edition on International Fascism 1920–45), *1*, No. 1, 1966

Laqueur, Walter, Mosse, George L. & Wistrich, Robert S. (eds.), *Journal of Contemporary History* on theories of fascism (Special Edition *11*, No. 4, 1976)

Larsen, Stein Ugelvik, Hagtvet, Bernt, Myklebust, Jan Petter, (eds.) *Who Were The Fascists?* (Bergen: Universitetsforlaget, 1980)

Lyttleton, A., *Italian Fascisms from Pareto to Gentile* (London: Jonathan Cape, 1973)

— 'Fascism in Italy: the second wave', *Journal of Contemporary History 1*, No. 1, pp. 75–100, 1966

McNall, S. G., 'Social Disorganisation and Availability: accounting for radical rightism', in *The American Right Wing* (ed. R. A. Schoenberger) (New York: Holt Rinehart & Winston, 1969)

Mannheim, Karl, *Ideology & Utopia* (London: Routledge & Kegan Paul, 1972)

Select Bibliography

Merkl, P. H., *Political Violence under the Swastika* (Princeton, N.J.: Princeton University Press, 1975)

Mosse, G. L., *Nazi Culture: intellectual, cultural and social life in the Third Reich* (London: W. H. Allen, 1969)

Mussolini, B., *The Political and Social Doctrine of Fascism* (London: Hogarth Press, 1934)

Nolte, E., *Three Faces of Fascism* (London: Weidenfeld and Nicolson, 1965)

— *Les Movements Fascistes* (Paris: Calmann-Levy, 1969)

Nugent, N., 'The Political Parties of the Extreme Right', in *The British Right* (ed. R. King & N. Nugent) (London: Saxon House, 1977)

Organski, A. F. K., 'Fascism and Modernization', in *The Nature of Fascism* (ed. S. J. Woolf) (London: Weidenfeld and Nicolson, 1968)

Papa, E. R., *Fascismo e cultura* (Venice: Marsilio Editori, 1974)

Parkes, James, *An Enemy of the People: anti-semitism* (Harmondsworth: Penguin, 1945)

Paul, Leslie, *The Annihilation of Man* (London: Faber, 1944)

Payne, Stanley G., *Fascism* (Madison, Wis.: University of Wisconsin Press, 1980)

Rhodes, James M., *The Hitler Movement* (Stanford, Calif.: Hoover Institution Press, 1980)

Saloman, E. von, *Die Geachteten* (Berlin: Rowohlt, 1930)

Seton-Watson, H., 'Fascism, Right and Left', *Journal of Contemporary History*, *1*, No. 1, pp. 183–97, 1966

Skidelsky, Robert, *Oswald Mosley* (London: Macmillan 1975,)

Sparks, Colin, *Never Again! The hows and whys of stopping fascism* (London: Bookmarks, 1980)

Stern, J. P., *Hitler: the Führer and the people* (London: Fontana, 1975)

Stigliani, Nicholas A., & Marzotto, Antonette, 'Fascist Anti-semitism and the Italian Jews', *Wiener Library Bulletin 28*, Nos 35 and 36, pp. 41–9, 1975

Strydom, Hans, & Wilkins, Ivor, *The Broederbond* (London: Paddington Press, 1979)

Talmon, J. L., *The Origins of Totalitarian Democracy* (London: Secker and Warburg, 1955)

Thadden, Adolf v., *Wille und Weg des nationalen Deutschland* (Hanover: Eine Rede des Frankfurter Parteitages der DRP, 1962)

Thayer, G., *The British Political Fringe: a profile* (London: Anthony Blond, 1965)

— *The Further Shores of Politics: the American political fringe today* (New York: Simon & Schuster, 1967)

Timerman, Jacobo, *Prisoner Without a Name, Cell Without a Number* (London: Weidenfeld & Nicolson, 1981)

Tomlinson, John, *Left, Right: the march of political extremism in Britain* (London: John Calder, 1981)

Tyndall, John, *The Authoritarian State* (London: National Socialist Movement, 1962)

Vander Zanden, J. W., 'The Klan Revival', *American Journal of Sociology 65*, pp. 456–62, 1960

Walker, Martin, *The National Front* (London: Fontana, 1977)

Weber, E., 'The Men of the Archangel', *Journal of Contemporary History, 1*, No. 1, pp. 101–26, 1966

— *Varieties of Fascism* (New York: Van Nostrand, 1964)

Wilkinson, Paul, *Political Terrorism* (London: Macmillan, 1974)

— *Terrorism and the Liberal State* (London: Macmillan, 1977)

Wilkinson, Paul (ed.) *British Perspectives on Terrorism* (London: George Allen & Unwin, 1981)

Winegarten, R., 'The Temptations of Cultural Fascism', *Wiener Library Bulletin 13*, No. 1 pp. 3440, 1968–9

Wolfinger, R. E. *et al.*, 'America's radical right', in *Ideology and Discontent1 (ed. D. Apter) (New York: The Free Press, 1964)

Zeman, Z. A. B., *Nazi Propaganda* (London: Oxford University Press, 1973)

Addenda

Horowitz, Irving, 'Left-wing Fascism', *Transaction Society*, Vol. 8, No. 4, pp. 19–24

Husbands, Christopher, 'The Past and Future of Urban Racialist Politics in England', chapter from unpublished MS, quoted by kind permission of the author

Robins, David, 'Growing Up: swastika style', *New Internationalist*, July 1982, pp. 18–19

Spoonley, Paul, 'New Zealand First! The Extreme Right and Politics in New Zealand 1961–81', *Political Science*, 33, No. 2, pp. 99–126, 1981

Timerman, Jacobo, *The Longest War* (London: Picador, 1982)

INDEX

Reference and information

☐	**A Guide to Insurance**	Margaret Allen	£1.95p
☐	**North-South**	Brandt Commission	£2.50p
☐	**Save It! The**	Gary Hammond,	
	Energy Consumer's	Kevin Newport and	
	Handbook	Carol Russell	£1.25p
☐	**Militant Islam**	Godfrey Jansen	£1.50p
☐	**A Guide to Speaking in Public**	Robert Seton Lawrence	£1.25p
☐	**How to Study**	H. Maddox	£1.75p
☐	**Pan Spelling Dictionary**	Ronald Ridout	£1.50p
☐	**A Guide to Saving**		
	and Investment	James Rowlatt	£2.50p
☐	**Career Choice**	Audrey Segal	£2.95p
☐	**Logic and its Limits**	Patrick Shaw	£2.95p
☐	**Straight and Crooked**		
	Thinking	R. H. Thouless	£1.50p
☐	**Dictionary of Earth Sciences**		£2.95p
☐	**Dictionary of Economics and Commerce**		£1.50p
☐	**Dictionary of Life Sciences**		£2.95p
☐	**Dictionary of Philosophy**		£2.50p
☐	**Dictionary of Physical Sciences**		£2.95p
☐	**Harrap's New Pocket**		
	French and English Dictionary		£2.50p
☐	**Pan Dictionary of Synonyms and Antonyms**		£1.95p
☐	**Pan English Dictionary**		£2.50p

All these books are available at your local bookshop or newsagent, or
can be ordered direct from the publisher. Indicate the number of copies
required and fill in the form below   7

Name_____
(Block letters please)

Address_____

_____

Send to Pan Books (CS Department), Cavaye Place, London SW10 9PG
Please enclose remittance to the value of the cover price plus:
35p for the first book plus 15p per copy for each additional book ordered
to a maximum charge of £1.25 to cover postage and packing
Applicable only in the UK

While every effort is made to keep prices low, it is sometimes
necessary to increase prices at short notice. Pan Books reserve
the right to show on covers and charge new retail prices which
may differ from those advertised in the text or elsewhere